Toad Leon is one of the most tru
many of the things you and I wou
rich lode of experiences makes him a great story teller.

Three character traits have greatly enriched Toad's life. His natural charm attracts admirers and respect from both sexes; his generosity is best displayed by his efforts to have everyone around him enjoy themselves to the fullest— and he stays ready to make the next interesting trip, investment or experiment at the drop of a hat. If you even mention an interesting new place or thing that should be seen, Toad's immediate response is, "Should we leave tonight or in the morning?" And he means it.

A good example of the Leon charm occurred a few years back when Toad and I were returning to Abilene from a trip to Dallas and he spied a tiny bar-becue restaurant in Putnam. Toad never passes up a chance for a good plate of 'cue so we wheeled into the little cafe and sat down. The lanky blonde waitress had a bad dye job, and apparently a bad day. She seemed to be put out that we'd interrupted her work (we were the only customers) and looked ready to toss us out if we didn't hurry up and order. That tough west Texas gal had seen a bunch, and wasn't impressed by a bit of it.

Before we left, the waitress had refilled Toad's tea glass 26 times, had brought him extra ribs and rolls that he had not asked for and was hovering over him like a mother hen. See what I mean?

Probably not all of Toad's mishaps, mule wrecks and accomplishments are included in this book, but there's enough to give you a very good insight to this man's life, and to keep you turning the pages until the end.

Jerry O'Bryant
Outdoor Writer for the Abilene Reporter News

What Made Wyatt Urp, *as told by Toad Leon, is a classic autobiography that should be read by one and all, young and old. It is a classic history of the life and times of the Depression Era.*

Now, it is with great pleasure that I call upon my almost 70 years experience in the news media, to make a few comments about this most interesting story of the 91-year-old Toad Leon—the youngest of seven children. This is more than an autobiography. It is a love story of Toad and his beloved wife, Donna McGowen. It reads like fiction of their career in the theatre business, beginning in Baird, Texas. The fiction involves their contact with many movie stars that came their way in the theatre business.

This colorful showman's career covers many fields starting with farming during the Depression and Dust Bowl days. It did not take him long, though, to realize he would make his fortune elsewhere. But, in the end, he returned to his grass roots beginning. It's hard to believe that the theatre business, which took most of his life, would eventually go out of existence. In the end, the drive-in theatres proved profitable because the land on which they were built became very valuable in places like Dallas and Houston.

The third adventure had to do with ranching in colorful New Mexico and establishment of an outstanding Appaloosa horse farm. This cagey Leon had the touch of knowing when to get out of the business, after three highly successful sales, which included movie stars in attendance and buyers. After building a herd of 300 Appaloosas (which was influenced by the late Carl Miles, a noted Abilene oil man and horseman), it is history that shortly after Toad's dispersal of all his Ap's, the legendary, colorful breed made famous by the Indians lost its golden touch. However, land values continued to advance which allowed him to sell the ranch at a nice profit.

After the theatre business had gone by the way of the boards, and the Appaloosa horse business lost its magic touch, Leon turned to other adventures. He had become a big game hunter, and that was his next venture. When he established his More or Less Ranch, south of Lawn, Texas, the best of Leon's sense of humor came to light. When asked how large the ranch was, Leon replied, "About 10,000 acres, more or less." Actually, the ranch was about 1,000 acres, but Leon explained in private that when asking about the size of one's ranch, you were treading on personal questions.

Along the way, he became interested in the food business and established one of Abilene's most prominent eating places, called Square's BBQ. It is interest-

ing to note that he and Donna left the fast lane of society in Dallas to return to Abilene to set up headquarters for their operations. That was when the early day training, as the youngest of seven Haskell County farmers, took over.

As a side light, we knew Clarence Leon, the elder of the children, as a successful ice man, through our acquaintance with the Arledge family, who were also ice men, and who were outstanding Hereford breeders from Nolan County. We knew Donna McGowen through Dʳ. Henry McGowen, who was our next door neighbor for 25 years. So, you see, we go a long way back with Toad Leon.

In closing, I want to congratulate Toad Leon for putting into words the life that most of us of the Depression Era knew quite well. Though we might add, that only with the touch of this most entertaining person, would you find history so interesting.

Sincerely,

Harry Holt
Former News Director of KRBC-TV

What Made Wyatt Urp?

The Life and Times of Toad Leon

as told by
his family, his friends and
the man himself

What Made Wyatt Urp?

The Life and Times of Toad Leon

as told by
his family, his friends and
the man himself

by Bob Lapham

illustrations by Merle Morrison

BARBED WIRE
PUBLISHING
LAS CRUCES, NEW MEXICO

Published by Barbed Wire Publishing
1990 East Lohman Avenue, Suite 225
Las Cruces, New Mexico 88001 USA

Cover font ITC Berkeley Oldstyle Bold
Text font ITC Berkeley Oldstyle Book and ITC Goudy Sans
All illustrations by Merle Morrison

ISBN 0-9711930-3-7

1 2 3 4 5 6 7 8 9 0

What Made Wyatt Urp?
The Life and Times of Toad Leon
as told by his family, his friends and the man himself

Acknowledgments ix

Introduction – What Made Wyatt Urp x

About the Author xiii

A Baby Toad Checks In 1

Rule School – 1916 4

Molasses? AGAIN!? 6

The Selling Game 8

How Not to Run Away from Home 9

76 Trombones, Minus One – 1925 10

Now He's an Orphan – 1927 12

Rule's Roaring '20s 14

Schreiner's Bull Ring – 1928 17

Artie's Car – 1931 20

Adios, Mother Earth 22

The Ice Business – 1932 24

There's No Business Like Show Business 26

The Life and Death of John Dillinger 29

The Love of His Life 31

The Belle of the Ball – 1935 34

Good Times in Graham – 1937 36

The Western Chase – 1939 39

Those Bloomin' Bloomers – 1939 42

The Fat Rats Rule Amarillo 44

The Great Peanut Caper of 1942 47

What I Learned in Dale Carnegie School – 1943 49

Film Row – the 1940s 50

Canadian Hunt – 1946 55

Alcan Highway – 1947 63

The Tab – 1949 68

Out of a Rut, and On to Abilene 70

Purchasing Pendaries 74

The Day the Japs Attacked Pendaries Ranch 79
Stores, and More 80
Memories of the Best of Times Never Fade Away 82
New Year's Eve – 1950 84
Smoking May Be Hazardous to Your Health 86
Save the Last Dance for Uncle Toad 88
How Much is That Hoggie... 90
Lots of Lost Sleep Over Sheep 92
OK, Toad...Let's See You Do It Again – 1950s 95
The Soap Tycoon – 1952 97
Polly and the Bouncer 99
Chasing the Uranium Dream – early 1950s 102
To Burger...To Burger Not 106
The New Mexico Caper 108
Donna's Surprise 111
How to Break a Haberdasher's Heart – 1956 114
Surprise, Surprise Charlie! – 1956 116
The Appaloosa Coat – Mid-1950s 118
Throwing Bull in the 1950s 120
Drive-In Picture Shows – 1950s-'60s 121
Psst! Want a Magic Bullet, Toad? 127
Golf is the Name of Toad's Game 128
Finding Friendship Through Party Golf 132
Bad Day at Broadmoor – 1955 135
The Toad Leon Get-Even Hole 137
Toad's Little Bit of Golf Heaven 142
Sale Day – 1960 143
Chief of Fourmile – 1961 147
High-Tailing It to the High Country 151
A Twist of Fate – 1962 155
Bon Voyage – 1962 157
Who Needs Pheasants? We've Got Lots of Ducks 162
The Colleyville Blues – 1962 164
Election Year – 1964 165
A Wild Bear Does What in the Woods? – 1964 166
A Chat With H. L. Hunt – 1965 169

The Easiest Money Toad Ever Made 171

The Plane Truth About Flying 172

Food Stamps Make the Woman - 1968 174

How Does Your Garden Grow in Lorenzo? 177

The Toad Leon Golf Classic 180

...And She Didn't Spill a Drop 183

Idea Men Often Leave the Details to Others 185

Toad's Trip of Trips – 1970 187

321 Hillside – Santa Fe, New Mexico 190

High Life at the Hyatt – 1975 192

The Barbecue Business – 1976 194

The More or Less Ranch – 1977 196

A Weekend at Vermejo Park – 1977 201

The Speech – 1979 203

Hang by Your Heels, Toad Leon...Oops! 205

The Ringers – 1980s 208

My Friend George – 1985 212

The Smartest Man in Rule, Texas 214

The Tax Man Cometh 216

How to Squelch a Toad – 1997 219

A Tale of Two Bulls and a Pair of Ostriches 221

A Birthday Party to End All Parties 223

Pointing the Southwind North – 1998 229

Call of the Open Road 236

The Think Tank – 1999 238

Toad's Tidbits 240

Two Who Know Toad's Wit Well 245

Get the License Number of That Truck! 247

Epilogue 250

Index 253

Toad Leon during his pool hustling days.

Acknowledgments

Either I read this somewhere or I dreamed it. But for some reason it has been on my mind since starting this endeavor. It seemed kind of appropriate:

Old folks dwell on the past
Because they have no future.
Young folks dwell on the future
Because they have no past.

My life has been blessed with good friends, good health and good luck. The luckiest day was when I met my wife, Donna. She was a helpmate and a soulmate and usually kept me on an even keel. We spent sixty-one wonderful years together. There isn't a day that goes by that I don't miss her. I think that she would have gotten a kick out of this book.

Many thanks to my children and grandchildren, who thought I had a story to tell and wouldn't leave me alone until I had told it.

Many thanks to Bob Lapham who listened to all my ramblings and, with his special writing talent, made sense out of them. He had the patience of Job.

Many thanks to Merle Morrison for her friendship and artistic renditions. She spent untold hours on "the cause."

Many thanks to the other contributors who added their memories and nudged mine. As the recollections flowed, the following little ditty seemed fitting:

As I go down life's crooked road,
Where she stops, nobody knowed.

We had fun putting this book together. Hope it brings you a chuckle or two.

C.D. "Toad" Leon
August 15, 2001

Introduction

What Made Wyatt Urp

Early in the summer of 2001, C.D. (better known as Toad) Leon finally caved in to pressure from his family. Particularly his daughters, Carol Ann Midkiff and Sandra Roberts. They had been begging their father to allow them to compile an overview of his life; and put to paper some of its events. To them and hundreds of others, Toad Leon continued to be one of the most colorful and popular homegrown entrepreneurs to come out of 20th century Texas and New Mexico.

"Nah," Toad kept telling them and his grandchildren, who soon joined the call for literary action. He simply wasn't interested. "Who am I to write a book?" he told Sandra, when she brought me by to discuss working with them on the project she and her sister kept pushing. "And if I did, who would want to read it?"

Finally, his daughters simply wore him down. "I agreed, just to shut them up," he said. "And since I'm ninety-one years old, if we're going to do it, I kinda figure we had better get on with it."

During the Golden Age of movies, and under the tutelage of his brother, the native of tiny Rule, Texas, was one of the most successful film exhibitors and theater owners in the Southwest. Next he became a pioneer in big-time drive-in theaters. Success in horse breeding, resort development, and real estate would follow him and his beloved partner in life, his wife Donna, from Dallas to New Mexico.

They would raise two daughters who established families of their own. Toad and Donna would enjoy close lifelong relationships with their offspring.

Leon's long and eventful life has been accentuated by humor. His razor-sharp mind has always enjoyed either listening to or telling a good story. So it stood to reason that chronicling his life first and foremost would have to be a fun trip.

Laughter usually didn't come from making money, nice as that's been. Leon has thrived on discovering humor amid life's little nuances. He has peddled ice from a mule-drawn wagon, run a bowling alley, been a dry-land farmer (however blessedly brief that misadventure was), struggled through failures in the hog and sheep businesses, prospected for uranium, been bewildered by the world of fast food franchises, survived the pitfalls of gin rummy and Texas hold-'em, and held off golfing foes' double-presses on their stroke holes. Among other adventures.

Along the way, the legions of Leon's friends steadily grew, even if by the turn of the century most of his and his late wife's party-going pals from Dallas to Abilene, through Harlingen and on to northern New Mexico (and most points in between) had passed away.

His was a life just screaming to be told in print.

The book's title came before the first word was written. It was an expression his daughters had heard all their lives. It surfaced outside the family in 1970 as a joke on some of his friends. "Not in my wildest dreams was I ever serious about writing a book. I was just having a little fun with the boys," Leon explained. He and Donna were dividing time between Pendaries Ranch, parts of which they had developed into a popular resort, and nearby Santa Fe, New Mexico. For years, Toad had enjoyed regular golfing. He even designed, paid for and supervised the building of his own course at Pendaries.

"This particular day, we were returning from playing in Albuquerque," he said. "Our foursome included Dandy Don Meredith, Nash Hancock, Mack Thomas and me." Meredith was the former Dallas Cowboys quarterback and popular original member of the NFL Monday Night Football telecast. Thomas wrote screenplays from his home in El Rito, New Mexico. He continues to do so. Their conversation centered around some stories Mack was working on, for Hollywood.

"As I recall, we stopped at a small cantina and had a few drinks," Toad said, adding that while the topic of Thomas' tales continued, "My mind began to wander. At this time, I was heavily involved with promotion, lot sales and the day-to-day running of Pendaries Village Golf and Country Club. I was obliged to wear many hats, the self-proclaimed mayor and sheriff among them.

"These were resort homes for the most part. During summer months, some husbands would spend the weekends with their families, then be off to the city during the work week. Remember the truism, 'When the cat's away, the mice will play'? This made my job considerably more tedious."

So, during a lull in the spirited conversation among the four well-relaxed golfing buddies, Toad said, "You know, I nearly have enough material for a book. In fact, I already have a title in mind."

"Oh, really, Toad? What could you write about?" one if them asked.

"Well, I could write about a few of my experiences at Pendaries and maybe a little about some of the businesses I've tried. I don't have all the ingredients yet, but the title fits." Leon said the four carried on like this for a while, with Toad patiently waiting for one of them to swallow the bait.

Finally Thomas asked, "OK, Toad. What's the title?"

"Well, I've always admired how the marshal of old Dodge City and Tombstone was able to keep the peace. At Pendaries, it's a challenge just trying to keep everyone in their own teepee. Since I want the title to have a western flair, it would be appropriate to call my book, *What Made Wyatt Urp?*.

"They cursed in unison," Leon recalled, smiling.

This book has sprung from hundreds of hours of taped conversations with Toad Leon. It is an attempt to get behind the scenes—the history, circumstances, surroundings, and special happenings that have come together in one man's colorful life during almost one hundred years.

The names that are used are real, "except for a few that we'll need to change, to protect the guilty," Leon proclaimed. The stories are true, though maybe they did get a bit polished in the telling. Toad himself has verified the places and the approximate dates he talks about.

Enjoy!

About the author

Bob Lapham is a former newspaper writer and editor who retired from *The Abilene Reporter-News* in 2000, after serving as sports editor, special sections editor, news editor and, from 1987 until 2000, arts and entertainment editor. He previously was sports editor of the *Brownsville (Texas) Herald*, and was sports director of the Rio Grande Valley Freedom Newspapers of Texas that included the *Herald*, the *Valley Morning Star* in Harlingen and the *McAllen Monitor*.

He is the author of one other book, *Twenty Years of Life Begins at Forty, the Story of a Unique Golf Tournament* (Lapham seems to favor long titles), and soon begins a novel, parts of which will be loosely based upon his days as a 1950s rock 'n' roll recording sessions singer, primarily in a trio called the Picks, that backed up Buddy Holly as the surreptitious voices of the Crickets.

Like Toad, he is an avid golfer. Like Toad, he attended Texas Tech (four and a half years, four majors) until giving up sans graduation. Like Toad, he was a struggling pilot (though he did manage to get his license).

He lives in Abilene, Texas with his wife, Mary. They have three grown children and one granddaughter.

For additional copies of this book contact:

Barbed Wire Publishing
1990 E. Lohman Ave., Ste. 225
Las Cruces, NM 88001
505.524.6808 (voice); 505.524.4813 (fax)
888.817.1990 (toll free)
e-mail: thefolks@barbed-wire.net
www.barbed-wire.net

or

Square's Bar-B-Q
210 North Leggett
Abilene, TX 79603
915.673.7182

A Baby 'Toad' Checks In

Claude Duval Leon was born April 24, 1910, in Rule, Texas. He was the youngest of seven children born to Henry Joseph de Leon and Margaret Ann Server Leon.

"My brother, Server, thought I looked like a toad frog at birth hence the name Toad," he explained. Leon rarely goes by C.D., and never outside government forms does he answer to Claude Duval. The name Toad has stuck since infancy, a moniker that obviously brings Leon considerable pleasure.

"When I was born my brother, Clarence, was 18, Server 14, Estelle 11, Carroll 9, Mike 6 and Mattie Lee 5." The age disparity between the older Leon children and their youngest sibling, as well as the absence of their grandparents and virtually all of their older aunts and uncles, prevented the family-conscious Toad from ever discovering very much information about his father's roots.

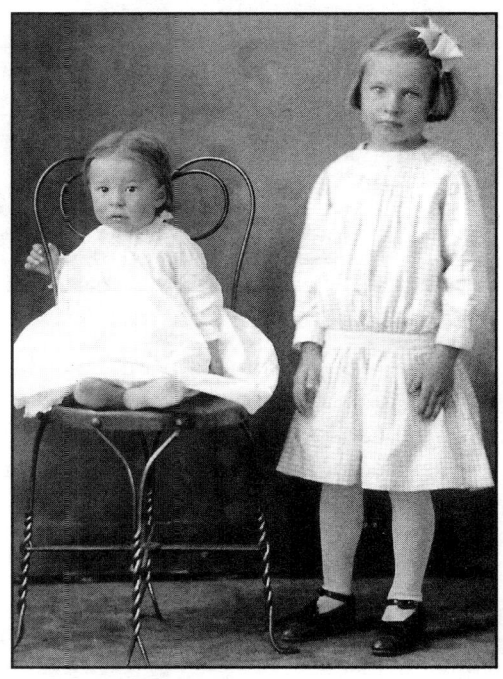

Toad and Mattie Lee in 1910

"My father's full name, according to church records we later found in Brownsville, Texas, was Henry Joseph de Leon (1861-1922). He was thought to have come from Spain, through Matamoros, Mexico. He was orphaned at the age of three, and was raised by an aunt, Cecilia Lively. He was fourteen when they moved to Ennis, Texas, and then to Haskell, where Mrs. Lively opened a café. My father drove a herd of sheep to Little Rock, Arkansas when he was nineteen.

"He met Margaret Ann Server (1868-1927) sitting in a peach tree in Davilla, Milam County, Texas. He always said that she was the prettiest girl he had ever seen. He was convinced he would marry her some day and told her so. They married in 1890, just like he predicted."

Toad is quick to note the parallel here. "Like father, like son. I felt the

1

Toad's parents-1890 photo

same way when I met Donna McGowen in Baird, Texas. She was sitting on a bicycle, and she was beautiful! We were married six months later, on June 5, 1935."

Toad said his father worked for the Server family and became adept at farming near Davilla, about 50 miles northeast of Austin. For several years, while six of their children were born, Henry and Margaret struggled with land that was quickly being worn out.

"In 1906, they moved the family by train and covered wagon to Haskell County, some sixty miles north of Abilene," Toad said. "This was fertile land and good cotton country." A half-section was purchased; located two miles south and a half-mile east of the small community of Rule.

Railroading had set the stage for the birth of the community of Rule, as it did in much of America's move westward. The area took some getting used to. Three tribes—the Kiowas, the Comanches and the Tonkawa—once used it as a continuous battleground. The plains could be bleak. Early

Henry Joseph de Leon and his mules, beginning the daunting task of breaking out the farmland shortly after the family's move to Rule, Texas.

white settlers recalled there being only a single tree in and around what would be Rule. And that was a hackberry, more bush than tree.

The Leon family in front of their Rule, Texas farmhouse in 1909, a year before "A Baby Toad Checks In." From left to right, father Henry, Mike, Mattie Lee, Carroll, mother Margaret Ann, Estelle, Server and Clarence.

Banker and farmer Jesse L. Jones is credited with founding the town shortly after the turn of the century and after the Kansas City, Mexico & Orient Railroad had surveyed the area. By 1902 the rail grades and beds had been established. The first train arrived in 1905.

The town was named for Kansas City Banker W.O. Rule, Sr. He had become treasurer of the KCM&O though there is no historical information to state that he ever visited the town.

"Papa broke out the land, built a house and barns, dug a well and put up fences with the help of his wife, children, a few horses and a couple of mules. We lived on the farm until 1919 and then moved to Rule."

Toad's father died when Toad was twelve. His mother passed away five years later, when he was seventeen.

Rule School - 1916

"It was my first year in school and I was six," Toad Leon recalled. "Back then there were no buses, so it was up to me to get the two and a half miles from our farm to school and back the best way I could.

"Sometimes I was able to catch a ride with Deputy Sheriff W.W. (Pot Leg) Kittley in his buggy, but mostly I was on foot. This gave me plenty of time to daydream and ponder the future. I always thought I was real good at daydreaming.

Rule School, 1916

"Each morning Mama packed my school lunch in a lard bucket. It was always the same—sausage on a biscuit wrapped in funny papers. The town kids brought their sandwiches on light bread. Sometimes they even had a banana or an apple."

It will come as no surprise to people of the next eight decades who would have dealings with Toad Leon that here the young whipper-snapper obviously learned quite early some valuable lessons in the field of commerce. "I'd say that a considerable amount of time was spent coaxing my fellow students to trade their lunches with me," Leon admitted.

By the time Valentine's Day drew near young Toad had his first sweetheart. Mildred Jones was the daughter of the Rule bank's president.

"The teacher told us that we could either buy or make each other valentine cards," Leon recalled. "I was frantic! I just had to give Mildred a real pretty one.

"On the way home that afternoon as I passed Westbrook Drug Store, I had a brainstorm. Not stopping to consider the repercussions I asked Mr. Westbrook if I could charge a valentine card to my father's account. Of course it was all right with him if I thought it would be OK with my father. I assured him Papa wouldn't mind at all.

"That evening, my sister, Mattie Lee, 11, helped me spell some of the words I wrote on this beautiful, store-bought valentine."

The end product was: Mildred, how pretty you ear. Oh how I live you! - Toad.

Mattie Lee never let her kid brother forget how his version of the card came out.

"I might add that Papa never let me forget charging that nickel valentine to his account either."

Mattie Lee (nee Leon) Weaver, with son Larry, husband Hilland, and son Leon, early 1940s.

Molasses? AGAIN!?

Waste not, want not. That has been the watchword around many a table, especially those closely linked to the U.S. farm. Wasting what was grown for your family was downright sinful.

So it was with the Henry Joseph de Leon family of Rule, Texas, in the years just before World War I when Toad's older brothers were in the process of dropping the "de" before their surname. By this time, Toad's father had acquired farm acreage other than the original half-section. One was located near the small community of Rochester.

"Mr. Clark farmed that place," Toad said. "He had set aside about 15 acres to grow cane. His yearly rent would be one barrel of sorghum molasses. Two barrels, if he had a good year." Now, molasses for breakfast in the morning isn't so bad - unless it's every morning, twelve months a year. And the stuff gets stronger with each passing month. "I don't like to admit this, but I grew to hate Mr. Clark during the time when I was grow-ing up," Toad said. "My brother Mike made sure I never wasted a drop of molasses. Can't stand to eat it to this day."

A shrink might think there was another reason for Toad's distaste. People tend to remember their first whipping, and Mr. Clark's syrup was smack dab in the middle of Toad's.

"We all ate our meals at the same time around this big table," he recalled. "Each one of us seven kids had his or her own plate with no two alike, of course. Mine had this picture of a fine lady with long, flowing hair. I was about six and I just loved her! She was the Queen of England, I think, though the vision doesn't fit Victoria."

Anyway, Toad was sitting there waiting for his food when someone served him a ladle filled with molasses. "Don't get syrup on my lady's hair!" he hollered, a request that was met with laughter. "I mean it! DON'T GET MOLASSES ON MY LADY'S PRETTY HAIR!" Then he began to cry and promptly was taken away to get a spanking.

Around the same time, Toad was rudely introduced to chores. "It was early one day," he recalled. "my father and my older brothers were getting ready to head for work in the fields."

"Toad," his father said, "you get those cows up and milked by the time we come home late this afternoon."

"Yessir!" the youngster replied, probably proud of the responsibility he had been given.

The feeling didn't last. A 10-acre patch of sudan was near the house, and that's where the Leon milk cows preferred to hang out. Toad knew it but when he went to looking not an udder-filled bovine could he find. The grain stalks were about three times as high as he was and they were pretty well over the cows' heads too. Later that day, his father and his brothers returned. "Toad, did you get all the cows up and milked?" his father asked.

"Nosir. I couldn't find 'em."

"What do you mean, you couldn't find them?"

"I just couldn't."

"Come with me, son, and I'll show you how to find cows," his father quietly said.

"He took me out to the barn and doubled up a buggy line and then proceeded to give me a real whipping," Toad said.

The licking served its purpose. Toad didn't recall ever getting another.

Looking for rain—young Toad with his parents.

And never again did he have any trouble finding cows.

The Selling Game

Toad Leon learned the fine point—or perhaps the fine print —of mastering the selling game at an early age.

"The year was 1920. I was ten," he recalled. "One day, I was reading *The Literary Digest*. On the inside back cover was a puzzle. The advertisement asked, 'How many squirrels can you find in the tree?' If I could circle all the hidden squirrels and pass the really simple test that accompanied the puzzle, I was told (or, I read) that I'd win...A SHETLAND PONY! I confidently mailed my completed puzzle to the company." Then began The Big Wait. Toad wondered how his pony would be shipped to him. By return mail? He doubted that. But there was no mistaking in the lad's mind—he had won!

"Instead of a Shetland pony, they sent me a dozen copies of *The Literary Digest*," he recalled. "It seemed that winning the pony would depend upon how many subscriptions I could sell. This was my first lesson in reading the fine print.

"At the very least, I felt duty-bound to sell the twelve copies they sent me. I screwed up enough courage to approach Mr. Joe Jones, the bank president and father of my first sweetheart, Mildred.

"When I entered the bank. Mr. Jones came around his desk and greeted me. 'Good morning, Toad. What can I do for you today?' "

"Mr. Jones, how would you like to buy a *Literary Digest*?"

"I've been waiting for you to come by. Of course I would, Toad."

"After more than eighty years, I still remember the kindness this well-known and respected man extended to a little boy. He made me feel as important as any of his big bank customers."

A few years later, Leon learned another tenet of the selling game—always stay focused, and keep tight grip on your wallet.

"It was a Saturday, sometime during 1926," he said. "Beans McCandless asked me to drive around with him while he tried to sell some lightning rods. We made several stops and while he talked to the homeowners, I sat in the car and waited.

"A few sales were made and we were about to call it a day when Beans decided to drive out and see Mrs. Kittley. I sat in the car and waited....and waited. Finally, Beans emerged from the farmhouse and walked to the car, a wide grin on his face.

"So, did you sell some lightning rods to Mrs. Kittley?"

"No," Beans replied, "but I'll tell you what I did do. I just bought the prettiest Bible you ever saw!"

How Not to Run Away from Home

Toad Leon learned a long time ago that running away from home is easier said than done.

"Back when I was in about the sixth or seventh grade in Rule, my best friend was Bill Fouts," he recalled. "In those days, you had to make your own entertainment. There was no TV and no radio. We were lucky to have a tin can we could tie a string on.

"Our parents would let Bill and me spend the night together. I'd spend the night at his house, then next time he'd stay over with us. His farm was about two and a half miles south and west of Rule. The railroad ran right through it so we'd always run down to the tracks when we'd hear a train coming and watch it go through. Maybe even put a penny on the tracks and watch it flatten out when the locomotive ran over it.

"This particular time, the train was going real slow through his farm because it was going uphill. Bill said, 'You know, there's an open door on that box car coming our way. Why don't we get on it? Fact of business, why don't we just run away from home?'

"He kinda challenged me on this thing, and before long I figured it wasn't such a bad idea. So we hopped on this freight train, went through Rule, and then headed for Rochester about 10 miles on down the tracks."

It may or may not have sunk in by now for our intrepid travelers that (1) they had not packed even a lunch, (2) they had no money, and (3) they didn't even have shoes on!

"Well, I decided Rochester was about as far away from home as I wanted to run, but Bill said no. The next stop was Knox City, so when we got there, I said, 'Bill, I'm gonna get off this train.' 'Oh?' he replied. 'Well, I'm not gonna run away by myself. I'll get off here, too.' The train was still going pretty slow, so we made it all right."

The two runaways finally figured out that a train coming along from the opposite direction would be going downhill, not up. In other words, it would be moving right along. Hopping it could be hazardous to their health. So they set out walking back to the Fouts' farm. About twenty miles' worth.

"For some reason, by the time we got back, Bill's folks hadn't even missed us," Toad said. "They never knew we tried to run away from home. So we wasted that effort; all for nothing.

"It was the last time I ever tried to run away from home."

A lesson everybody's got to learn, Wyatt said.

Seventy-Six Trombones, Minus One—1925

Well, maybe if Brother Toad Leon wasn't yet ready for the pulpit, he could contribute to society with the gift of music that must be hiding somewhere in his youthful soul. At least, that's probably along the lines of what Mama Leon was thinking when it came to her youngest child. Toad's brush with performing music could've inspired Meredith Willson's "The Music Man."

"I was a sophomore in high school when the Rule Chamber of Commerce saw fit to assemble a marching band," Leon recalled. This was to be an elite ensemble designed to visit other towns in the area and proudly promote the community.

"A new band instructor, Mr. Humphries, was hired. His duties included encouraging the businessmen to sponsor the endeavor, to enlist band members and give private lessons to the musically challenged," Toad said. "I fit in the last category, in particular.

"My mother was contacted. 'Yes, of course Toad would be interested,' she said. By this time, Mama had given up on my becoming a preacher, and was looking for other ways to broaden my horizons.

Toad Leon, age 15, second trombonist, Rule High School Band

"The band needed another trombone player, so Mama bought me a shiny trombone and a brand new band uniform. Knowing I required considerable help, she also signed me up for a series of music lessons."

Huh? Did Prof. Harold Hill really exist, not only in composer-writer Willson's Gary, Indiana, but in Rule too?

"I was selected to play second trombone," Toad continued. "Now, the second trombone carried no tune. All I was required to play was 'too-tah...too-tah.' After several weeks of lessons, Mr. Humphries thought the band was ready for its first concert. We eagerly met on the high school campus Sunday afternoon.

A rather nervous Mr. Humphries pulled Toad aside for some hush-hush, last-minute instructions. "Toad, since you haven't had many lessons and haven't as yet become proficient on your instrument. It would be better if you just pretended to play. you might 'too' when you need to 'tah.'" What a day!

"We marched off down toward the water tower where the bandstand was located. The band played loudly and I puffed my cheeks in and out in what I hoped was a convincing manner," Toad recalled. "Behind the band walked a little boy leading a Jersey milk cow. She sported a banner that proclaimed in bold letters, 'Rule, Texas—The Biggest Little Town on Earth!' Below, in smaller letters was printed, 'And this ain't no bull!'"

The trombone? Toad never got the hang of it.

I wonder if Wyatt ever did?

Now He's an Orphan—1927

It was 1927 when Toad Leon experienced a shock all too familiar to children born late in the lives of their parents. His mother, Margaret Ann Server Leon, passed away. She was fifty-nine. His father, Henry Joseph de Leon, had died five years earlier at the age of sixty-one. Toad, seventeen, was an orphan.

Toad (left) with nieces, Polly (center) and Mildred (right) in 1924

"I was a senior in high school. The main topic of discussion among my brothers was what they were going to do with Toad. It was decided that I would live with my oldest brother, Clarence, his wife, Nora Cloud, and their daughters, Mildred and Polly."

Clarence was eighteen years older than Toad. He owned the Leon Ice Plant in Rule. "Clarence thought just like my father. That is, a person should always stay busy. A milk cow and a push mower were purchased so I could do just that. I was to milk the cow twice daily, keep their extensive lawn mowed, and work at the ice plant on weekends. I developed a way to dry up a cow in three months. But Clarence always found a farmer with a fresh cow for sale.

"About this time Mildred broke her arm and the doctor suggested she carry a bucket of rocks in order for the arm to heal properly. I was instructed to give her a ride to school each day on my bicycle. This embarrassed me to such an extent that I asked her to get off my handle bars a block or two from school. This allowed me to pick up my sweetheart, Margaret Brooks.

"Clarence and Nora occasionally played dominoes with other couples, sometimes away from home. Once I was told to baby-sit Mildred and little Polly. It grew dark and I became increasingly bored with the job. The girls were sitting on the living room floor, absorbed with cutting out paper dolls, when I sneaked outside, pulled a pillow case over my head and scratched on the window screen.

"I really wasn't prepared for my niece's screaming reaction. I had scared the living daylights out of them and, naturally, they couldn't wait to tell their daddy and mother."

But there was one bright spot to his continuing ordeal. "I was never asked to baby-sit again," said Toad.

And Wyatt was equally relieved.

Rule's Roaring '20s

"It would have been hard to find a better little town to grow up in during the late 1920s and early 1930s than Rule, Haskell County, Texas," said Margaret Brooks Holder in 2001 as she reflected on the town's version of the "in-crowd."

"If we were deprived of anything back then, we didn't know it and since we were all in the same circumstances, it didn't matter."

For a while, Rule's wide main street was shared by buggies and automobiles. By 1920 it was still a dirt thoroughfare, down the middle of which stood gas lights. Now, however, the street was used mostly by autos.

"The Depression was no deterrent to our having fun," Margaret Holder said. "Young people had to make their own entertainment but that posed no problem even if there were no club houses, no golf courses or tennis courts to play on, no TV to watch, and no radios to listen to.

"Most of us played basketball on a hard gravel court. If the rocks didn't get you, the stickers would. I remember Toad was quite a basketball player in high school. At least," she added, "when the 5-foot 6-inch dribbling ace filled the position of play-making guard. For some reason, he wanted to jump center," Holder said. "When Toad asked the coach how much taller he would have to be, coach thought a while and replied, 'At least a foot, Toad.' I don't recall it being mentioned again.

"We had no school cafeteria but most of us lived close enough to walk home and back in the lunch hour. And, of course, there was always the brown paper sack.

"I think Toad had the only bicycle in town. It was quite a treat for any of us girls to get pumped by him. The bike sure came in handy during lunch hour.

"Toad was our star baseball player. But if he ever missed a grounder, especially when the game was on the line, he would throw his new glove as far as it would go. The younger boys knew this and stood around waiting for Toad's tantrum to happen. They would actually fight over who got to keep Toad's leather glove. Most of them had what we called 'cotton picking gloves' stuffed with their mothers' kitchen hot pads. A leather glove like Toad's was a prized possession.

"Toad usually could wheedle one of his four older brothers into letting him use his car on Saturday night. There would always be six, maybe eight, high-schoolers ready to pile in. To drive around Rule was the highlight of the week. Sometimes we had enough gas and money to drive the twenty miles over to Stamford and have olive Cokes curb-serviced from the drug store. Boy! That was living!

"Then there was the picture show Toad's brother, Server, owned. We all tried to make the Saturday matinee. The girls stayed for the double feature if it was Mary Pickford or Shirley Temple, but the boys would only stay for the second show if it was a Tom Mix western. But whether we were all together for one feature or two, it was fully noted and passed around school the next Monday as to who sat by whom!

Ruby Smith (left) and Margaret Brooks Holder (right) share memories of Rule's Roaring Twenties with Toad on his eighty-eighth birthday in 1998.

"On Halloween we kids were really kept under surveillance, especially the boys, who seemed to take delight in pushing over out-houses. It wasn't difficult to guess which boys would pitch in for such mischief. Their families were the only ones who had out-houses left standing the next day.

"We thought it was great fun to swipe watermelons during summertime. The boys made quite a production out of who could find the largest one that was just ripe enough. We girls would stay in the car, scared to death and just knowing the boys were about to be caught.

"Later, all the fun was taken out of our escapades when we learned that most of the farmers knew the kids would be out to get melons. They would leave several large ripe ones near their fences, easy for us to find. I guess they were remembering when they were young and did the same thing. Anyway, those watermelons sure were good eating. Nothing seems to taste that good now. I wonder why?

"We didn't have football in Rule until Toad was off to school at Schreiner Institute. He would come home for some of the games though. He looked so dapper in his military uniform. We all thought he had it made.

"Most of the ol' gang are gone now," Margaret Holder concluded. "Those of us who are left probably celebrate happy hour with a nap, and burn the midnight oil until about 9 p.m. We learn to start the day off with a smile, just to get it over with.

"However, looking back to Haskell County seventy-five years ago, we thought the whole world revolved around Rule High School. And I'm not so sure it didn't."

Of course, Toad's reflections broaden when taken from the eyes of a prim young lass from Rule. Sometimes, when the older free spirits around Rule who craved a little action would schedule a cockfight, Toad and his pals would sniff out the plans and join the crowd. Usually these illicit duels to the death—at least for the roosters—were held among the cedar brakes along the Salt Fork of the Brazos River. Invariably, if the boys got wind of the cockfights, so did the law.

"We'd look up and see the sheriff's car bouncing along coming after us," he said with a chuckle. "It was a sight, all these men and some boys high-tailing it on foot in different directions with the deputies in hot pursuit." This despite a usually dry river bed famous for its many rattlesnakes which would hide among the breaks.

"About the only thing the Salt Fork was good for was having a cock fight," Toad said.

Schreiner's Bull Ring—1928

How Toad Leon, eighteen, wound up at Schreiner Military Institute in Kerrville, Texas the fall of 1928 takes some explaining. Perhaps someone saw in the dashing free spirit of Rule High School the settling in of a dangerous pattern during the 1926-27 school year. Life had turned into fun and games for Toad.

Shortly after his senior year in high school, but before Toad would walk the plank at Kerrville's Schreiner Institute or venture into an engineering degree plan that fell short, Toad got his first taste of Dallas. "I went there to spend the summer with my sister, Estelle, and her husband, Jack Jackson," Toad recalled. "But what I really wanted was a job. Actually a career. These two guys from Rule High I knew had told me Dallas was the place to find a job. They had been kicked out of high school for beating up the superintendent. But I didn't care. They were friends of mine.

"One of them had an uncle who was dispatcher for the Dallas transit system. Now there was a career, I figured. I could spend my life conducting on a streetcar, wearing that little bill cap and collecting money. I was ready."

*Cadet C. D. Leon,
Schreiner Military Institute, 1928*

Estelle wasn't though. Toad didn't get a job on the streetcars, and Estelle made sure his interests focused elsewhere. Jack, her husband, was dispatcher for the Dallas Fire Department, and Toad thought this was pretty neat too. Still, before fall he was back in Rule with his brothers trying to figure out how to keep their word to Mother Leon about Toad's education.

Martha Roundtree's success was measured by her ability to right the 5-foot 6-inch party boat that had become Toad Leon. How well she succeeded is still open to interpretation to this day. But for Toad her efforts in 1927 were a shock.

"Martha was my Spanish teacher at Rule High," Leon said. "I thought she might cut me some slack since she was my cousin. Also, she lived with us.

"It came time for our final exams, and I was having too much fun to prepare. The result was a dismal score of forty (out of a possible one hundred). So Martha proceeded to flunk me. Graduation ceremonies were held, and I was handed a blank diploma.

"Mother had stipulated in her will that I was to go to school. My older brothers decided a regulated military environment would benefit my education. So my brothers had me enrolled."

"Not only was I the fourth man in the rear rank of the squad, meaning I was lowest man on the totem pole, but also my weekly allowance was only three dollars, which wouldn't quite cover expenses."

By now, Toad had established an affection for various games of chance, so he figured poker and dice would help supplement the meager stipend his brothers had established. Toad's best friend from Rule had been Waddie Hill. "He taught me what I figured was all I needed to know about shooting craps, and even gave me lessons in how to false-cut cards." Sure enough, Toad was caught shooting dice during the first week at the institute. "My penalty was two weeks restricted to campus, and twenty demerits. For each demerit, one was required to walk five miles around what they called the Bull Ring.

Toad had not learned the lesson in life that Martha Roundtree had attempted to teach him. Foster L. Jones, son of the wealthiest man in Haskell County, had been going to Schreiner Military Institute in Kerrville since the fifth grade. Foster Jones by now was a cadet major. Once again I thought Foster might cut me some slack. Foster not only didn't help me out any. He made an example out of me. So much for slight edges."

It was enough to make Wyatt urp.

"About halfway through working off those demerits, someone suggested that instead of Sunday church services, we go see 'Dr. Woods'. Going to see 'Dr. Woods' was unofficial code for slipping down to the Guadalupe River and playing poker."

Somebody squealed. The card players were caught, and Toad latched on to thirty more demerits. Only once during that demerit-scarred school year was Toad permitted to venture off campus and go down town. But the operational word here is "permitted."

"My other experiences in Kerrville were limited to drinking beer in

Mexican town after 'lights out' had been ordered. From our dorm room on the second floor, my roommate, Jax M. Cowden Jr., and I could shinny down a rope ladder tied to the radiator.

"Once Jax hired a taxi so he could go home to San Angelo to see his girlfriend. We stuffed his bed and I hollered 'All in!' that night during at inspection." However, Jax's romantic interlude didn't last just the night. He wasn't back on campus by breakfast, nor lunchtime either. His absence was duly noted, along with the fact that young Mr. Cowden had been assisted in his escapade by young Mr. Leon. Back in the late 1920s, most of Schreiner's cadets were working their way through school. "If Jax and I hadn't both been full-pay students, they would have kicked us out," Toad admitted.

"At any rate, I did actually graduate that time, even though my family didn't let me send out any graduation notices—again!

"Along the way during my nine months at Schreiner, including other more minor infractions, I figure I walked more than 350 miles around the bull ring. I can't be sure, but I may hold some sort of record at Schreiner Military Institute for walking off the most demerits in a single school year."

Toad's sister, Estelle, left, her daughter, Sibyl, and her husband, Lester (Jack) Jackson in December, 1944, during a Leon Family Reunion.

Artie's Car—1931

As the Great Depression settled in on parched West Texas, Toad returned to Rule from his Schreiner Institute days in Kerrville. By 1931, the brothers had passed Toad around some. "I lived with Clarence a while, then Server a while. Now they said it was Carroll's turn," he said. Carroll and his wife, Artie, lived in Rule, where they had the Magnolia Gasoline agency.

"Two of my best friends, E.B. Wharton and Waddie Hill, approached me during the holiday season," Toad said. "They wanted to get dates and go to the big Christmas dance over in Seymour, almost 50 miles to the east."

"Do you think you can get a car?" one of them asked Toad.

"My mind began to explore the possibilities. Since our dates were real nice girls, we needed to borrow a real nice car. I zeroed in on Artie's brand new Chevrolet. It was a beautiful thing—jet black, with wire-spoke wheels and adorned with an abundance of chrome. The plan was executed. The six of us drove to Seymour in style. It was a festive occasion, and we danced the night away. A good time was had by all.

Pictured from left to right are Wilbur Leon, Barbara Leon, Carroll Leon (whose car was wrecked in this story!), Linda Leon, and Mrs. Artie Leon in 1944.

"About 1 a.m., we started for home. Since the girls hadn't joined us three guys in the partaking of a bit of bathtub gin, one of them asked if she could drive. I thought that was a fine idea. About 20 miles out of Seymour was the small community of Goree. The highway curved sharply as you pulled into town. Our driver somehow failed to negotiate the curve and ran off the road. The car bucked and bounced, and finally rolled over a couple times. There was momentary bedlam as the six of us careened around the inside the car. My brother Carroll carried a 36-inch cast-iron Stillson wrench on the floorboard. It whirled around and hit each of us a time or two. It was a real wild ride, but the results were only minor bumps and bruises. We caught a ride and got home about 2:30 a.m. I woke Carroll and gave him the bad news."

"Was anybody hurt" Carroll asked his kid brother.

"No."

"Where's Artie's car?"

"It's still back there in Goree. It won't move,"

"You and Waddie go back there and stay with that car," Carroll ordered. "Somebody is liable to strip it clean."

Waddie drove the two of them back to the scene of the accident in his little Ford. "It was freezing," Toad recalled. "We sat out there with Artie's car until morning. A nice couple down the road took pity on us and fed us breakfast."

The wreck didn't hurt anybody much, but none of the girls' parents was ever quite as friendly to poor ol' Toad. "Looking back, I think they had been led to believe that I had been driving," he said. "I had the car fixed, and life settled back to normal."

In the mean time Server beckoned Toad from nearby Haskell to run the town's bowling alley while Server continued to invest in the movie theater business around the area.

All's well that ends well, they say. Until the next bump in the road, that is.

Wyatt may have been wondering
if young Toad Leon was all bumps along about now.

Adios, Mother Earth

Fortunately for the C.D. Leon clan of the future, its patriarch did not establish a lifelong relationship with Lady Luck based upon their first serious fling. That was in August of 1931. Picture yourself just turning twenty-one. It is time to make your mark. You pick farming and enter into partnership with your older brother, Mike. You and he begin working a section of land twenty miles north of Lubbock. It's in the heart of the fertile South Plains—fertile when Mother Nature is in a good mood, that is.

This particular year, she wasn't. In fact, as bad luck would have it she was embarking on the worst period the area has known, before or since. The great drought that led to the infamous Dust Bowl had just begun. Still, the two Leon brothers had the makings of what probably would be the last decent crop

Toad's brother, Mike, and his wife, Morea, 1940s

for a while. But for Toad Leon it made no difference. He had tried farming and farming just wasn't going to work for him.

"Listen, Mike, this is not for me," he told his brother. "You take my share of the crop, whatever you can make this year. I'm leaving."

According to Virginia L. Barnhart, Toad's niece (the daughter of Clarence Leon), Mike gave only a half-hearted argument to his young brother's decision. While Mike really liked working the land it was obvious that Toad was no farmer. Nor would he ever be. Mike figured he might be able to eke out a crop this year even without Toad. Hell, for that matter, he might be able to do better without his little brother.

"Well, Toad, a man's gotta do what he's gotta do," Mike said. "Where are you going?"

"Dunno. Haven't really thought about it. Maybe Rotan, for the time being." Toad had helped another brother, Clarence Leon, run his ice business there a while back.

Toad hurriedly packed his gear in his balky Model T Ford. For once he didn't mind having to jack the damn wheels up so when he cranked it the car would start. Toad didn't mind because he was about to put Lubbock, Texas, in his rear view mirror; just like songwriter Mac Davis would do 30 years later.

As the sun began to set, "Off he sped down the dirt road, spraying a cloud of red dust behind," Virginia Barnhart would write in late 2000, shortly before her death. "He nearly made it to Slaton, 15 miles southeast of Lubbock, when, with a loud bang and a swerve, the car experienced a blowout.

"Not having a spare," Barnhart continued, "he doggedly chugged ahead because he was afraid that unless he kept his Model T pointed southeast, he might be tempted to return to the farm. On three tires and a rim the remaining 120 miles to Rotan were a slow go. The night was pitch black. The threat of another blowout loomed. The road was long and lonely. The only living things around seemed to be the howling coyotes.

"Toad pulled up to Clarence's house at 7 a.m., as his brother was stepping outside to check on what that loud crunching and clanking from the just-arriving Model T was all about."

"Toad? That you? What're you doing here?"

"I gave Mike my half of the crop and promised the Good Lord I'd never hit Mother Earth another lick!" Toad replied.

"Well, get your stuff out of the car and come on in. Nora'll fix you some breakfast. After you get cleaned up, come on down to the ice plant. I'll see what I can find for you to do" So Toad began his second stint of delivering ice for his brother, piloting a horse-drawn wagon on home deliveries in and around Rotan. Still, for Toad sitting up there behind Dick the wonder horse, was a heap better than hoeing cotton that was coughing and gagging for life in topsoil that soon would be hitching a ride on hot, dry winds headed for Old Mexico.

The Ice Business—1932

By the mid-1920s some of the Leon boys were cornering the ice plant market in rural West Texas from Rule on west for 50 or so miles. Many folks in the rural areas didn't have electricity, but they all had ice boxes. Slip a fifty-pound chunk into the well-insulated enclosures and you could keep your perishables cool for a week. You could even chip off a piece or two for some good old ice tea during summertime.

Clarence Leon gave his youngest brother, Toad, his first meaningful business experience in 1932 selling ice in Rotan, Texas. Clarence is pictured with his wife, Nora, (center) and daughters Polly (left) and Virginia (right) in 1944.

But times, they were a changin', two decades before Bob Dylan was even born to chronicle them in song. "My oldest brother, Clarence, had a thriving ice plant business at Rotan," Toad Leon said. "But by 1932 electricity was spreading to the hinterlands and with it came new household appliances.

Enter Frigidaire refrigerators and the monopoly West Texas Utilities Company enjoyed. "WTU began offering Frigidaires as replacements for the old-fashioned ice boxes. A substantial sales force was sent to blitz Rotan and surrounding communities touting the merits of owning one of the new electric driven refrigerators," Toad said.

Clarence Leon had seen the handwriting on the wall. "To head them off for a year or two, Clarence offered 'ice contracts' to his customers. This allowed them to receive their regular ice deliveries for twelve months for $25. Of course, those who signed up wouldn't need a new refrigerator for at least a year." Clarence didn't stop there. Peach and apricot orchards were found on many farms. The trees did fine. Their fruit often didn't; however, due to late freezes or killing frosts.

"He convinced a lot of them to sink a 100-pound block of ice at the base of each tree, in order to postpone spring bud blooms. Clarence was an innovator and a man of various interests. From retail to service to ranching and farming. That season he had contracted with several farmers to custom-combine their wheat," Toad continued.

"During harvest I managed the ice plant along with his right-hand man, Jim Kelly. He was a black man with numerous talents, from making ice to making home brew. Jim had been a loyal friend of the Leon family for many years. He was a hard worker who expected the same from his workmates," Toad said.

"If you wants to be successful, Mr. Toad you must s-t-a-a-a-y on the job," was a little ditty he sang to his young co-manager as they pulled blocks of ice. "Once Jim was arrested for bootlegging and was sent to prison at Huntsville for two years," Toad said. "he worked on the state-run farm during his stint. He was in charge of the horses and mules.

"One cold mornin', dem mules wouldn't take to th' bridle," Kelly told Toad one time when they were working with their own delivery animals. "Dey jus' turn and kick at me. Den along come th' boss man. 'Jim, can't you bridle dem mules?' he say. No, suh, I cain't. 'Jim, gimmie that bridle and I'll show you how to do it,' Boss man say."

"So, Mistuh Toad,, he took that bridle and whumped me up side of my haid with it! And guess what? I done bridled dem mules after that."

Toad was in charge of home delivery routes in and around Rotan. He worked them six days a week. "If our customers needed ice they would put a card in their front window, denoting whether they required a twenty-five-pound block or a fifty-pound block. My wagon horse was a big dappled-gray Belgian named Dick. He was one of the smartest horses I have ever known, and I've been around a few, believe me. I tell the story about how Dick would look over the houses as we rode up to them. If there was a card in the window, he would stop the wagon."

Hummm!? One wonders if that tale
just might make Wyatt urp.

"Well...this could be stretching it just a bit," Toad conceded.

There's No Business Like Show Business

The year 1932 was pivotal for not only the country, but also for Toad Leon. Franklin D. Roosevelt was elected to hopefully lead the U.S. out of the Great Depression. And Toad was still looking for his niche in the business world. He was about to find it, working with his third older brother in just two years, but first there was some business to take care of back in Rule.

His mother, Margaret Ann Server Leon, had died four years earlier. The four older Leon brothers had received their share of the family inheritance, and put it to work. "My Daddy had an estate worth in excess of $100,000 when he died in 1924," Toad would say seventy-seven years later. "That wasn't bad for a Spaniard who came to the U.S. from Mexico as an orphaned baby with nothing. He had little more than that when he took his young and still growing family to Rule. Daddy raised cotton at five cents a pound with back-breaking work and built an estate that today would be worth millions," Toad was proud of saying.

But Toad's share and the shares of his two older sisters, Estelle and Mattie Lee, were still held in trust. Together, they owned three buildings in Rule, plus a section of farmland. "Ready to spread his wings, Toad urged division and the older siblings, the trustees, agreed," wrote Virginia L. Barnhart in the year 2000.

"We flipped a coin to see who would get which building," Toad recalled. He sold his to a grocer for $1,500. With the sisters agreeing, the 640 acres of land were sold for $35 per, "not a bad price in 1932."

"Toad now had a nest egg of $8,600, which he carefully hoarded," Barnhart wrote. "Having had his fill of dry land cotton farming in the Dust Bowl, and then hauling ice on his back, Toad accepted brother Server's offer of employment at Server's movie theater in Sweetwater about 40 miles west of Abilene. His pay was $5 a week, and room and board.

"They ran the theater for a year. Server sold it to Robb and Rowley Theaters, took the money and bought two theaters in Haskell, about 10 miles from their hometown of Rule.

"As part of the deal, Toad wound up with a Baby Austin automobile that Server had won in a poker game," Barnhart continued. "He gave up his Model T without regret, and moved with Server to Haskell."

Server, ever on the lookout for a deal—a trait Toad obviously would court with lifelong passion—bought a bowling alley in Haskell. Toad was just the man to run this hot new fad.

"Conscious of the need to whip up interest in his new enterprise, Toad hired a boy to set pins and scheduled a series of bowling contests," Barnhart wrote. He would act as the challenger, and would take on anyone ready to show how good he was at the sport. Challenges always drew a crowd, especially if somebody stood to win a buck or two. And the more people who came to kibitz, Toad figured, the more who'd come back later and learn the game. Besides, he didn't lose as often as one might suspect.

Toad wouldn't swear that the pin setter didn't kick over a few pins in his boss' favor—accidentally of course. So Toad made a little money and bought the bowling alley in Rotan. Soon, he moved it to Rule.

"These were hungry, ambitious young men," wrote Virginia Barnhart. "Server was in his mid-30s and Toad, in his early 20s. Server was married and had a young daughter. He was full of ideas and drive. Server had a major resource in his youngest brother, who was single, free, mobile and raring to go.

"The early '30s were tough years in Texas," Barnhart continued. "The Dust Bowl was ravaging the northern part of the state, the Depression was in full swing, a buck was very difficult to come by, the veterans of World War I had marched on Washington as Cox's Army, and Roosevelt had just been elected. It was not a time for the faint of heart.

"Together Server and Toad had guts and drive and a little money. Server had a progressive attitude. He was looking to the future and investing in it. Toad was still tentatively feeling his way, holding on to his inheritance while working for and learning from Server."

By now, Server Leon was convinced that moving pictures that talked had a real future. He eyed Moran, a tiny ranching community between Albany and Cisco. At Server's urging Toad sold his bowling alleys and moved to Moran to organize the opening. He was excited to have an operating interest in this new venture.

"Cannily, he found second hand theater seats and a used projector," Barnhart wrote. "Toad rented an old building and splash-painted the walls himself. Always conscious of the need to make an impact, he bought a new white suit, a convertible and a megaphone. He drove all over Moran and its surrounding area advertising the 'Grand Opening' of the new theater."

Opening night featured the film "We're Not Dressing," a musical comedy starring Bing Crosby, Carole Lombard and Ethel Merman. "What a sight Toad must have been, this handsome young man in his snazzy white suit and splashy convertible!" Virginia Barnhart wrote.

Everything was geared up for success. Ideas on how to promote the venture were flowing. The Leon Brothers had a monopoly. And townspeople had pledged support for their very own picture show. Alas, the latter ingredient to this recipe for success dried up quickly.

"Bank night had proved to be the making of many small town theaters," Barnhart wrote. "The holder of the winning ticket won $25 if he or she was

Server Leon with daughter, Madge (left) and wife, Jerene in 1944

present at the drawing. If not, the bankroll was carried forward and added to next week's total."

Toad got ready for a sellout the first night he "banked" in Moran. He was at the theater early, ready to welcome the crowd, sell tickets, and run the projector. And not a single Moranite or Moraner or whatever people in the town that today has all but disappeared called themselves, showed up. For all these years since 1933, Toad has refrained from referring to them Morons. But just barely.

Devastated, he called Server, who was never slow to make a decision. Server told him to move Bank Night to Saturday, close up, cheer up, and come back to Haskell to help run the two theaters there. He could drive to Moran on Saturdays until that operation could quickly be sold.

Toad wound up making not one nickel from his hard work and grandiose plans in Moran.

> *It would've been enough to make Wyatt urp, if not for the fact that things were about to look way up for Leon Theaters.*

Also, the major turning point in Toad's life was about to occur. Ironically, it would happen just over the hill a few miles west of Moran.

The Life and Death of John Dillinger—1934

People were scrambling in early 1934 to survive the nation's Great Depression and West Texas' horrible Dust Bowl. The Leon Brothers were out there scrambling too.

This was the era of America's notorious bank robbers. Bonnie Parker and Clyde Barrow, Pretty Boy Floyd and, of course, John Dillinger vied for the dubious distinction of becoming the FBI's Public Enemy No. 1.

Dillinger had terrorized banks in Indiana, Illinois, and Ohio before being betrayed by his "woman in red." She helped the FBI set up an ambush on the streets of Chicago. Dillinger was gunned down by agents as he left a movie theater. Server Leon somehow had landed distribution rights from a film company to "road-show" a two-reel short subject called, "The Life and Death of John Dillinger." Not only could he show it in Leon Theaters. He could hire it out to other venues. Server was assigned the area in Texas between U.S. Highway 80 and the Red River,

"Server booked it in various theaters around, and I was chosen to be the 'ballyhoo' man," Toad Leon recalled. "An artist dressed up the side panels of our Model A pickup with depictions of John Dillinger robbing banks and his bloody body lying dead on a slab. Back then this was powerful advertising.   "My job was to drive around the selected town a day or two before the film was to be shown in order to drum up business. My first assignment was in Lubbock, Texas. The beginning of the film, about the life of John Dillinger, had arrived in Haskell. Now we waited for the second half, dealing with the gangster's death, to show up.

"The film company promised us that the second half was in the mail and would arrive 'any day now.' But time was running out. Server had already booked both halves with the owner of the Lyric Theater in Lubbock for the coming Friday and Saturday."

Server instructed his younger brother to take the first half of the film on to Lubbock. "I'll mail the last half to you. When you get it, just splice the two reels together. Everything will be fine. You'll see." Server promised.

"So I was sent ahead with only half a movie," Toad said. "In between my 'ballyhooing' runs, I'd go back and forth to the Lubbock post office. But no film package arrived.

"I was frantic. I called Server and told him I couldn't bring myself to admit my predicament to the Lyric's manager. He was a big, redheaded, short-tempered man and I knew he wouldn't be pleased. And that's an understatement, believe me."

Friday night rolled around and still no last half to the film. Toad wanted to disappear, but Server remained confident—safely back in Haskell, almost 100 miles away. While the younger Leon feared for his scalp, Server wanted his presence for the showings. "We get fifty percent of the gate, so you be sure and catch the tickets both nights," he told Toad. "You know how those picture show people are," was Server's parting shot.

Friday came and the Lyric was sold out. People were standing in line to see "John Dillinger"—his life and his death.

However, opening night came and went with only the life of the gangster portrayed on screen. The story simply came to an abrupt and obviously incomplete end.

"You can imagine the disappointment of the crowd and the fury of the manager," Toad said. "He ranted and he raved, but he didn't whip me, even though I knew he had considered it."

And Wyatt cringed.

However, things looked brighter Saturday. The U.S. Mail finally delivered the missing reel. Toad spliced the two halves together, and another sold-out audience gobbled it up.

The Love of His Life

By 1934, Leon Theaters so far had survived the Depression and managed to grow. The company owned by Server Leon was positioned to make profitable moves, especially in small towns. Despite his disappointment at Moran, Toad Leon figured he had found his calling as Server's right-hand man.

Server was thinking expansion. Baird, Texas looked appealing to him. It was a railroad "turn-around" town, with plenty of Texas & Pacific workers over-nighting there. Others were permanent residents. Baird was a good twenty miles east of downtown Abilene, which had become a bastion of Interstate Theaters' venues. Although permanent Baird residents were

The Plaza Theater in Baird, Texas, 1936

not unlike those mostly ranching folk in Moran, less than twenty miles to the northeast, there were more of them. And contrary to Moran's rather remote location, busy U.S. Highway 80 ran right through the heart of Baird.

So that little West Texas town became the expansion target and Toad was excited. For the first time, he was ready to invest his own money in partnership with his brother.

"We moved our equipment from Moran to Baird," Toad recalled. "Mike Segal was still showing silent pictures there so we were able to give Baird a new deal on picture shows. When I first got there we started our Bank Night which we held each Tuesday night. I walked every street in town, first one side and then the other, selling special bank night tickets."

Toad gave the T&P turn-around people a special break. They could buy a ticket to the movie even though they might be overnighting in Fort Worth or Big Spring the coming Tuesday. He'd hold their stubs and if they won they'd get the money when they returned to Baird. You might have called it the Toad Leon Raffle, or the Leon Brothers' Lottery. What made our Bank Night so successful—it didn't cost us a dime."

He sold five merchants co-sponsor space for $5 each. "We bought a building that had begun as a theater from Mayor Swartz. He later put in a haberdashery there. While we were remodeling we found 25 brand new pairs of ladies' high buckle shoes in the attic. We advertised giving away those, too, by drawings. It was the keenest thing I ever did. We made 25 ladies very happy by giving away those shoes."

He didn't know it, but the best was yet to come. Baird would be where Toad would find a princess who would turn his life into romantic royalty. "He moved to Baird full of spit and vinegar and, with energy and ambition, opened their new movie house," remembered Virginia L. Barnhart, Toad's niece, in the year 2000.

From the beginning, the theater was a success. Toad was comfortable with exhibiting films. He had decided that this was his kind of business. "It challenged his sense of creativity and showmanship, and provided an avenue for his considerable management skills," Barnhart wrote.

It was late summer in 1935 when Toad was changing posters at the front of the theater. A pretty young lady and her friend rode by on their bicycles. Toad did a double take. Beyond a doubt, the petite blonde with dancing blue eyes was the prettiest female Toad Leon had ever seen.He was smitten on the spot. Quickly engaging them in conversation, he discovered that the one who had caught his eye was Donna McGowen. She had graduated the previous spring from Simmons College in Abilene, and had just returned home after spending the summer in Denver, Colorado. That explained why he hadn't met this Baird beauty before.

In short order, Toad asked Donna for a date. She accepted. Six months later, they were married.

Donna's father, Harvey Carroll (Boy) McGowen and his brother, John, co-owned the prospering McGowen Brothers Grocery Store. Just six months after the wedding, Donna's father passed away. And only four months after that, John died.

"Toad and John McGowen's son-in-law, W.O. Wylie, bought the grocery store and Toad undertook the management of that business in addition to the theater," Barnhart wrote. "These were totally different enterprises, each requiring a very different management style. Toad now found he was working from dawn until the last movie ended near midnight."

The biggest adjustment was in tallying receipts. Toad was accustomed to the daily cash flow of the movie business. He quickly learned that credit was the name of the game in groceries—at least back in the cash-strapped 1930s. With Baird being a railroad town, Toad was obliged to give grocery credit to T&P employees. They were extended up to $30 a month, payable every month on payday.

The adjustment for dealing with farmers and ranchers was even more extreme. Many of them didn't have monthly paychecks. Some got paid only once a year, when their crops came in or their calves sold. By 1936 the Dust Bowl was still blowing much of the area away and the Depression was far from over.

Toad decided his funds were too limited to underwrite yearly credit tabs so he sold his interest in the grocery business. With those proceeds Toad became a full partner in Leon Theaters. He and Server looked to further expansion. Their company was off and running. And best of all, Toad was a very, very happy married man.

Baird had been good to him.

And Wyatt smiled.

The Belle of the Ball—1935

Donna McGowen, School Beauty, 1933 Simmons College yearbook

On July Fourth Donna Leon was introduced to Toad's kin and friends from the old hometown who hadn't made it to their wedding in Baird a month earlier. The occasion was the annual Texas Cowboy Reunion Rodeo in Stamford, about thirty-five miles north of Abilene and about the same distance south of Rule. Clearly, the diminutive beauty was the belle of the

Reunion Ball. Gov. Jimmy Allred would be there. So would socialites and ranch people from all over West Texas.

Toad, twenty-five at the time, had always seemed ready to dance the nights away throughout the region, though his dancing escapades were not without pitfalls. When he lived in Rule he wrecked his sister-in-law's car on a trip to Seymour for a holiday season dance. When he first got to Baird, before he met the lovely Donna, he had taken a young lady 60 miles to a dance in Rotan.

"I was in my little convertible. Boy, I loved that car! We had no sooner arrived in Rotan when this guy backed out and hit me. I tried to get my car re-started, but it wouldn't go. My brother, Clarence, lived in Rotan. I called him and he loaned me his car until mine could be fixed. I found out later that my date didn't have too good a reputation in Baird, something Donna quizzed me about when we started going out together."

Toad had even suffered a mishap in Stamford shortly after going to work in the theater business for his brother, Server. "He had this panel truck. We'd put posters from the movie we were showing at the time on the sides, and I'd drive up and down the streets of nearby towns. I was out at Stamford Country Club for some reason one night. I remember the name of the film we were showing, whose posters I had on the truck, was 'Flying Down to Rio' starring Delores Del Rio. Anyway, I missed a turn and drove the truck into a lake on the golf course. I don't know why things like that always happened to me."

But that July Fourth evening all went well. People from Haskell, Rule, and thereabouts delighted in confronting Toad's bride with, "My gosh! You married him?"

Then they'd gleefully step over to Toad and ask, "You mean, she married you?"

Finally, Gov. Allred arrived, signaling the start of the dance. Most people there figured he would ask one of the beautiful Seale girls, authentic cowgirls from Baird, to be his first dance. But the governor looked around the hall, spied Donna, walked over, smiled, and held out his hand to her.

Toad was not surprised.

Nor was Wyatt.

Good Times in Graham—1937

Expansion! That's what appealed to the new partnership in Leon Theaters. If one looked hard enough, he could envision that—like the man, or not—FDR may be right in proclaiming, "Happy Days are Here Again." If not yet accomplished at least the end to the Great Depression now was more than a distant hope.

"I was operating the theater in Baird, Texas, when my brother Server came to visit," Toad Leon recalled. Server talked about the oil town of Graham, some seventy miles northeast of Baird, as being a prime target for picture show expansion.

"There were already two theaters in town," Toad explained. "But on the west side of the square, between the two existing theaters, was a vacant store. We made a deal to buy the building. It would be up to us to remodel it."

Toad and Server were about to bump heads with local politics and the good ol' boy game played by its practitioners.

"In visiting with Mack Williams, a good friend of mine and a close friend of the mayor, I learned that Mr. Larmour, owner of one of the shows, was on the Graham city council. He had persuaded the council to pass a new ordinance that read, "No new theater is to be built in Graham, Texas, within 300 feet of any store selling liquor, lacquer, paints, or varnishes."

That pretty well boxed in the Leons' plans.

"Mack, what am I going to do?" Toad asked his pal.

"Toad, I'd go to City Hall and apply for a building permit anyway. After all, Graham is still in the United States of America," replied Williams.

Larmour and his friends at City Hall knew the ordinance couldn't stand so they didn't oppose the permit. Four months later the Leon Theater opened. "Back then, theater owners had yearly contracts with specific movie companies, in order to have access to their films," said Toad, who had moved to Graham with Donna and their infant daughter, Carol Ann, so he could manage the new Leon theater. "There were three companies that hadn't contracted with my competitors in Graham—Republic Pictures and Monogram, both who made westerns, and Universal Pictures. With these three companies we made a good showing on Fridays and Saturdays. The kids loved Gene Autry and Roy Rogers.

"Although we were limited on product throughout the rest of the week, we made up the difference by building false fronts on the theater, advertising extensively, and working very, very hard." They gave away dishes every Wednesday night. If a patron came often enough, he or she eventually would complete a set. Dining room furniture, living room sets, and even a car were given away.

"I had forgotten all this until recently," Toad said, from the living room of his large home overlooking the second hole at Fairway Oaks Country Club's golf course in Abilene. "While drinking coffee with my good friend, Irving Townsend, one morning at Fairway Oaks, he mentioned that his mother had won a car back in 1938 in Graham. I smiled. 'Know who gave your mother that car?' It really is a small world, sometimes."

Actually, the Leon brothers gave away three cars that year—one at Albany and one at Haskell, in addition to the one in Graham. "We made arrangements with the Chevrolet factory in Flint, Michigan, for us to get three cars. We paid $640 each for them and saved $75 by picking them up." Server, a driver, and Toad drove to Flint and towed the new cars back to be displayed in the three towns.

"We sold chances in books of five tickets." Toad recalled. "A book of five cost $1, or 20¢ a ticket to the movie. That saved a nickel over the regular price. I sold these up and down the street. I'd even match people double or nothing."

Depression-era movie prices were 25¢ for adults and 9¢ for children. "If you charged a dime or more, you created a federal tax. Not long ago one afternoon, I took Sandra and her daughter, Noel, to a film in Abilene. It cost us $4.50 each, and that was the matinee price. They bought the biggest popcorn, and I threw in a buck more for butter. Then cokes. By the time I left the theater, it had cost me $40 or so. And the movie wasn't very good either."

By now his personality and his patented toad-prince good looks were making him a well-known figure in West Texas. Their uniqueness soon would be underscored. "When Carol Ann was two, she and Donna were in a Graham dry goods store. 'I'm not sure who you are, but that has to be Toad Leon's daughter,' the owner told Donna. She looks just like him.'

"That same year," a proud Toad Leon continued, "Donna, her mother, Johnnie McGowen, and Carol Ann took a trip to California. On the way back, they stopped in a small cafe in Needles California for breakfast. To keep Carol Ann from getting down and running around, they sat on stools at the counter. The waitress kept looking at Carol Ann and wiping the counter. Looking and wiping. Finally she said, 'I'm from Texas. In fact, I used to live in Haskell. Actually, I know Toad Leon.' Small world again."

In Graham Donna sold tickets during matinees "while some of the best friends I ever made shot pool and played dominoes at the local pool hall," Toad said. "Donna didn't like this very much. I had to persuade her that since we were new in town, I needed to meet influential people. She never was convinced."

It was in Graham that Toad Leon's love of the outdoors was rekindled and that set in motion his lifelong passion for hunting. "The fall of 1937 rolled around and it was duck season," he recalled. "My friend, Claude Kennedy, had the tailor shop next to our theater. He asked me if I'd like to go hunting the next morning. I had a shotgun and thought that was a good idea. We got up early, while it was still dark, and drove to the lake. We could hear the ducks quacking. We got on our hands and knees and crawled very carefully toward the sound. Every so often we raised up to look. Finally we saw the pretty little quackers bobbing in the water. 'This is close enough,' I said. 'Let's shoot! ' So we let them have it. Suddenly, another hunter stood up. 'Hey! Those are my decoys you boys are sinking!'"

"Another new business venture making the rounds in those days was miniature golf," Toad said "There was a large vacant warehouse on the south side of the square. I had the brilliant idea of introducing 'indoor miniature golf' to the world. Weather wouldn't affect it. We could run it twelve months a year. The warehouse had a concrete floor, so we built runways with 1x4s. We packed them down with cottonseed hulls, which actually made a fairly decent putting surface."

The concept was born and died in Graham. "Looking back, I doubt if it made any money," Toad said. "But it operated a year or two. And I was gaining more experience."

The C.D. Leon family closed out the '30s in Graham and it turned out to be a profitable year as well as an enjoyable milestone in Toad's career.

Now, he and his brother were ready for the big time.

Next was Amarillo,
and Wyatt was already shaking in his boots.

The Western Chase—1939

The Leon clan is famous for its trips. They often took them in tandem or in some form of a group outing. One of these occurred in 1939, when "the country was still gripped in the jaws of the Depression, and war clouds were gathering over Europe," as Toad Leon's niece, Virginia Leon Barnhart, said in recounting the adventure. Her recollection follows:

"Clarence, my father, and Toad were the oldest and youngest of seven children. They had prospered, Clarence with his ice plants in West Texas and Toad with the string of movie houses he and my uncle, Server Leon, owned. Both Clarence and Toad had new cars. They decided this might be a good time to make their long-dreamed-of trip to the West Coast and on up to Canada. En route, they would take in the World's Fair being held in San Francisco.

Clarence gathered up Nora, my mother, and their two younger daughters, Polly, seventeen, and me. Toad loaded up Donna, Carol Ann, three, and Donna's mother, Johnnie McGowen. In only three days after the brothers had hatched the plan, we were packed and ready to go.

Logic demanded that we go to California first, and add Aunt Jerene, her daughter Madge, my oldest sister, Mildred, and a third car to our entourage. All three Leon kin had spent the summer in school at UCLA.

We raced to the Grand Canyon and then continued across the desert with wet cup towels hung in the open windows and pans of ice at our feet in fruitless efforts to moderate the intense heat. We indulged ourselves every night in the marveled convenience of the newly developed motor hotels someone had begun calling 'motels.' Mother preferred those with neat little separate cottages. These were much too subdued for my eight-year-old tastes. I liked the converted train cars and the carefully decorated cement teepees.

After a couple of days in Los Angeles we took Highway 1 heading north. That afternoon we stopped for a leisurely picnic, after which Toad and Clarence decided to get a couple beers from one of the cars' trunk. 'I'll go ahead and you can catch up,' Mildred told the brothers, who seemed to be rearranging the trunk but obviously were popping the caps on more beer. Soon, however, we were on our way again.

Mildred had driven off with Jerene and Madge. Daddy was leading Toad's car. He drove at a leisurely pace for a while, but the black Ford did not appear ahead. He sped up more to his usual illegal speed, but still no Mildred and Company in sight.

'Where the hell are they?' he growled. 'I didn't think Mildred would drive this fast.' I stood in the back seat behind his right shoulder watching as the speedometer climbed to seventy-five, then eighty, then to eighty-five. It was now growing dark. Daddy kept up a running commentary on the impossibility of Jerene's car outrunning us, frequently asking mother if she could see Toad in the rearview mirror. She couldn't.

By now, the picnic was a distant memory. I'm afraid I was whining a bit about being hungry. Using this as an excuse, though in truth his ulcer probably was acting up, Daddy said, 'Now, Nora, there's a town up ahead. I'll take Jinny in and get us both some milk. You watch out for Toad and stop him when he gets here.'

Mother agreed. So when we got to a small grocery store, Daddy jumped out, grabbed my hand, and we rushed in to get milk and cookies. We were back in no time.

'Where's Toad? Did you see him?' Daddy wanted to know.

'Well-l-l, Clarence…I'm not sure,' Mother replied.

'What do you mean, you're not sure! Did you see him, or not?'

'Well, a sort of yellow streak went by, but I don't know if it was Toad.'

Daddy threw the car in gear and we took off, scattering gravel in our wake. We were now swerving around Highway 1, with mountains rising to our immediate right and the Pacific Ocean, glistening in moonlight to our left, far below precipitous cliffs. I was still standing behind Daddy watching his every move and staring with muted horror as the speedometer climbed. The headlights jerked from the mountains to the ocean.

75…'Clarence, slow down!…' 80…'Clarence, you're scaring the girls and me half to death!' 85… "Clarence, for heaven's sake!' I could feel and hear Polly beside me, clasping her hands and murmuring a prayer as the speedometer reached 90!

'CLARENCE!'

'Hell, Nora, now we've lost not only Mildred but Toad, too. Looks to me like you could've at least flagged him down.'

Our speed had topped out at ninety-three, but now had subsided to a less-harrowing eighty. And on we drove. Even Daddy didn't know exactly where we were but the time was approaching midnight. The lights of a town glowed ahead, and after a bit a flashing 'motel' sign. Our speed dropped off still more.

'Well, I don't know where the hell they are or whether Toad is ahead or behind, but I've had enough,' Daddy announced. 'I'm going to bed. Let THEM find ME for a change!' Now Mother was worried. She paced the room once we had piled in.

'Clarence, I don't know what to do. But we've got to find them!'

'Tell you what I'm going to do, Nora,' Daddy replied. 'I'm going to sleep.' He turned over and did just that.

After a few more turns around the room, Mother opened the door and went out into the night, disappearing in the direction of the motel office. When she returned, Polly asked, 'What did you do?'

'Well, I couldn't think what to do except call the highway patrol. I gave them the license numbers of the two cars. And I asked them to stop them if they saw the two cars and tell them where we are staying. They've probably already stopped Toad for speeding.'

Soon Polly and I fell asleep, lulled by Daddy's soft snoring. But we were awakened almost immediately, it seemed, by Toad and Daddy talking. Sure enough the police had stopped him about sixty miles up the road, and just as mother had hoped, directed him back to this obscure motel. They were still talking with some chagrin about Mildred outrunning them when we fell asleep again.

It was just growing light in the east when we awoke again, this time to the sound of a slammed door. It was my sister, Mildred, followed by Jerene and Madge. Never meek or retiring, she was nevertheless usually soft-spoken around Daddy. But now a stressed Mildred was backed up by her aunt and cousin and she was livid.

Toad and Donna, awakened by the raised voices next door, came in as the story unfolded.

A few miles up the road from the picnic site Mildred had found a shortcut. She had pulled into the side road to flag us down, but hardly had time to raise her hand when we whizzed past, followed by Toad. For the past twelve hours or so she had been trying to catch up with us.

The police had stopped her about three hours ago about a hundred miles back. Now, indignant and exhausted, she, Madge, and Jerene had finally caught up with us. The indignation and ire finally subsided into an uneasy silence as Daddy and Toad looked at each other shamefacedly with raised eyebrows. Then a giggle escaped Mother's carefully pursed lips and one by one, we were all overcome with laughter.

Soon, we resumed our trip north, up the California coast. Would our quest for a normal trip by the Leons be reinstated? Of course not! But that's another story.

NOTE: *In 1999, not long before her death, Virginia Barnhart said the story of the Great Western Chase had been told with glee at Leon gatherings hundreds of times during the previous sixty years, 'heard by aunts and uncles, then first and second cousins, both once and twice removed. Until my father's death in 1959,' she said, 'he still looked shamefaced at the telling.'*

Today, she said, her Uncle Toad bears the painful guilt alone.

Those Bloomin' Bloomers—1939

You'd think, after the hair-raising Great Western Chase of 1939, Clarence and Toad Leon and their families and in-laws would have it nice and easy the rest of the way. The Leons don't do routine.

It had been a long day's drive, but now the three-car Leon Caravan was en route home from the West Coast and Canada. They had come to rest outside Missoula, a smallish town of maybe 25,000 inhabitants in western Montana. That night's accommodations were three motel units constructed of railroad Pullman cars. "To my eight-year-old eyes, these were pretty classy," said Virginia, Clarence's youngest daughter, sixty years later.

They had eaten earlier at a restaurant on the road, so after checking in everyone had gone to their respective quarters and collapsed into bed; some with a book, others obviously intent on a good night's sleep. As Clarence dropped into bed he told his wife, Nora, that the car seemed to be pulling to the left. He thought the wheels needed realignment. He then promptly turned over and went to sleep not aware that Nora was busy with her own tasks and not paying particular attention to him.

"This was the time of day when Mother rearranged the luggage, straightened up the suitcases, and planned breakfast," Virginia recalled. "Having finished these domestic duties, she turned to the task of washing our underwear. Polly, 16, was expected to do her own each night but Mother still indulged me by washing mine along with hers.

"Finishing this small job, she looked around for a place to hang her bloomers. Hers modestly came down her legs and were elasticized just above her knees. Mine were a tiny size 8 panties. No suitable place came to her eyes, so she went outside the cabin, looking for a clothesline in the brightly moonlit night. Nothing. Then she spied the new Chrysler Daddy had bought for the trip. On the front chrome bumper were two short perpendicular decorative posts. She carefully hung her bloomers on one and my panties on the other, came back inside, and climbed gratefully into bed."

The next morning Clarence was up early and dressed before Nora stirred. He told her to sleep for another hour while he and Toad took this opportunity to run into town and get the wheels aligned. They drove around looking for the Chrysler dealership. Then they circled the court house square, peering down the side streets for the familiar auto emblem. Since it was about the time when most people came to work, there were many milling about. Clarence noticed that more than a few were looking at them, smiling and waving at the new car with the license plates from the Lone Star State.

"What a friendly town," Clarence told his younger brother. "I'll bet not many people from Texas get up this far north.'

Not spotting the Chrysler place they began a second circle of the square. By now lots of people were lined up at the curb pointing, smiling, and waving. Clarence and Toad, being friendly men, smiled and waved back.

"Good-humored too, for this early in the morning," Toad added.

At last, a couple blocks down a side street they spotted the Chrysler logo. As they turned through the wide double garage doors into the service area, a man wearing a big Stetson and driving a pickup was leaving. He glanced at their car, did a double-take, threw up his hands, and laughed. "Mister," he hollered out his window, "I've seen lots of flags in my life, but yours takes the cake."

"What the hell...?" Clarence jumped from the car and walked around to the front of it. There flapping gaily in the breeze hung Virginia's small panties on one post, and Nora's long bloomers on the other. Face flaming with embarrassment, Clarence grabbed the offending lingerie and threw them in the back seat. He gunned the car in reverse, exited the garage, and with a screech of tires beat a hasty retreat. His mood wasn't helped by his younger brother sitting beside him and convulsing with laughter.

Arriving back at the cabin, the still red-faced Clarence sought out Nora who was putting out the breakfast foods.

"Looks to me like you could've found somewhere else to hang your damn bloomers!" he barked.

As the rest of the family assembled and the story was retold even Clarence finally began to see the humor. Still, after the group had packed up and left the cabins, with Clarence leading the caravan, Toad couldn't help but notice that his brother drove 30 miles out of the way in order to avoid circling that court house square one more time.

The Fat Rats Rule Amarillo

By the late 1930s, the two Leon Brothers had developed the magic managerial touch with Server as head of the growing chain and Toad as second in command. Just as Baird and then Graham had become important places in the Leon Theaters' early history, Amarillo was no less significant The move into the hotly contested picture show competition in the Panhandle city came as World War II heated up for America.

Film fans flock to the Leon Theater in Amarillo in 1943 to see Jane Russell in "The Outlaw."

"Server came by one day and said, 'Why don't we go to Amarillo and see what we can find there?' So, in 1941, we leased a building in a choice location that took almost five months to remodel." The already established competitive edge belonged to Interstate Theaters. Toad was named manager of the new Leon Theater, and found that he would be second run. The others would get to show prime features such as "Casablanca" and "Mrs. Miniver" first, then pass it on down the pecking order. But with soldiers coming into town at all hours of the day and night, "we were able to do pretty damn good," Toad said.

He developed the marketing strategy that called for advertising slogans such as, "A picture is first run until you have seen it. We were open from

11 a.m. to 11:30 p.m., seven days a week, 365 days a year," he said. "That's how you did it back then."

Toad did a little bit of everything in addition to overseeing the operation. Donna sold tickets. Husband and wife often would see each other for the first time each day around midnight when they met in the projection booth with the day's receipts.

"One day, the fellow who owned the Star Theater came to us and wanted to know if we'd be interested in purchasing it. We were, and we did. Two or three weeks later the Rex Theater on West 6th Street became available. So we bought it, too."

Soon, Toad and Donna discovered they were going up against rats. Not in their competitors who, like it or not, had to make way for the Leons. These were real rats.

"It seemed like the whole city of Amarillo was infested with the things," Toad recalled. "These rats were as big as cats, with whiskers. They'd rummage for popcorn on the floors of our theaters late at night. You could look down at people watching the last show and they'd be lifting their feet up as these things ran down the aisles. Donna and I might be in the projection booth counting the day's take when she'd say, 'Toad, here they come!' You could actually hear the rats romping up the stairs. Donna would hop up on a desk while I took a broom and tried to sweep them back downstairs."

The rats knew a good thing all right. In late 1941 popcorn was added to the nation's growing list of shortages. But even that was turned into a marketing ploy. "Server had this farm south of Amarillo about 120 miles between Lubbock and Abernathy. He asked the guy he had farming it if he thought he could raise popcorn. 'We can try,' came the reply."

Well, it worked like a charm. The first crop wasn't of the bumper variety but it provided plenty for Amarillo's three Leon theaters and then some. While the price of popcorn rose and its availability declined, the Leons were able to advertise, "Come to a Leon Theater near you and try our home-grown popcorn!"

Toad found other ways to flex his marketing muscle. When he discovered that Milton Barker, one of the managers of his Amarillo venues, was adept as a cameraman, an idea was born. This was long before video cameras. Barker's expertise was in 16mm and 32mm film—the grind 'em out and edit 'em down variety. Toad green-lighted a motion picture laboratory and the purchase of new sound and film equipment. Barker put together a crew from among Leon employees in Amarillo and oversaw a local shooting schedule that called for 1,000 feet covering local events. Television hadn't even thought of this yet.

45

From the 1,000 feet per week came 600 feet of what Amarillo children and adults were up to in their town. These snippets would show on a rotating basis as short subjects at the three Leon theaters on Thursdays, Fridays and Saturdays.

It proved successful for almost a year and made headlines in the Amarillo newspaper.

While Toad, Donna, and their young daughter, Carol Ann, were in Amarillo, Toad was turned down for U.S. Army duty. So he joined the Home Guard. It was a civilian corps that trained regularly to be ready to protect women and children, were there to be an invasion or other war-related emergency. Training sessions were designed to be as realistic as possible.

"One night, I had just gotten home from the theater," Toad said. "It was about 1 a.m. when the phone rang."

"Private Leon?"

"Yes."

"Report to the water tank. It looks like they're attacking."

Toad, still in his business clothes, reported as ordered. Much like a regular army bivouac, the Home Guard unit was ordered to crawl up to the tower through underbrush caught in an early ice storm. "It cut my brand new leather shoes to pieces!" he said.

"At least we saved the water tower. Neither the Japs nor the Nazis ever attacked it while the Amarillo Home Guard was on guard," Toad used to like to brag.

After almost two years in Amarillo Server sent word to his younger brother. "I believe it's time you came into the Dallas office and learned the business from this end."

"At that time the speed limit was thirty-five mph. From Amarillo to Dallas took us two long, full days. I'll never forget. When we left, it was a cold, miserable day. We got from Amarillo to Claude, about twenty-five miles, and Donna and I were so cold both our hands and feet were aching. I pulled into a filling station and asked the guy to check my heater that didn't seem to be working. 'What you need is to put a sheet of cardboard in front of the radiator,' he said. Don't know how, but it worked."

Unknown to everyone except Server was that he was dying. He put Toad on a crash course for learning how to run the company, "And it was a good thing he did," Toad added.

The Great Peanut Caper of 1942

Toad strikes an innocent pose—about this time he and his partner/brother, Server Leon, were working on their secret project—a hot-peanut dispensing machine.

Whatever happens to those really great-sounding ideas that fizzle? Sometimes they seem to drift out in space, folded up in some sort of eternal, two-dimensional envelope, silently screaming to be let out again. Only no one hears. The Leon Brothers' great plan to corner the hot peanut market might be out there somewhere, just screaming to be heard one more time.

"We heard about this guy in Duncan, Oklahoma who had built a machine in his garage with pliers and a screwdriver that kept peanuts warm and dispensed them in a cup when you put a nickel in," Toad Leon said. "It was the cutest thing you ever saw." To Toad and his brother, Server, both now working their theater chain out of Dallas, this sounded like an idea that couldn't miss. Not only for their movie houses, but other theaters as well. And just think of owning the patent for such an invention, then putting them in bus stations, bowling alleys and on street corners across the U.S.!

They took the prototype model to Macknic Company, a manufacturer in Tulsa that made parking meters. Could they mass-produce the machines? Not in its Rube Goldberg style, the Leons were told. It had about 200 working parts and would be too expensive to duplicate. But the manufacturer could re-design the basics and come up with a streamlined model they could live with.

Hush-hush! Don't let the word out about our million-dollar deal. But did they have a lock on the idea? A juke box convention was due to be held in Chicago so Server and Toad made plans to attend to sort of look over the coin-operated machine industry, right in the heart of a city controlled by (gulp!) the MOB, which was infamous for moving in on fledgling loose-change industries. To their relief, the patent they had purchased from the guy in Duncan seemed to have a lock on hot peanuts.

So they called Tulsa and ordered a first batch of 10 machines to put out on a trial basis in and around Dallas. They bought several barrels of peanuts, and a new business lifted off.

In no time, the great peanut caper turned on "our boys" with a vengeance. "It was my job to service the machines," Toad said. "I'd get a call from a pool hall in Oak Cliff telling me to come out here quick. A guy put in a nickel and the machine wouldn't stop. They had peanuts all over the floor. Then I'd get a call from a bowling alley in North Dallas. Better come fast. This guy put in a nickel, didn't get any peanuts, and now he's trying to tear up the machine."

The Leon brothers called in their ten hot peanut dispensers and prepared to send them to Tulsa for re-tooling. But the World War II effort had put the company into making ammunition, so the ten peanut machines were stashed away. Where?—no one was able to find out. "They just disappeared," Toad said. "They'd have been a collector's item, if nothing else."

Yes, those hot peanuts made Wyatt urp, all right.

What I Learned in Dale Carnegie School—1943

The rough edges soon were coming off young Toad Leon after he moved from Amarillo and joined his older brother in the Leon Theaters' new home office in Dallas. Server decided it was time to put even more polish on his brother's skills. His own, too.

"About this time, a Dale Carnegie course, 'How to Win Friends and Influence People,' was being offered to the Dallas business community," Toad recalled. "It was geared primarily to sales personnel, so Server thought the course would be a good education for me, our office manager, and himself. Among other things, we learned how to remember people's names by the use of association. When you met someone, you were advised to think of something about them that would remind you of their name later on.

"A few months after completing the course, Donna and I took a trip to Colorado and New Mexico. We were accompanied by our good friends, Joe and Nell Jack. Nearing Santa Fe at noon, I asked, 'How does fried chicken sound? There is a wonderful place up Pecos Canyon called Arrowhead Lodge that serves great food.'"

"But Toad, they require reservations," Donna said.

"Aw, we know them well enough. I'm sure it'll be all right," Toad responded.

They were greeted warmly at the door. "Using my new Dale Carnegie 'association' technique, I made the introductions. 'Joe and Nell Jack, I would like you to meet the Arrowhead's owner and my good friend, Dave Fox.'"

The owner glared at Leon. "Toad, you S.O.B., my name is not Fox. It's Dave Wolf."

In spite of the faux pas, *one that surely would have made Wyatt urp*, Toad said the group was served a delicious meal.

Film Row—the 1940s

A two-block area in downtown Dallas was known as "Film Row" during the golden age of movies. The intersection of Harwood and Jackson streets was the heart of the movie community. Distributors, theater chains, film advertising and public relations firms, transporters, concessionaires and equipment dealers, were among those who serviced the film industry throughout the Southwest.

"It was not unlike a small West Texas town," Toad Leon recalled with a certain fondness. "We all knew each other on a first name basis, from secretaries and salesmen to top executives and owners. In short, Dallas was where the action was, in our business.

"As we accumulated more theaters, Server had known a move of our headquarters from Haskell to Dallas just made good business sense. So Leon Theaters went to Dallas in 1940 and established our home office on Film Row. We were at 200-1/2 Jackson Street. On the first floor was Republic Pictures. On the second floor were Isley Theaters, Colonel Cole who was head of Independent Theatre Owners of America, McLendon Theaters, and Leon Theaters.

"My brother Server was the deal-maker and I was the man in the field, moving from town to town for openings, revamping and establishing newly acquired movie houses. Ours was a partnership made in heaven! However, all good things come to an end," Toad Leon said, a somber tone to his voice. "Without telling me why, Server suggested I move my family from Amarillo to Dallas in 1943. He wanted me out there to learn the film buying and booking end of the business. In other words, his end.

"I was soon to learn that my brother's health was failing. Not yet fifty, he died in 1945, a victim of cancer. I have often said that Harry S. Truman's job after FDR died was not much more difficult than the one I faced. I was only thirty-five and had some really big boots to fill while a lot of people were depending on me.

"In addition to taking over the business, I was to be trustee and

Toad (front row, third from left) and his theater managers at the grand opening of a Leon theater in Slaton, Texas.

administrator of Server's estate for the next ten years. That in itself was a considerable responsibility. I was in a unique situation. For one thing, I had advice coming at me from all sides. Some were of the opinion that I should let more experienced people take over Leon theaters."

In fact, Server had warned his kid brother that this would be the case shortly before he died. "Toad, you will get plenty of advice. Just consider the source each time and remember that some of it will be self-serving."

"I was just hard-headed enough to think I could continue the operation as Server had taught me," Toad said. "Jerene, Server's widow, couldn't have been nicer and more supportive. Her never-wavering faith in my ability was a mainstay."

The first hurdle in the upheaval, Toad figured, was to travel to theaters in the Leon chain and meet with their managers, all of whom had been hired by Server. "Most were older than I, and some had doubts about whether a young man my age could capably run such a far-flung operation," Toad said. "At this time, we had twenty movie houses from East Texas to Amarillo to El Paso to Brownsville. But things smoothed out in a short while. Most of the managers stayed with me, some for many years."

One of the benefits of being on film row was staying in close contact with booking agents. This enabled Leon Theaters, known for its preponderance of small-town houses, to bring stars such as Roy Rogers, Gene Autry, Tex Ritter, and Monte Hale to their stages as live acts. This thrilled people in those tiny Texas towns.

1948 Film Convention, Adolphus Hotel, Dallas. Dale Evans, Toad Leon, Donna Leon, Roy Rogers.

"Lots of information was passed around in the local café on Film Row," Toad said. "After five p.m. each weekday we gathered and discussed the current events over a beer. It was here that one was apprised of who was in town, who had theaters for sale, who wanted to buy a theater or theaters, how a particular movie was grossing and so forth.

"In fact, it was while I was in the café one evening that, sight unseen, I bought two theaters in Slaton from Hershel Crawford. A few weeks later I drove to Slaton, about fifteen miles southeast of Lubbock, to see what I had purchased.

"What I found were two rundown movie houses in dire need of renovation. It seems the city fathers of Slaton had urged Hershel to upgrade and improve his theaters. Having no luck some of them decided to go in together and build a new one themselves. As I drove into town I saw there a pile of bricks on the town square, ready for construction to begin.

"Now, Slaton was a good town, but I didn't think it was large enough to support three picture shows. I met with the city fathers and assured them that a major overhaul of the buildings I now owned was a high priority. Slaton soon would have theaters of which townspeople could be proud. In the mean time, I had run into a friend from San Antonio who had once lived in Slaton. I filled him in on the situation."

Toad's friend met with some of the movers and shakers of Slaton, including the group thinking about building a theater. He later told Toad that he had advised them of the difficulty they would encounter with having only one theater in Slaton, competing against the two Toad was going to fix up. Since Leon Theaters had a sizable circuit they wouldn't be able to compete for pictures.

For Toad Leon, this only underscored the old adage, "It's not what, but who you know. With him being a mutual friend, both parties wound up satisfied. They stopped construction, and we proceeded with our renovations."

1948 Film Convention, Century Room in Dallas' Adolphus Hotel.
From left: Donna Leon, Chill Wills, Betty Wills, Margaret Falls, Horace Falls,
and Toad Leon.

An audience participation venture called "Test Your Horse Sense" was a copyrighted deal. Toad had purchased local rights and ran it weekly in Slaton. He gave prizes to people who could answer the evening's questions that were flashed on the screen. It worked, but also came with built-in overhead. So, to help make "Test Your Horse Sense" cost-effective, Toad let the theater in Post have it each week, the night after the Slaton showing. Pretty soon, the same person was winning the weekly contest at Post, some thirty miles southeast of Slaton. The guy was going to the movies there to try his hand at the game, then to Post next day after learning the answer. Test Your Horse Sense" didn't hang around very long.

Joe Jack, who owned a film transport company, would become one of Toad's closest friends in Dallas. Jack was located a block south of the Leon Theaters' building. In the rear of his office complex was a room they called "The Butcher Shop." It was a gathering place for afternoon poker games.

"The name Butcher Shop was appropriate," Toad added. If the regular group wasn't at the Butcher Shop, they probably could be found at the Variety Club playing gin rummy. Toad remembered that Joe Jack had his favorite table in the back from which he held forth. His favorite saying was "I'll play any man, from any land, any game that he can name, for any amount that he can count."

Joe Jack and Toad would remain close friends for years to come even after Leon and his family left the pressures of Dallas. The two would buy a ranch together and Jack would advise Toad on other cattle dealings.

"Joe was one of the smartest men I ever knew," Leon said. "He could make a million dollars (doodling) on the white border of a newspaper over his morning coffee.

"We used to talk about going into the consulting business since in all probability between the two of us, we had been in just about every business you could think of at one time or another."

The card games would begin most every working day along about 1:30 p.m. or so. They would start following lunch and a cocktail. Toad tells of his own rule of thumb at Variety Club card game sessions, "Around six p.m., if I happened to be winning, I'd tell the boys, 'I need to go home. Donna has supper waiting.' Around six p.m., if I happened to be losing, I'd call Donna and ask her, 'Why don't you come down and we'll have dinner at the club?'"

For Leon the afternoon poker and gin games finally got close to becoming an obsession, one which he would finally force himself to confront. But not yet, not in the mid-1940s.

"Looking back, those were heady days," Toad reminisced. "Hollywood was in its heyday, and we were along for the ride."

Canadian Hunt—1946

Toad Leon developed a love for nature and the outdoors at an early age, as had so many other youngsters born in rural communities a few years either side of the birth of the twentieth century. The Salt Fork of the Brazos River ran near his home in Rule, Texas. As a boy, he learned of rattlesnakes and rabbits, polecats and badgers, coyotes and deer, and a plethora of fowl; of .22 rifles and .410 shotguns.

As success in the business world blossomed so did a revitalized attachment to the outdoors. His love of the wild went far beyond that morning near Graham, Texas, when he mistakenly blasted a neighboring duck hunters decoys out of the water! Toad's love of wildlife would carry him through his nine-plus decades with his financial success allowing him to purchase the More or Less Ranch in West Texas and stock it with exotic game from Africa and elsewhere.

Toad and his mount become close acquaintances during a lengthy Canadian hunt in 1946.

Without a doubt though, a hunting trip in 1946 to the edge of civilization in British Columbia, did more than anything to reconnect Leon to nature. Anticipation of this great adventure that he would share with a friend and one of his brothers prompted Toad to keep a diary-like journal. It follows in its entirety and, I believe you will find, speaks volumes through its observations:

8/25/46: Trinidad, Colorado

This afternoon Clarence (Toad's brother) and I joined Dr. E.F. (Doc) Hudson from Stamford, Texas. Tomorrow we start on our trip where we hope to get moose, bear, big horn sheep and mountain goats, (in addition to) doing a little fishing along the way.

8/27/46: Athabaska, Alberta, Canada

We crossed into Canada yesterday after leaving Great Falls, Montana where we had spent the night. The country from Great Falls northward is mostly rolling hills and deep valleys (before) ranch land gives way to wheat fields. After entering Canada we passed through Calgary, a thriving, bustling city of about 100,000 people, then northward to Edmonton, and then into scrub brush country. Soon after entering Canada the roads became noticeably bad—crooked, winding, full of chug holes and unpaved in places. On leaving Edmonton, the roads turned to gravel— very dusty and rough.

Tonight we are staying in a tourist cabin. The weather is quite cool, the first we have encountered that necessitated a fire. Clarence, Doc and I have a good time traveling together, jollying each other and wondering if we will get a bear or if the bear—a grizzly of course—will get us. I hope the mountain climbing will not be too hard on Doc.

9/1/46:

The hunt begins - We shoved off this morning from Dennis Murphy's, near Hudson Hope. We traveled through brush all day, mainly small jack pine and aspen. Hornet nests were encountered frequently, giving the horses fits and always causing a commotion. Our party now also includes the outfitter, Jim Ross, and two guides—Gary Powell and Mac McGarvey —a horse wrangler, Ray Pitts, and the cook, Pat Sloan. We have seven saddle horses and twenty-two packhorses. When strung out, our pack train covers about a quarter mile. Looks like we are a small army on bivouac, with all the tents, artillery, ammunition and food. Pat even has a packhorse just for his cast iron stove. We made about seventeen miles today.

9/2/46:

Lost three pack horses during the night. Gary went back to hunt for them. After lunch we continued on and made about thirteen miles in three hornet-filled hours. I demonstrated my marksmanship today by killing one grouse in about fifteen shots with a .22 revolver. No other game or wildlife has been seen. We camped tonight along a small stream where Clarence took a bath, the rest of us not needing same.

9/3/46:

Traveled in rain most of the day through much low timber. We had to cut our way through some of it but we made 25 miles, maybe more. However, it was tough on both men and horses.
We arrived at W.H. Simpson's Trading Post. He freights in all his supplies, mostly by sleigh, from the small frontier town of Fort St. John, British Columbia. His trade is mostly with trappers and Indians, who swap furs for supplies. Simpson keeps a small herd of polled Angus and raises horses to sell to the Indians. I happened to look up and see a small doe wander into camp. Now we have fresh meat, for a change.

9/4/46:

Only made 15 miles through scrub pine and aspen today. Camped on the Halfway River where Doc and I caught some rainbow and bullhead trout both of which are large and plentiful. Soon after making camp, it began raining. It even snowed some but our tents kept us warm and dry. This morning we made contact with our first Indian. Pete Butler only wanted some whiskey. He traveled with us all day. We asked him to spend the night in camp but he said he had to take 20 pounds of sugar to his father. It would be a trip of several days through bush and forest with only his tarp and saddle blankets for cover in weather that was freezing. He was of the Beaver tribe, spoke very good English, and was fairly clean. He was riding a small palomino pony that had a nice running walk and he rode a good saddle. It was nearly dark when he took off in the rain without a slicker.

9/5/46:

It was a hard day; cold and cloudy and much of it traveled through a burned-off region of small spruce. The going was difficult and tiring. Passed Brady's place about noon. He is a squaw man with a dozen children. All look like full-blooded Indians. His squaw had died of tuberculosis a few months before. The children were very dirty and had no shoes. He is a small active man of 63 who lives by trapping, raising a few head of cattle and selling ponies to the Indians.

9/6/46:

It was rather cold last night and the ground was frozen this morning. My woolen underwear has come in handy. We now have been traveling six days. The trail is quite plain and is largely used by trappers. It is surprising how little wildlife we have seen with the exception of that one doe I shot and a few bush chickens and willow grouse.

9/7/46:

The going today has been good. It's open country at times and we are just now entering mountainous country, with a little snow on the highest peaks. No sign of sheep, goats, or bear yet. Jim Ross, the outfitter, left us after the first day to join up with a hunting party already in the mountains. He is supposed to rejoin us; soon, we hope as he is the only one who knows this country or is familiar with the location of game. We camped on Cypress Creek about 100 miles from our starting place. For the last four days we have passed old abandoned Indian camps with their uninhabited lean-tos and teepees. The Indians evidently cleaned out all the game, down to the birds and rabbits, and moved on.

9/8/46:

We made only a few miles yesterday; camped at 2:30 p.m. and rested all of today. Clarence killed seven ptarmigan this morning. They are white-breasted, brownish-colored birds, about the size of a prairie chicken. We ate them for dinner but they were tough old birds. Jim Ross came into camp during late afternoon. He still hasn't located his other hunting party and he's going back to search for them. Last night was mild. Today has been warm and pleasant. I took a bath in the creek and washed clothes.

9/9/46:

Doc killed four more of those ptarmigans this morning as we broke camp. Finally we're beginning to see signs of game—bear tracks, caribou, deer, etc. We traveled over rough muskag country and were glad to make base camp on the forks of Halfway River and Rebb Creek. We will hunt out from here. Since this is so soon after World War II no hunters except Indians have hunted this area for 10 years. The nights are now cool and frosty, but our air mattresses and down-filled sleeping bags make good, soft and warm beds. We have missed lanterns the most. Neither we nor the guides thought to bring them along. None of us packed a shaving mirror either, but the lens of our binoculars serve that purpose. Doc seems to be making the trip OK.

9/10/46:

I got a 29-inch curl and 22-inch spread bighorn sheep today. Started down a shale slide to get him and couldn't stop. I hunkered down and tried to dig in, which slowed my descent just enough to wedge myself between two boulders before falling over the precipice. Felt like the whole mountain was moving. It was all very, very exciting but actually scared the hell out of me at the time. Clarence killed a 600-pound grizzly. Doc drew a blank but still has high hopes.

9/12/46:

Doc lost his balance trying to cross the river on a log and landed in rocks some eight feet below. He badly sprained his ankle and I'm afraid he is in for a painful time. Gary and I got back to camp about dark with two caribou. We had climbed a high mountain and found them near the top. Mac reported seeing four mountain goat billies and three grizzlies on a nearby mountain.

9/13/46:

Doc spent a miserable night with his ankle and was still in bed when the shooting broke out. A grizzly had approached the cook tent. Gary got him and gave him to Doc who was delighted. Of course he would rather have gotten the grizzly himself. We are having nice meals with plenty of fresh meat in camp—sheep, caribou, bear, an occasional grouse, etc. Pat,

Toad and his guide admire two grizzly bears killed on the hunt.

the cook, is a typical witty Irishman who has the typical Irish brogue. He loves to talk and tell stories and has quite a stack of them. By cooking all over the northwestern states and Canada, he is rich in experience. He told this story: A girl went to mass and prayed. "Hail Mary, Mother of God, I want to marry Tommy Todd." A deep voice responded, "N-o-o!"

"Jesus Christ, I wasn't talking to you. I was talking to your mother."

9/14/46:

Miserable weather with clouds covering the mountain tops. A bear prowled all through camp last night and ate half of the carcass of the bear killed Friday. The carcass was dragged about a hundred yards out of camp, across a stream and onto a knoll. We are hoping he will come back to finish it so we are watching for him. We had bear roast for supper last night and I have never eaten more tender or better-tasting meat.

The weather cleared about midday and Doc hit the jackpot. He brought two caribou back to camp. Mac, who had been out scouting, came back to camp and told of being chased by a grizzly. He said he rode up on him and the bear showed fight. It was all his horse could do to keep out of the bear's way until he could fire. Then the bear wheeled and ran.

9/16/46:

Clarence and I located goats today, but we didn't climb the mountain, deciding to save this for later. On the ride back to camp, we saw a big moose down in muskag. We tied up our horses and stalked on foot. Since he was getting close to deep timber we decided it was now or never. On the count of three we both pulled down on him. Clarence's gun jammed so I got off the lucky shot. Clarence estimated the distance to be at least 350 yards, maybe as much as 400. The moose had a tremendous head. He was the biggest any of us had ever seen including the guides. Must have been the bull of the woods. I think he would make a good showing in Boone & Crockett.

9/17/46:

Doc got his bighorn sheep ram today. He is finally clicking.

9/18/46:

We went goat hunting today. Doc started out with us but soon went back to camp having no inclination to climb the high peaks. At one point we located a small herd. When I urged Clarence to hurry he responded with, "Toad, right now you are young and wiry. But I want you to come back in 20 years and say that." At this time I was 36, Clarence was 56, and Doc was probably in his mid-60s.

9/19/46:

All we lack now is a bighorn sheep for Clarence. After a long ride I gave it up and headed back to camp. Then Clarence came in just at dark with the biggest ram yet taken. He had a curl of 40 inches, more than a complete circle from base to tip. Clarence killed him with one shot at 150 yards while the ram was running.

9/20/46:

It rained all last night and snowed in the mountains. Miserable day. We are afraid that winter weather may have set in. Incidentally, we have seen the Northern Lights several times. The guides spent all day catching the horses, rounding up supplies, fleshing out Clarence's ram, and generally breaking down camp.

9/21/46:

Started on our way out amid good weather. With the sun shining brightly the panoramic view was beautiful. The gray and brown valleys ran up to the green mountainsides that were covered with spruce, which finally gave way to the snow-capped peaks. Around noon the weather changed to a slight snowstorm, but it was not too disagreeable. We intended to go home by a different route via Beatty's, who is Gary's father-in-law, but Gary was unable to find the trail since only two horses have gone over it this year. We spent two hours looking, then camped on Graham Creek. It was plenty cold that night.

9/22/46:

It got down to zero last night. Hoarfrost is over everything, and the wet ground is deeply frozen. We're off to a poor start this morning due to losing eight horses during the night. Ray had to make a 10-mile ride to get them back. We traveled 24 miles in spite of it all but it was a tough day on everyone—especially Pat the cook.

9/23/46:

Made nearly two days travel in one today, and stopped at Brady's place. Everyone is very anxious to get out of the bush.

9/24/46:

Today was very hard on Doc but especially on Pat. His horse went under a log and dragged him off causing a deep gash in his head and bruising his chest. Pat has plenty of nerve but he's just too old for a trip and a job like this. We made it to Simpson's Trading Post after covering 22 miles.

9/25/46:

The going has been arduous, and we are all happy to be back on the fringe of civilization. We stopped at Colb Creek.

9/2646:

At last, after putting it in high gear, we arrived at Hudson Hope. Here we said farewell to our guides and spent the night in a real hotel. We expect to reach Grand Prairie tomorrow and Edmonton the next.

9/29:/46:

Arrived back in the good old USA at Great Falls, Montana around 7:30 p.m. What a trip of a lifetime this has been! We will all look back, even on the hardships, with pleasure. We left home a little more than a month ago, packed horseback 140 miles into the most fantastic country imaginable and amassed memories to treasure. A good hunt with good friends in the beautiful wilderness—it doesn't get any better than this.

Alcan Highway—1947

Leon Theaters had an in-house weekly newsletter that was circulated among the theater managers. They took turns writing about happenings in their small towns and exchanged ideas for theater improvements and film promotions among other topics. By now Toad Leon's exploits as a big game hunter were bordering on legend among the Leon company. When Toad's turn came, he headed his epistle thusly:

Leon's Weekly Bull-e-tin
September 24, 1947
Dallas, Texas

A condensed version follows:

It seems that I have had a lot of pressure put on me from several different directions to write the bulletin this week describing our trip to Alaska. I know of no way out of it.

This Alaskan trip really started about a year ago when my brother, Clarence Leon, Dr. Hudson and I went to British Columbia on a big game hunt. As soon as we returned home, they immediately began talking about another trip for this year. I wasn't the least bit enthusiastic and told them so. I felt I had seen enough of the wilds to last me a lifetime, but as time went on and hunting season approached my fever came up in proportion.

I contacted both Clarence and Dr. Hudson but both were too busy. I put all the pressure I could on both and even went so far as to drive 200 miles out of the way to contact Dr. Hudson on his ranch in Colorado. But to make a long story short they both fizzled out. So I left Dallas July 26 with my wife Donna and our two children—Carol Ann, twelve, and Sandra, four. We loaded up in my Lincoln automobile with a Higgins trailer attached.

We went through Colorado where we picked up my sister-in-law,

Jerene Leon. She accompanied us through Yellowstone Park and into Montana where we crossed over into Canada at the Waterton International Peace Park. From there, we went on to Kootenay and Yoho parks, and to Banff and Lake Louise.

It is understated to say these parks were beautiful. The streams, lakes, trees, snow-capped mountains, and glaciers were everywhere. The Chateau Lake Louise Hotel was out of this world both in accommodations and service. And, I might add, prices. Thank heavens, we only stayed two days.

Sandra Leon (left) and Carol Ann Leon (right) with Aunt Jerene, 1947, on Alcan Highway trip.

After leaving Jasper National Park it was on to Calgary, Alberta, where we left Jerene and the two children. They returned by train through Winnipeg and St. Paul. Donna and I headed north to the "tall and uncut."

In Edmonton, we were told it was impossible to get permission to travel the Alcan Highway unless we had definite business in Alaska. No tourists were allowed. This was overcome by putting on my most sincere look and telling the Northwest Mounted Policeman who was in charge that we were going to Alaska to prospect for gold. He seemed convinced, but of course there were certain requirements that had to be met and certain supplies we had to carry. Among these were a six-day supply of food, two extra tires and tubes for the car, an extra tire and tube for the trailer, ten extra gallons of gasoline, an extra fuel pump, water pump, a fan belt, extra spark plugs, distributor, condenser, mud chains, tow ropes, and various and sundry other items.

He also warned us that the speed limit was thirty-five mph and on bridges it was five mph. We were to pick up no hitchhikers and we would be checked further on down the line. It was 550 miles from Edmonton to the beginning of the Alcan Highway at Dawson Creek. This was an all-dirt road and we were traveling it during the rainy season. It was by far the worst road of our whole trip. It would take us three days to make the 550 miles.

The second night out we stopped in the only hotel in Grand Prairie, British Columbia. It was a small two-story affair and a little rough around the edges. After looking at the bed linens Donna suggested turning the sheets over, but we weren't the first to have had that idea.

Being Saturday night, the little town was full and the locals were celebrating. They were still at it early Sunday morning. As we packed to leave, from our second story window we heard one rowdy group discussing our rig.

"Look at that car. Those damn Texans, let's just turn it over," etc. Since we needed to hit the road, it was decided to make the proverbial "run for it." In approaching our car, we were surprised when the men who just minutes before had been an angry mob now cheerfully greeted us and began a friendly conversation. Regardless, we were soon on our way.

Out of Dawson Creek, we spent a few days with a friend whom I had met the previous year. Mac McGarvey had been a member of our hunting party. He lived at Peace River Crossing, a beautiful place, where we hunted bear two days. No luck and the mosquitoes were terrible.

We talked Mac into going with us through British Columbia and acting as our guide so we could hunt. This took us eight days. Donna and I got a black bear each but this was about all the luck we were to have, outside of camp meat which consisted of a mountain goat of the wrong gender. Those eight days were very interesting, because Mac knew several of the old sourdoughs thereabouts. In fact, we camped four days with a trapper who had worked all over the Yukon Territory and Alaska. He had eight of the prettiest husky dogs I had ever seen. These dogs were used to running his trap lines in the winter, either packing them like horses or pulling a sled.

We hated to leave this beautiful place. It was wonderful hunting country. But by this time we had been gone for about three weeks and felt we had better make tracks. We left Mac at the Yukon Territory line and forged on north to White Horse which was noted for the Yukon gold strike of 1904. Incidentally, White Horse (pop. 1,500) is the only town of any consequence on the Alcan Highway.

It took three days to get to Fairbanks. We saw wilderness and more wilderness along the route. We'd often go five hours without seeing a car either coming or going, however numerous bear and moose crossed the road.

It was impossible to get a place to stay in Fairbanks, so we went on to Central City 169 miles on down the highway. Situated on the Yukon River, it was only twenty miles from the Arctic Circle. Sadly, we had just missed the annual caribou migration. A native told us there were possibly as many as 5,000 in the herd.

We returned to Fairbanks where we tried to get boat reservations to Vancouver. Due to a longshoreman's strike it was next to impossible to get the car and trailer loaded on board. But we ran into a very nice fellow, Lou Severance, who operated the Moose Track Lodge that also included a little gambling enterprise in the back.

Lou liked the looks of my automobile. After spending all of 10 minutes bargaining, I doubled the price I had paid in Dallas for the Lincoln. It was Sunday morning. Lou must've had a profitable night Saturday since he paid me in $10 and $20 bills. We slept that night on a sack of money with my pistol cocked. First thing Monday morning I was at the bank exchanging cash for a cashier's check.

So Lou now owned a Lincoln automobile and a Higgins Trailer and Toad and Donna Leon were now afoot in Alaska. He was nice enough to take us down to Haines, Alaska, 650 miles to the southwest where we were to catch a ship on Wednesday. However, the ship didn't come, so we stayed in this village of 300 people until the following Sunday. Before we finally sailed we knew practically the entire population of Haines by their first names. We even attended their Chamber of Commerce meeting.

On Sunday morning we boarded the Princess Louise and sailed to Skagway, fourteen miles across the bay. Here we had a thirty-six-hour layover. Skagway was a very interesting place. We attended a "Days of '98" dance while laying over there.

Soon, we were on the move again, down the Inside Passage toward Juneau, another small place or two, and finally to Vancouver five days later.

The scenery from the ship was beautiful. A senatorial party from Washington D.C. was on board. We made friends with a young man who had climbed Mount McKinley—quite a feat, since up to that time there had been only about four parties to reach the 20,000-foot summit.

We had no reservations whatsoever in Vancouver. The only way to get to Seattle was by bus. Fortunately we had shipped the bulk of our stuff back to Dallas so we had only eight bags to wrestle.

From Seattle we flew to Portland and visited my cousin, James Server, whom I hadn't seen in twenty years. He and his wife had a nice little fishing boat and insisted we go salmon fishing on the Columbia River. We fished all day in the rain and nearly froze to death. People all around us were catching thirty-pounders. We must've been using the wrong bait.

We boarded the Union Pacific and, after bidding the Servers farewell, were on our way to Denver. We changed there to the Burlington and headed to Dallas.

To sum it up: We had a most wonderful time, but it was not a trip I would recommend to those who need hot and cold running water and all the modern conveniences. It is definitely a trip only for the big outdoor types.

A footnote:

At every stop along the way we heard about some Texans who were on the Alcan Highway about three days ahead of us. Years later we found out they were the parents of our good friends from Muleshoe, Texas. Bill and Irvin St. Clair said their folks had two other couples with them. It remains a mystery to me how six people were able to make the Alcan trip in a single car carrying all their gear plus the extra "required" items.

When I sold my Lincoln, I never dreamed how much trouble it would be to replace it. This was just after the war and cars were hard to come by. I phoned my general manager, G.S. Hill, while we were still in Fairbanks and apprised him of the situation. When we arrived back in Dallas he still hadn't located one. Long waiting lists were the norm. In fact cars were so scarce, dealers practically demanded a trade-in. Not having one made it tough. After several weeks of searching, my friend, Horace Holly, owner of an automobile dealership in Abilene finally found me a replacement.

The Tab

Virginia Leon Barnhart knows all too well how much fun Toad has making people squirm. She gives us the following first-hand example:

I was a senior at the University of Texas and was looking forward to a big football weekend.

Not only did I have a weekend date with John Barnhart, my latest heartthrob, but my sister and her husband, Mildred and Bob Blackshear, along with Aunt Donna and Uncle Toad, were coming to Austin for the game. During phone calls we had made plans. My family had invited John and me for dinner after the game at a fancy restaurant that college students and young lawyers rarely had the means to enjoy.

John had graduated from law school a year earlier, and at age 24 was newly elected to the Texas Legislature. As the result of some serious lobbying by the University of Texas John had been given fifty-yard-line seats. It was a great game and afterward we hurried to dress and meet my family at the restaurant.

We arrived just in time, as the place was filling up. After a couple of drinks at the bar we moved to our reserved table. There was considerable conversation about the game plus some family stories. Mildred and Toad were pumping John for personal information probably with an eye toward protecting my welfare. In turn they were telling John more about my family than than I wanted him to know.

As the evening progressed the stories grew taller and Bob and Toad were feeling no pain. But John seemed to be enjoying them so I finally began to relax.

Then the steaks arrived, rare and delicious, and the noise level in the restaurant rose to just under deafening levels. Since I assumed Uncle Toad was paying I ordered the most elaborate dessert and the rest of the table followed my lead. After a couple of hours everybody was about ready to leave. The waiter arrived with the check and I realized that Toad and Bob were not at the table. Since no other man was visible the waiter gave John the check. He was surprised, to say the least. Aunt Donna insisted that he give her the bill and that Toad was going to pay for it. John gallantly demurred. Mildred insisted. John furtively glanced at the bill but did not relinquish it to Donna. By this time, I was embarrassed to my very soul, and felt that my face was burning red.

I nudged John. "Give it to her!" I hissed. 'They invited us."

John shook his head. We waited. Toad and Bob did not return and Mildred and Donna were growing as embarrassed as I was. They were whispering loudly to one another.

"I can't believe they're doing this." and, "They're drunk!" were replaced by "I'm gonna kill him!" Although I shared their growing anger I was trying to remain cool and sophisticated a difficult task for a nineteen-year-old confronted with appalling behavior of her family—not only in public, but toward her impoverished beau.

"John, why don't you go to the men's room and tell them we're ready to leave," Aunt Donna finally said. But John continued sitting there.

"Well, I'll sure go get them!" Mildred said.

Just before she stood, Bob and Toad emerged laughing from the closely watched men's room. But when they arrived at our table they discovered their hilarity was not shared by their wives. Finally when we began moving toward the cashier I noticed Toad was clutching the check. John, obviously much relieved, was laughing with Toad and Bob.

As John drove me home, for what I expected would be the last time I learned that the bill was $74.38, without tip. John had exactly $75 in his pocket.

Note: Virginia should've had more faith in John. She would become his bride, after all.

Out of a Rut and on to Abilene

With Leon Theaters comfortably making the transition from dying downtown auditoriums to drive-in shows, why would its leader decide to bid farewell to the fast times in Dallas and move his headquarters west 200 miles to the sleepy little city of Abilene? "Frankly, I was in a rut and I didn't like it," Toad Leon replied. He had a top-notch staff that oversaw the operation, but that left too much spare time on his hands.

Several of his fellow film, distribution, and exhibitor executives found a fun way to solve that problem. "We got to where every day, we'd go to the Variety Club around lunch time, have a cocktail, and play gin rummy until evening. When it got up to playing Hollywood-style gin for 10¢ a point, that could get into several hundred dollars a day. I'd wake up in the middle of the night and lie there wondering why I had thrown the seven of spades the previous afternoon, or something like that."

Toad made the decision to try somewhere else for a change. He could see what the pressures of the big city were doing to his friends, healthwise and otherwise. A move back to the real world, out of the hectic traffic and frantic pace, was in order.

He faced his wife with the news. "Donna, I have decided to move out of Dallas and I hope you and the children will come with me."

"What!?" she replied, initially in shock. This was news to her. She would miss her home and her good friends but being married to Toad for nearly twenty years had prepared her for the unexpected. She had always suspected her husband might be part gypsy. "Where?" queried Donna.

"I'll let you make the choice," Toad offered. "Abilene, Amarillo, Wichita Falls, Albuquerque, Lubbock, San Angelo or Santa Fe."

"Well, since you came from Rule and I came from Baird and we already have friends in Abilene, I choose Abilene."

Of course Toad always suspected her choice might have been influenced by the fact that Abilene was about the closest city to Dallas.

Toad would move his entire office from Dallas, leaving only film booker and buyer Harold Brooks in Big D's theater district. Leon's first problem was finding suitable office space in Abilene where a resurgence of oil drilling had seen a huge influx of exploration companies. "We leased a building at South First and Sycamore streets for a few months,"

Toad said. "At that time, the location wasn't too great. A few flophouses dotted the area and ladies of questionable reputation hung around the corners. This became a concern of the office staff I had moved from Dallas with us.

"Malcolm Meek, president of Citizen's National Bank, asked if I would like to lease office space in the bank's new ten-story building in the heart of downtown. Construction was almost complete. Naturally, my office staff was delighted," and looked forward to getting a green light to move.

At the same time Toad had fished around for a suitable family dwelling, "but right away I got the feeling the real estate agents had seen me coming." He purchased two lots in the new Tanglewood addition of Abilene, and built the first home there. The Leons moved in shortly before his office space in the bank building was ready.

"Maxine Tadlock of Dallas was a wonderful commercial and residential designer," "Toad recalled. "She and Rufus Sively, the builder, had recently performed their magic on our house in Tanglewood. Again we called on Maxine's expertise to 'do' our new office. The end product was beautiful. Natalie Burnstein, a loyal friend and my secretary for more than thirty years was ecstatic. She commented

Donna bids the family home in Dallas goodbye as they prepare to move to Abilene.

71

GITTINGS · CARAGONNE

"He cleans up well!" said Toad's friends in 1953 as his successes in the theater business increased.

that we had surely gone 'from rags to riches.' The location was perfect for her coffee breaks. She made many friends from other offices."

On seeing Toad's own office within the complex for the first time, with its new furniture and oriental accessories, his down-to-earth brother, Clarence eyed with particular suspicion "that long couch and all those damn pillows."

But when Clarence saw the wet bar, "he approved," Toad said. "The bar soon became a gathering place. Our motto was, 'Don't be late to suite 408.'"

The heart of Toad's staff consisted of G.S. Hill as general manager, Ed Fleming as head of advertising, and Burnstein as executive secretary.

Fleming would become one of the most popular of Leon's entourage. One morning he came in late. As he arrived Toad chided him with a pseudo-threat of docking his pay unless Ed had a good excuse. The office staff gathered, wondering what Fleming was going to come up with this time. It seemed that as Fleming headed downtown and approached the intersection of South 14th and Butternut streets, famous for the Dixie Pig Restaurant on its southeast corner, he failed to see that a lady was about to run a red light. She broadsided him. He jumped out and ran over to her car. "Are you all right? Are you hurt?" he asked.

"Oh, I'm OK," she replied. "But whose fault was it?"

"I'm sorry, ma'am. It was my fault. When I left the house this morning, I could have gone to town several different ways. But I elected to come this way."

"I thought so," she said.

"Ed Fleming was a great friend of mine," Toad reflected. "He had been district manager for Conoco Oil Company in Wichita Falls before he joined Leon Theaters. When we moved the offices to oil-active Abilene he again wanted to dabble in his past profession. He was able to sniff out twenty-one farm-out leases from major oil companies that we picked up. We sold some interests, kept some interests, and managed to drill twenty-one dry holes.

"Fini for me in the oil business," said Toad.

Wyatt (burp!) agreed!

Purchasing Pendaries

"Toad, how did you ever find Pendaries?" was a question Leon has been asked many times. And rightly so. The legendary New Mexico ranch was to become ever more of a storied spectacle under the Leons' ownership.

The Pendaries Ranch headquarters house in 1962.

"Donna and I lived in Dallas at the time," he explained. "A big hat, boots, maybe some chaps, and a horse had always appealed to me. Perhaps playing so many western films in our small-town theaters had conjured up a fascination with ranch life."

Actually Toad already had done a little ranching. A few years earlier he and Joe Jack, who owned a movie film transport company headquartered in Dallas, together bought a small spread near Bledsoe, Texas. It was located in the semi-arid plains 60 miles west of Lubbock. Toad's interest in ranching thus born, he and Donna lit out looking for their dream spread. It was the winter of 1949, and the time seemed right. The film business was booming.

"We drove part of Wyoming, and most of Colorado," Toad recalled. Nothing. "We finally ended up in Las Vegas, New Mexico, and stopped by to see an old friend. Harold Anderson was in the oil distribution business. "During our visit, I told him what we were up to and what we had in mind—a place in the mountains, with a valley, lots of trees, and plenty of water. Also we wanted this place to have at least a chance of being self-sustaining. The closer it was to Dallas, the better."

To the Leons' surprise, Anderson said he knew of something that just might fit all of their requirements—so long as his area in northern New Mexico was near enough to Dallas. He offered to show them his idea of their brand of dream ranch the following day. So you can imagine what the rest of the evening was like. Toad and Donna could hardly sleep.

"Next day after breakfast, we drove north 12 miles to a small village called Sapello. Then we turned west for another 10 miles," Toad recalled. "As we drove, the land began to fall away and open into a wide, magnificent valley that was surrounded by the snow-capped peaks of the high Sangre de Cristo Mountains. We were truly awe struck." Toad paused as he recalled his late wife's reaction. "To this day, I remember hearing Donna murmur, 'How green was my valley!' The next words out of my mouth were, 'How big? How much? Is it for sale?'"

Anderson helped Toad and Donna get in touch with the owner who, by coincidence, lived not too far from Dallas in the Texas Hill Country ranching community of San Saba.

"Two weeks later we had the Pendaries (pronounced PAN-DA-RAY) Ranch under contract," Toad said. The beautiful, bountiful acreage soon turned into a home away from home for the Leons and their daughters, Carol Ann, then thirteen, and Sandra, five. Before long, the ranch would become a major interest in all their lives.

"I could hardly wait for school to be out back in Texas so I could gather up Donna and the girls, get to the ranch, and ride my horse," Toad said later in life. "Then I looked forward to getting there and riding over Pendaries in my jeep. Finally, I looked forward to being there and driving around it in my Buick. I guess that's just another way to say that life marches on—just like time does."

The historic Pendaries consisted of considerable land, not counting extensive grazing rights in adjacent federal lands and national park areas. It was named for a French settler who began developing the spread in 1870, four decades before New Mexico became a state. He originally claimed ownership of the entire valley which is also named in his honor. The elevation ranges from 7,500 feet in the valley floor to the 10,000-foot high Hermit Peak, which served as a guidepost for 50 miles to wagon drivers on the old Santa Fe Trail.

Jean Pendaries came from Gascony, France, and settled in Las Vegas, New Mexico, where he built, operated, and eventually sold the Plaza Hotel. In 1875 he began to acquire property at Rociada which still bears his name. He raised his family in the valley, and one of the daughters, Margarita, married a well-liked young man named Jose Baca.

Sandra Roberts, Toad's youngest daughter, has continued a life-long interest in the area in general and the Pendaries Ranch in particular. "The story of Baca's life and operation of the ranch is delightfully told in Oliver LaFarge's book, *Behind the Mountain*," Sandra Roberts said in the summer of 2001. "The book was published in 1951 not long after Toad and Donna purchased Pendaries. Oliver had married one of the Baca daughters,

Consuela, so the book is an authentic account of that period."

Jean Pendaries went to work developing his newly acquired ranch and quickly became one of the substantial citizens of the area. An 1883 photograph shows a grist mill and a large sawmill both powered by the Manuelitas river, a commissary, a home, and a cluster of barns. No record is available to indicate the sequence in which these were constructed but it stands to reason that Jean built the sawmill first so he could manufacture lumber to build the other necessary structures.

The grist mill was built in 1875. There were few flour mills in the area—two at Mora, one at La Cueva, another at Sapello, and a large one at Las Vegas. These mills took a portion of the grist as payment; the percentage could run as high as fifty percent. Jean recognized the need for a mill closer to home that would provide milling at a more reasonable price both for his neighbors and for his own operation.

He designed and supervised the construction of the mill which took a year to complete. The foundation was made from huge, hand-cut rocks. The walls were eighteen-inch adobe put together with lime mortar and the exterior was hard plastered. The original water-powered wheel was eighteen feet in diameter and

The historic Pendaries Ranch Old Mill in 1950 before its restoration.

was constructed entirely of wood as were all the component parts of the mill. Water was brought in from the acequia (ditch) by a 250-foot wooden overhead flume and then fed into the huge troughs of the wheel. The massive drive shafts were multi-laminated, octagonal in shape and were precision-made, hand-fashioned by skilled foreign craftsmen who also were migrating to New Mexico. Some of the original wooden gears were two feet in diameter. All the equipment could simultaneously operate throughout the three-story structure and, in addition, separate processing equipment could be run independently. The entire inner structure of the building was made of large timbers, every one mortised and doweled.

About the only materials brought in for the mill operation were the massive grindstones and the sifting screens. The six millstones were three feet in diameter, sixteen inches thick and weighed 300 pounds each. They were transported from the Missouri River over land by teams of oxen from what was then known as Westport Landing but which later became Kansas City. The milling screens, made of a heavy silk material and the most expensive of the equipment items, were imported from St. Louis.

The first miller was Jose Maria Trujillo, a small man who seldom spoke. He constantly made rounds lest something go wrong. During his later years Jose became deaf. Still, he could tell from the vibrations if a certain hopper was empty or if one of the huge belts was slipping. The millers lived in the mill. The main room was an elevated section where they had a bed and other furnishings. During the busy season they worked around the clock as teams.

The mill was of great interest to the community year round. While customers waited their turn during the harvest (and even during off season) they shared news of deaths, births, marriages, crop failures and raids by the Corras Blancas (white-hooded mounted raiders).

With the changes of time—horse-drawn wagons to gas-powered trucks, high wages in the beet fields of Colorado, sheepherders drawing $200 a month in Wyoming—emigrations from the area began. With less

UPI photo dated May 20, 1963 shows the destruction by fire of the historic ranch house.

wheat being grown, less milling was needed, and the mill at Pendaries finally ceased to function.

"What wonderful memories the old walls must hold," Sandra Roberts said. "The gala occasions when the mill was swept clean and dusted, the floors waxed with corn meal and dances held. Many dignitaries from the territory and later from the State of New Mexico were wined and dined there.

"One building situated near the mill was called the 'post office.' Originally it housed the commissary items necessary to outfit the herders and workers on the ranch and also their mail. The operation was successful and soon expanded to serve the local communities of Rociada, Upper Rociada, and Gascon. The items carried included food, tobacco, liquor, hardware, and clothing. Typical prices were shoes, $1.25 a pair; bib overalls, 75¢; calico fabric, 15¢ a yard; coffee, 15¢ a pound; lard, 7¢ a pound; pinto beans, 2¢ a pound."

During the early 1930s, operations of the mill and commissary/post office were discontinued. The buildings fell into disrepair. When Toad purchased Pendaries in 1949 he immediately began restoration of the mill, post office, and the original Baca home. "Bill Lumpkin of Santa Fe supervised the restoration of the old headquarters while we took up residence in the foreman's house," Toad said, summing up his and Sandra's recollections of the purchase of Pendaries.

During their 25-year ownership the Leons zealously guarded the natural heritage of the ranch while Toad tried to settle on a money-making cattle breed. Herefords, Angus, Brangus, Brahmas and Simmental cattle took their turns as featured livestock trying to make their owner a profit.

Not until introducing the beautiful Appaloosa horses to Pendaries would the ranch reach its highest potential. But that would not come before a couple other ill-fated experiments.

The Day the Japs Attacked Pendaries Ranch

Not long after he and Donna purchased beautiful Pendaries Ranch, Toad Leon confronted a problem that no one had been able to solve. Several hundred acres comprised the most beautiful rolling meadows you ever saw. But upon closer inspection, you realized that it was about the most worthless territory as well. "We had some boggy meadows," he explained. "The sub-irrigated ground was so wet, you couldn't even ride a horse over it."

Toad listened to all sorts of suggestions, like "Why don't you drain them off?"

"Because," Toad replied, "it is so boggy, you can't get any equipment in there. A tractor would just sink out of sight."

"Did you ever consider using dynamite?" someone finally asked.

"No. How?"

"Just punch a hole, stick in a piece of dynamite, take a step, punch a hole, another stick of dynamite, another step, and so on. Then you eventually blow the whole meadow at one time."

Hummm. Toad had run dozens of westerns on his movie screens where both villains and white-hats alike had hooked up dynamite to that neat little box with the whizbang handle on it. "I always wanted to do that," he mused.

All of the particulars, including enough sticks of dynamite to blast through a good way to China, were assembled. Hundreds of feet of explosives, all in rows, were buried, and connected to the control box gizmo. The area was cleared. Toad took his position at the box, put both hands on the handle, and pushed.

BLAM!!!

"Rocks, clods, and best of all, water, flew everywhere. It was a chain reaction that blew a drainage ditch across the meadow, at least a quarter mile," Toad said.

Meanwhile, Toad had a friend from his old hometown of Rule, Texas, visiting him. He was driving up and had just come around the toe of Goat Mountain when the meadow erupted. The World War II veteran of the Pacific Theater ran to the meadow, found Toad, and exclaimed, "My God! I thought we'd been attacked by the Japs!"

"But you know what?" Toad added. "It sure solved our wet meadows problem."

Stores and More

About the time the Leon family became active New Mexicans part of the year, Toad's wife experienced how confusing the dual state citizenship with its ethnic color can be to a foreigner. For example, a sales clerk at Titch's Department Store in Dallas had the following exchange with Donna.

"It was December and Donna was shopping for Christmas gifts for our ranch hand's seven children," Toad recalled. "Until you get used to them, names some-

Leon residence at 4336 Versailles, Highland Park, Texas, 1944.

times can be very confusing. After the gifts had been selected, the usual questions followed."

"Where do you wish the items to be shipped?" the clerk asked.

"To Eufracio Silva at Pendaries Ranch in Rociada, New Mexico."

The clerk was non-plussed at the information. "Will you spell them, please?"

"E-U-F-R-A-C-I-O S-I-L-V-A.

"P-E-N-D-A-R-I-E-S Ranch.

"R-O-C-I-A-D-A, New Mexico."

The clerk winced, but carried on. "Billing name and address?"

"Toad Leon, 4336 Versailles Street, Dallas, Texas." Donna didn't even hesitate, knowing what the look on the clerk's face meant. "T-O-A-D L-E-O-N, 4336 V-E-R-S-A-I-L-L-E-S, Dallas."

"Fast forward fifty years to Abilene," Toad said. "I had long ago sold the house in Dallas. One evening I was invited over to E.G. and Juanelle Cockerell's home for dinner. Now E.G. is a dermatologist of repute who—and I'm here to testify—can mix a mean margarita. After a couple of his concoctions, the subject of Dallas came up.

"I have an uncle who lives in Dallas," Dr. Cockerell remarked in passing.

"Really," Toad replied, "we lived in Dallas for ten years. But that was a long time back."

Toad in Dallas, 1946.

"My uncle lives in Highland Park."

"That so?" We lived in Highland Park."

"My uncle lives on Versailles Street."

"You've got to be kidding!" Toad replied, "We lived on Versailles Street."

"He lives in the second house from Armstrong Street."

"What!? We lived in the second house from Armstrong."

"His address is 4336 Versailles"

"That was our address!" Toad exclaimed.

"Well, I'll be damned! His name is Ed Grafton."

"Yes! That's him! We sold him that house!"

Another case of "It's a small world…"

Toad also recalled a Sunday evening at their home in Santa Fe, when he received a call from a lady in Denver identifying herself as being with the regional credit manager's office of J.C. Penney Company. "Mr. Leon, I don't know if you are aware of this or not, but your wife is considerably over the limit you established. Would you ask your wife not to charge anything to her Penney's card for a while?"

The Leon clan had gathered for the holidays in Santa Fe. Both daughters had married and begun families of their own.

Carol Ann laughed at her father's reaction. "That particular Christmas, Mother had done all her shopping in Santa Fe, and Penney's was about the only large department store there at the time. She rarely used the card otherwise."

"Well, she had run up $2,000 worth," Toad replied. "The lady who called was pretty new at it, you could tell. 'Would you please talk to your wife?' she asked. 'Oh, I would be glad to,' I told her, 'but it's a lost cause. I've been talking to her for nearly 35 years, and I haven't reined her in yet.'"

The next time Toad saw Bill Bucholz, who was then Penney's regional manager in Santa Fe, he just had to tell his friend about the dun from Denver. "Bill turned kinda white, as he apologized," Toad said. "But I told him that young lady from Penney's was certainly looking out for my welfare. Nobody from Neiman Marcus had ever called me at home on a Sunday night to caution me about Donna's spending habits in their store."

Memories of the Best of Times Never Fade Away

Toad Leon and Betty Freeman Slaughter have been friends for almost sixty years. She had been one of Donna Leon's closest friends and he had been pals with Betty's first husband, Wayne Freeman. The couples didn't miss a beat when it came to having a good time.

A speaker-phone connection from her home in Dallas to Toad's home in Abilene brought a wealth of information about the long ago but not forgotten fun times they shared. "We used to go out a lot together in Dallas didn't we Toad? To the University Club, the Baker and Adolphus hotels downtown, and the Cipango Club out on Turtle Creek," Betty said.

"You know, Jane Black and I always relied on you to be kinda our escort in reserve. We felt we could depend on you to be the most sober of the men in our bunch. One night, after an especially good time we were leaving Benny Bickers' University Club. As we began the walk down the long stairs to our car, Jane asked, 'Where's Toad?' I said I didn't' know. We looked up and down the street and just happened to look up a light pole. There you were. You had climbed to the top. Right then and there Jane and I decided maybe we had better reconsider your escort role."

When Betty asked Toad if he remembered that night his delayed response was, "Uh, yes I do, Betty. But just barely."

"I have lots of Toad stories," Betty continued. "Toad, do you remember the night at the University Club when Wayne couldn't get the car started? You suggested we call a taxi and get the driver to push us home."

"Yes, I remember. The cabbie wasn't too sure about it at first but he finally came around. The highlight of the whole evening was when we got out of the car at your house and discovered Wayne hadn't even turned on the ignition switch in the first place. There was just one Wayne-e-e Bird."

The Cipango Club in Dallas had an awning at the front entrance held up by steel ribs. "After one nice dinner, when you were feeling no pain, you jumped up, grabbed the awning ribs, and swung Tarzan-style all the way down to the parking lot." "It was the first time Johnny Black had been around Toad," Betty continued, "and we had told him that you were this sort of sedate, older fellow and to try to be on his best behavior around you."

Toad grinned. "Well, I can be sedate on occasion. Anyway we took a lot of great trips together, didn't we?"

"We sure did. Remember the play, Toad? Wayne had decided he wanted-ed to invest in the upcoming Broadway production of 'Men of Distinction.' You did too, but I think Wayne had talked you into it. We decided to go to New York for the opening. We stayed at the Waldorf and were wined and dined by the production company. They sent flower bouquets, fruit baskets, champagne, caviar, and pate', which you referred to as potted meat, to our rooms."

"I remember. I remember," Toad said, in between spasms of laughter. "There was just one little hitch. The play opened and closed the same night."

"Well that just makes for more fodder for the book," Toad added philosophically.

Close friends, Wayne and Betty Freeman (left), with Donna and Toad at the Copacabana in New York City, 1952

The two aging compadres had revived for one another some of the lasting memories of the times spent as couples.

"Good luck on the book. It should be a good one," Betty said.

They rang off, leaving Wyatt in a nostalgic mood.

New Year's Eve—1950

Toad Leon spent much of his long, productive, active and interesting life trying to get one-up on his wife, Donna. But as quick and sly as he was, it rarely happened. And if he did luck out, it seemed like the price was always too steep to pay.

It was enough to make Wyatt...you know.

An example was New Year's Eve, 1950. "The Variety Club of Dallas was organized by the motion picture industry," he explained as a preamble to the night he kissed Alice Faye and lived to regret it for all the wrong reasons. "Membership included all phases of the industry—from exhibitors, distributors and the businesses that serviced them, to actors and directors of the film world. Our club was located on the seventh floor of the Adolphus Hotel in downtown Dallas. Here was where most of the business deals were really made."

The club also was active as a charitable organization having dedicated the Boys' Ranch in Bedford, Texas, in 1949.

Each year the club hosted a festive New Year's Eve party. This year was no exception. Donna and I were having a wonderful time with good friends. The band kept playing and the cocktails kept flowing, but when 1:30 a.m. rolled around, Donna was ready to call it a night and go home. Toad's reply was, "Wait a minute, Donna. I haven't kissed Alice Faye yet." He used the excuse several times, and was able to stretch the evening.

"I had a whole lot of fun. A whole lot. But you can imagine Donna's frame of mind by the time we finally headed home," Toad said. "She was giving a running commentary on the probability of my being stopped and arrested. It was at the corner of Knox and Fitzhugh that I retorted, 'OK, I'll stop the car and you can

Donna and Toad, New Years Eve 1950, before the party turned a little ugly for Toad.

drive.' As I stepped out, she quickly slid under the steering wheel and drove off. There I stood in total disbelief—wearing my tuxedo with no hat and no topcoat while six inches of snow swirled around my shoes."

The streets were empty as he began trudging home. Just when he thought he might freeze to death, a police car pulled up.

"What the devil are you doing out here?" The officer demanded.

"Trying to get home. I live on Versailles."

"You have a long way to go. Get in."

Toad has since insisted that Highland Park's police are the nicest in the world. "We nearly beat my sweet wife home. I might add that this was the first and last time I ever kissed Alice Faye," he concluded.

Smoking May be Hazardous to Your Health

For Toad Leon in the early 1950s life away from his beloved Pendaries Ranch included fun and games with the boys at the Variety Club in downtown Dallas. The club was a gentlemen's hangout deluxe. Membership included distributors, exhibitors, and others in the business of showing movies.

Frank Sheffield, a fledgling theater man with the Interstate chain who would become a lifelong friend and often an aide to Leon, remembered as a young person just starting out getting to go behind the closed doors of the club that took up a floor of the Adolphus Hotel. It was in the heart of downtown Dallas and near the theater district. "I wasn't a member or anything like that," Sheffield recalled. "You had to be an executive or an owner to belong. I don't know why I was there on this particular day. I was just a guest for some reason."

Even if he wasn't able to peek behind the inner set of closed doors he could tell this was a fun place for businessmen and their womenfolk. Slot machines lined the walls of the outer bar for one thing. And Sheffield knew they were playing high stakes card games in the back. In other words, somebody in the Variety Club knew the right people in law enforcement.

If Dallas had such a mecca for well-heeled men then you know Houston wouldn't be far behind—not to mention ever admitting that it had been behind at all. But it was. So the Rice Hotel dedicated a floor for the private and exclusive enclave to become the second Variety Club in Texas. And if you belonged to the first Variety Club you would be extended privileges while visiting the Bayou City.

"This was a big deal for us in Dallas so we chartered a special train to accommodate our contingent that would attend the grand opening," Toad Leon said. "For some reason, this was strictly a male event. No wives went with us."

The official ceremonies included meetings, speeches, cocktails, and a sit-down dinner. Afterwards some of the new Houston Variety Club members and the Dallas visitors began a poker game.

"Many drinks and several packs of Chesterfields later, I finally went to bed exhausted at 5 a.m.," Toad said. "To top it off, I had lost my fanny playing poker." When he finally awoke, not feeling much better than when he had piled into bed, Toad discovered to his dismay that he had missed the chartered train back to Dallas.

"I caught the next train home and rode by myself. I was feeling sick...Sick...SICK! My head hurt, my stomach hurt, and my chest hurt. It crossed my mind that I might be having a heart attack. Could it have been all those drinks?" he asked himself. "Or all those non-filter cigarettes? Or the lack of sleep? Or maybe a combination of all of the above?" It was a lonely, painful reflection as he watched the pine trees whiz past outside his train window.

"I said a silent little prayer," Toad recalled. "If the Lord would just let me get over this one hump, I wouldn't smoke another cigarette for as long as I lived."

Donna's cheerful greeting, "How was your trip? Tell me all about it," as he dragged himself, pale and wan, inside their Highland Park home around mid-afternoon, didn't help Toad's mood.

"She followed me upstairs, continually chatting. Donna, being nobody's fool, knew what was going on. She had decided to help me stew in my own juices. I wondered how many times I had uttered to others in like circumstances, 'If you dance you have to pay the piper,' or, 'if you play, you pay.'

"Donna, I can't talk now," Toad told his wife. "If you will just let me go on to bed, I'll tell you all about it later—if I survive!"

Looking back at the incident fifty years after the fact Toad said, "Thankfully, I never had to attend another grand opening of a Variety Club—especially in Houston."

His promise to the Lord, about the Chesterfields? "I nearly kept it. I didn't smoke another cigarette for ten years."

Save the Last Dance for Uncle Toad

Toad Leon is a people lover. Especially if they are kinfolk. And likely as not, his brand of familial affection will be wrapped in humor, not taking life all that seriously. Sometimes, humor won't cut it. And Toad is adept at deeper bonding.

One of his nieces, Linda Leon Zachary, heard about Carol Ann and Sandra's plans to push their father into permitting his life story to be put to print. She asked if she could participate. What follows is Linda's recollection of a traumatic time in her life and how the Leons of Pendaries Ranch got her through her tough summer of 1952. Especially Uncle Toad. It's Linda's story:

My father, Carroll Leon, third oldest of the Leon brothers, had been killed in a farm-related accident in June of 1952. I was fourteen at the time and the summer months stretched before me, long and lonely and hot. I had been brought home from camp in cool New Mexico when the accident occurred and my mother thought it best that I not return to camp. However, I was not coping well with our loss and my mother didn't know what to do with me, or for me.

Miraculously, out of the blue, someone decided that I should go to Pendaries Ranch to spend several weeks with Uncle Toad, Aunt Donna, Carol Ann, and Sandra. Carol Ann was sixteen and seemed very grown-up to me. She had invited a number of friends to the ranch. I believe a few of them had come from Dallas to attend the party. I did not have an appropriate dress so she loaned me one of hers. She gave me some pointers on what to say and how to act. One of the boys took a little special interest in me. He probably did not know that I was only fourteen, but it certainly made me feel good anyway. I had not started dating yet so the party scene was unfamiliar, but very exciting.

The party was outside the house with the dancing inside on the Mexican tile floor. I was sitting in a chair off to the side, by myself, when suddenly Uncle Toad was standing before me. He wanted to know why I wasn't dancing.

"I don't know how," I replied.

"You can't dance? Well, you're getting ready to learn."

With that remark he reached down, took my hand, pulled me out of the chair, and led me into the main room. I felt so self-conscious I thought I would faint. All I really wanted to do was to run out of the room. But I was more afraid of what my mother would say later had I been rude, than I was of facing the impossibility of learning how to dance while in the company of strangers. Uncle Toad put his arm around me. He told me to relax. Then he told me something I have never forgotten and to this day I truly believe.

"Linda, it's a woman's job to keep out from under her partner's feet. If you get stepped on, it's your fault, not your partner's."

Barbara Leon Scheef (left), Linda Leon Zachary, and Wilbur Leon, 1996.

Then we began my first dance. We danced and danced and danced! And the better I got the more confident I became. Before the evening was over I was dancing with some of the boys who had come to the party. I remember Uncle Toad telling me sometime during the party that every young woman should learn how to dance. It was an important social activity.

After I returned home to Lubbock I was allowed to take ballroom dancing from the Arthur Murray Studio. And because of Uncle Toad's lessons I was really rather good. My instructor told me so.

That first dance, with a very special uncle, was many, many years ago but I remember it as if it were yesterday. . I have since danced to all kinds of music. I thank Uncle Toad Leon for giving me the beginning of a life-long hobby, one that I still enjoy.

How Much is that Hoggie...

If Toad and Donna thought the cattle business in the high country was a struggle,especially Toad, his next experiment in searching for something to make Pendaries pay a dividend would become a nightmare.

"When I bought the ranch the old Baca House was being used for grain storage," Toad recalled. "The first floor was filled with wheat up to the window sills. However, it was of such poor quality I couldn't sell it. What was I going to do with it?" Enter again old Rancho Bledsoe pard', Joe Jack. He suggested that Toad fatten up some hogs on the inherited grain. "I bought six registered Hampshire sows and one register boar," Leon said. "My foreman, John Rackley, built some nice farrowing sheds.

"The sows started having litters, and those litters had litters. So it wasn't long before we were out of feed and in the hog business. There wasn't much grain being grown in our area back in 1951 either."

Clickety-clack went the wheels in master entrepreneur Toad Leon's brain.

"I remembered my friend in Plainview, Texas, who raised popcorn. During the cleaning process the cracked kernels were separated into what they called screenings. I sent for a couple truckloads of these."

He and his hands found that popcorn screenings at their best are "hard as rocks. They had to be soaked, boiled, steeped and manipulated into mush to even be digestible. But our hogs kept multiplying, and so did the feed bill. We made it our top priority to sell some hogs."

The nearest market was Clovis, New Mexico, a 300-mile round trip from Pendaries. "It was summer. John and I drove at night so the hogs would stay cool. We arrived at the Farmers and Ranchers Market just as the sun was coming up. It promised to be a hot day and already trucks and trailers were jockeying for position in the long line.

The biggest, tallest cowboy I had ever seen impatiently motioned for us to back up and unload. There he stood in a big black hat with his pants tucked into high-topped boots and a quirt in his hand. He proceeded to gate-cut the hogs sorting some this way and some that way.

I asked him what he was doing.

"I'm grading your hogs," the cowboy replied. "Some are number ones and some are number twos." The number ones brought more money, of course.

"Well, all of my hogs are number ones," I told the cowboy. "John, load 'em up. We'll take them somewhere else, where people appreciate good hogs."

I crossed the street to a phone booth and called Swartzman Packing Company, only to be informed that they didn't buy hogs in Clovis any-more. We would have to back-haul them to the company's Albuquerque facility if we wanted to sell to Swartzman. Was there no place in Clovis to sell our hogs? Only Farmers and Ranchers, Toad was informed.

"Oh, my god!" Toad told himself. The sun was getting higher, the day was getting hotter, and the hogs were now panting and thirsty. The situation was critical, hog-wise. Toad swallowed his pride. He and John got back in line at F&R and waited their turn. As they backed up there stood the cowboy with his hands on his hips.

"Mister, do you want to sell your damn hogs or not?" he barked.

Toad meekly nodded. This time, grading was not an issue. Hogs came off the list as products of Pendaries Ranch.

And Wyatt urped.

Lots of Lost Sleep Over Sheep

About ten years later the Pendaries Ranch had gone through its various breeds of cattle and the hog nightmare. Toad was finally about to hit on a winner—raising prize Appaloosa horses. But before he would become nationally known for the brightly colored breed, northern New Mexico style, Leon had one more ill-fated animal experiment to suffer through.

"My foreman and cutting horse trainer, Gayle Bourland, suggested that we get some sheep," Toad explained.

Bourland told his employer, "I understand you can make some money on sheep. The wool will pay expenses and the lamb crop will be clear profit."

Years before, Jose Baca had raised sheep on Pendaries so the idea had a certain amount of historical significance, Toad figured. "Of course, back then ol' Jose actually had shepherds who, for all intents and purposes, lived with the sheep. They even drove them to the high mountains for summer grazing.

"Anyway Gayle and I went to Vaughn, New Mexico, in the heart of short grass country. I bought 3,500 head of ewes and some rams. As was the case in most of my prior livestock ventures, we bought on the high—$26 per head." Right about now Toad figured he should've remembered an old Leon family story. "Years earlier, my brother, Server, also had some dealings with sheep. He put an ad in the paper that read, 'Sheep for sale.' His partner's wife, Mrs. Clark, was home alone one day when a man drove up to the farmhouse.

"What kind of sheep are you selling?" he asked.

"I really don't know,"she replied. "All I've ever heard them called are those DAMN sheep!"

Toad should've remembered. But he didn t. "We never thought to ask when the ewes had been bred. They started lambing just before Christmas. In northern New Mexico lambing too early is risky at best. As it happened, we were in for an extreme winter."

It snowed early and profusely. The old hog farrowing sheds were hastily reconditioned into lambing quarters. "At least, now we had a lamb crop," Leon said, even if it was somewhat abbreviated. Spring came and with it the lush meadow clover. "Sheep love clover. Ours just gorged themselves, then bloated and died. The Rociada town dogs formed packs and for sport chased the survivors which usually got too hot and died. Those that didn't got up on Goat Mountain where the thick oak brush pulled their wool off."

Still some came through these horrors more or less intact - only to contract wool worms. To add insult to injury, the shearers showed up late.

"Between the clover, coyotes, dogs and various other maladies, the sheep herd dwindled considerably," Leon sighed, recounting his three long years wrangling with his woolies. "One summer there were so many dead sheep, the funeral pyres littered the meadow. Years from now, when archeologists excavate the area they will assume it was the site of some sort of massacre."

Miraculously a couple of falls later the ranch produced some lambs from the original herd. "About then down came a 25-inch snow that stayed on the ground for weeks. We were forced to feed by jeep and mule sleds. By the time we were able to get ready to ship those 80-pound lambs, they weighed only 60 pounds. We had discovered the hard way that sheep need a whole lot of maintenance."

It was time to bail out of this venture Toad figured. So he put in a call to Ike Wiggins over in Wagon Mound. "Ike was a big, likeable man who dealt in sheep. He came to the ranch the next morning for a look-see. Ike ran them through the chute and toothed them.

"Toad, some of these sheep are gummers," he told Toad "They are so old, I wouldn't be interested. But I'll take your younger ewes. I'll pay $5 a head, and that's a good price, my friend."

Toad blanched. "Will you come get them?"

"Nope. You'll have to deliver them to Wagon Mound," Ike replied with a shake of his head. "Why don't you drive them over? It shouldn't take more than a couple days."

So a deal was struck. "My brother Mike, Jack Roberts, Clyde Pickett, Ernie Rogers, a couple other local cowboys and I set off early one morning to trail the herd cross country."

At least Toad went in style. He rode his big prize-winning Appaloosa stallion, Quanah. "The first night we camped just on the other side of Mora. Mid-afternoon the next day we arrived in Wagon Mound and delivered the herd."

Ike, with his substantial belly jumping from laughter, used to like to tell the story of "the funniest sight I ever saw. Up the road came Toad riding his $25,000 stud horse, driving those $5 sheep."

At least, Toad Leon was now out of his three-year-long livestock failure.

"I have come to believe that a sheep enters this world looking for either a place or an excuse to die," he said philosophically.

And Wyatt urped.

OK, Toad...Let's See You Do It Again

On that lazy summer afternoon at Pendaries Roy, Gene, Johnny Mack Brown, Lash LaRue, Wild Bill Elliott, Bob Steele, and even ol' Duke himself—all those B-Western heroes the Leon Theaters used to feature on Saturdays before the 1950s—would have been proud of Toad; if not more than a little awestruck. Just like Toad himself.

Toad Leon's one and only attempt at being a trick shot artist came during another movie-like scenario—this one akin to the 1995 movie "City Slickers."

"We used to drive our cattle up to graze in national forest land for ninety days then bring them out just before hunting season," Toad recounted. "This particular year I had invited my niece, Virginia',s husband, Johnny Barnhart, and his brother Joe to join in on the cattle drive. Being 'flat-landers,' this was a whole new experience for the Barnhart brothers.

"First off Johnny put in his request for a 'spirited mount.' So I pointed at the horses in the corral and told him to take his pick. He chose the prettiest and flashiest one in the herd. Bonnie was Carol Ann's black and white paint mare. Being a parade horse she strutted and pranced all the way up the mountain and all the way down the mountain. Much to Johnny's chagrin and discomfort, I might add."

The group included Johnny, Joe, Toad, Jack Roberts, Toad's brother, Mike, and three or four ranch cowboys. They were on the trail two days, resting the cattle the first night at the mouth of Sparks Canyon in preparation for the steep climb the next day. Mid-morning of the second day Joe came up missing. Toad was half worried since he didn't think Joe had ever been in the woods a day in his life. Toad asked Johnny what had become of his brother.

"Well, Joe lost some of his personal things so he has gone back to search for them," Johnny replied.

"We found a kinda wide spot on the trail and held up the whole herd for an hour or so hoping Joe wasn't lost," Toad said. "Just as I was about to send someone back down the trail he rode up. Joe had backtracked and found his silver brush and comb set and his toothbrush so all was well.

"Finally, we made it to the grazing area and got the cattle milling and situated on water and salt. I was in the cabin trying to get a fire started for supper when I heard gunfire."

Toad went outside to see Joe, Johnny, and a couple of the guys shooting a pistol at tin cans.

"C'mon over, Toad, and see if you can hit 'em," one of them called out.

"Oh hell, anybody can hit those cans. Gimme the gun. Johnny, see that little pebble by your foot? Pitch that up in the air. I'll show you something." So Johnny threw the rock in the air and Toad did a quick-draw imitation, firing nearly from the hip. The rock disintegrated into a puff of dust.

Toad blew smoke from the pistol's barrel, smiled, turned and walked back to the cabin as the rest of the party stood around with their mouths wide open.

"Hey! Come back and do that again!" Johnny called.

"Sorry, boys. I don't have time. I need to start supper." Inside, Toad promptly leaned against the wall and nearly died laughing. "I was more astonished than they were," he said years later. "I could have tried that shot a thousand times more and never come close to hitting that rock."

A man after Wyatt's own Dodge City and Tombstone heart.

The Soap Tycoon—1952

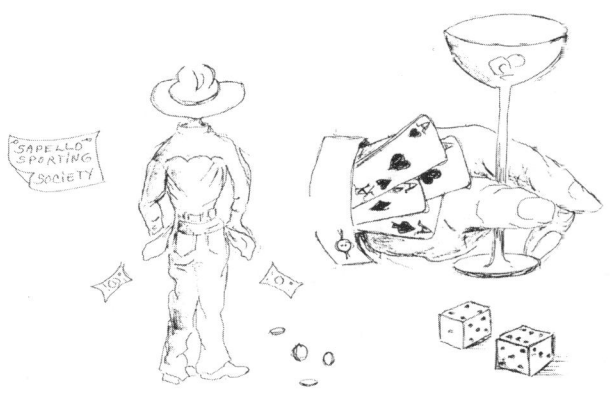

Back when the C.D. Leon family took up semi-annual residence at Pendaries Ranch, The Reader's Digest had a section called *The Perfect Squelch*.

Toad and Donna fell in with a group of local residents who called them-selves The Sapello Sporting Society. "This was a loosely knit group of ranchers and businessmen in and around Las Vegas, New Mexico, initiated in the early 1950s by Jim Arrott," Toad recalled. "Jim lived up Sapello Canyon with his wife, Tattie. Sapello Canyon is just over the mountain from Manuelitas Canyon where Pendaries is located.

"Jim, being the founder, was called Chief Sport. The sole function of the society was to gather for cocktails, conversation and a little poker. Most of the members were transplants who had migrated to the beauty of the Sangre de Cristo Mountains of northern New Mexico, either from back east or from Texas. We would take turns hosting the events. The ladies played poker in one room and the men in another.

"One evening several of the fellows were standing around in conversation. In the group was Col. Bill Salmon. Now Bill lived in Houston and was prominent in the maritime shipping business. He was a self-made man having begun his career as a stevedore and through foresight and fortitude he had amassed a fleet of freighters. He also owned a 50,000 acre ranch close to La Cueva, New Mexico. He was very prosperous and knew everyone of any consequence in the state of Texas, and most of the rest of the U.S. These included people from legislators to newspaper tycoons." In other words, Bill had been known to drop a name or two, on occasion.

"I asked him at one of these occasions," Toad continued, 'Bill, do you know Gordon Fugg? I think he's from Houston.'"

"Well, Toad, I don't know. The name does kinda sound familiar. What does he do?"

"He just came out with a new type of soap." Toad responded.

"Oh yes, now I remember. I do know Gordon," Bill replied.

"How do you like his new television commercial? The jingle is great and very effective, don't you think?"

"Huh?"

"You know, If Rinso won't rinse it, and Duz doesn't do it, then just Fugg it!"

Women of the Sapello Sporting Society kick up their heels-1952. Donna Leon in center.

Col. Bill Salmon stared at Toad a moment, as if to wonder if he really had been squelched, and if anyone else had noticed. Then realizing he had, and they had, he rolled his eyes and muttered, "Toad, you S.O. B."

"Jim and Tattie Arrott were wonderful friends," Toad concluded. "Both originally were from Pennsylvania. She was an heir to Pittsburgh Glass and he was an heir to American Standard. They revived the reunion of the last remaining members of Teddy Roosevelt's Rough Riders. The reunion was held for years at their ranch, then at Pendaries when Jim became too ill to host it," Toad said.

Polly and the Bouncer

Toad Leon can be the most giving, thoughtful and resourceful friend and member of the family that you can imagine. To a fault sometimes when his mind relies on his non-stop ideas, but lets his heart assume that the details will take care of themselves.

His niece, Polly Denton, found that out in the late 1960s. Polly, the daughter of Toad's brother, Clarence, was mulling over ideas for something neat to do with her husband, Buck. The El Paso couple decided a long weekend in Dallas would be great—especially if it would fit around the raucous Texas/Oklahoma football game played each October in the Cotton Bowl.

"Our plan was to invite Willodine and Gene Pressnell from Carlsbad, New Mexico, to be our guests," Polly said, in recalling the weekend. Gene and Buck had become fast friends due to their common interest in potash mining. The two couples had taken more than a few trips together including plenty of quail hunts. Polly wanted this trip of almost 650 miles to the east to be special. And who other to help her make it so than good ol' Uncle Toad!

Toad and Donna had left Dallas for northern New Mexico, but they had kept their contacts handy for regular trips back to Big D. So Polly called Toad for suggestions on how to make the UT-OU weekend extra special.

"Toad, we thought you could suggest a really elegant place to go the night before the game," she said.

"Well, Polly, right off hand I'd say that would be the Cipango Club on Friday and you might want to go to Brook Hollow Country Club on Saturday. I don't think you would be disappointed in either."

"Do we need to make reservations?"

"Of course," Toad replied as he fished out the phone numbers for her to call. "Just tell them you want to reserve a table for Toad Leon."

"But Toad, don't we need to present a card or something to identify us?"

"Why no! You won't have any problems."

"But…"

"Trust me, Polly. You and Buck just walk in with your friends. Tell them you are my daughter, Carol Ann, and there won't be a problem. On Saturday be sure to go to Brook Hollow. They always have an all-day party during UT-OU weekend. They start with bloody marys and brunch in the morning, a bus ride to the game after lunch, then a return ride to the club following the game for a dance that night."

"Oh, Toad, you're a lifesaver, as usual. Thanks," Polly said. "Now, how will we take care of all the expenses?"

"Don't worry about that," Toad replied. "They will send me a bill and then you can reimburse me."

"Toad, I can't thank you enough! This sounds like a once in a lifetime weekend."

The wheels started turning. The Pressnells were ecstatic over the plans. Willodine and Polly planned their wardrobes in detail via phone while agreeing that they would leave for Dallas on Thursday, spend a good part of Friday morning shopping at Neiman Marcus, and then get ready for their big night at Cipango.

And it all began working like a charm. "Friday night arrived. Willadine and I were decked out in our Neiman 'specials.' We drove to the club where the red carpet stretched from the massive door to the curved driveway. Two attendants rushed out, one to open the doors and the other to park our Chevrolet, which we noticed was one of a kind among the Lincolns, Cadillacs, Rolls Royces and stretch limos.

"Not the least intimidated we strolled to the door. It opened immediately, and we were suddenly surrounded by bright lights, beautifully clad ladies who obviously had also done some shopping at Neiman's, and sheer elegance everywhere we looked." Leading her party of four, Polly walked to the desk where a lady sat checking the arrivals.

"Reservations?" she asked Polly.

"Yes. Toad Leon."

After staring at Polly "for an interminable length of time," she said, "And who may I ask are you?"

Polly instantly got the idea all might not be going well. "I became somewhat nervous when I noticed the guard—or more likely a bouncer—walked to the desk and gave us the cold stare. In my most resolute voice, I told the lady that I was Toad Leon's daughter, Carol Ann."

"Really?!" the lady said, her eyebrows arching. "I DON'T BELIEVE SO! Carol Ann has just left the club, and you certainly are not her!"

Oh no! Polly thought to herself as she felt her face turn flaming red. Now what? With all this taking place in front of the Pressnells, our beautiful weekend is about to be derailed.

"Well…to tell you the truth, I really am not Carol Ann, as you already have noticed. Toad Leon is my uncle. He is the one who told me to call and make the reservations. He assured me we would have no problems. He thought spending an evening here would be a special occasion for my husband and me—we're from El Paso—and our friends who are from Carlsbad. But I guess this is one time he was wrong."

The lady nodded. "I see." Then, as if perhaps thinking better of invoking a power play that might not be worth the trouble it could cause, she turned to the hostess nearby and said briskly, "Seat them at Mr. Leon's table."

"As we walked past the bouncer, or whatever he was," Polly recalled, "I heard him say, 'I don't like the looks of this one bit! For sure I will be watching them all night.'" And he did.

"Even after all of our identity problems, we did have a grand evening of dining and dancing," Polly said. "We left in the wee hours of the morning in high spirits, looking forward to the excitement ahead at Brook Hollow and the Cotton Bowl."

The following month Polly got a call from Toad. After a brief chat, he said, "Polly, from the looks of your bill that I just received, you must have had your dream weekend. I hope, with the figures I am about to read off, you will think now that you had as good a time as you had then."

They laughed and Polly said, 'Oh, we did We did!"

And Wyatt seconded the motion.

Chasing the Uranium Dream—early 1950s

How many people do you know who once had an idea—good, bad or indifferent—and rode the dream of striking it rich into the ground? Sure. A bunch. And more than likely when the bitter pill of failure was force-fed to them they vowed never to drink at that trough again.

Not Toad Leon. Within this book, you can count more than twenty hot ideas he hatched that fizzled. His leaping into the uranium-chemical mining madness of the early 1950s is a prime example. It also displays his rare knack for picking himself up and dusting off his dream machine so he can be ready for the next wild ride while not allowing himself or his partners to take defeat all that seriously.

"A man in Utah, a Mr. Stein, had recently made a fortune in uranium," Toad explained. Many uses for the highly active and often radioactively unstable uranous compounds were being developed. The U.S. would convert properties found in pitchblende into mixes of artificially produced uranium 233, 237 and 239. Three-quarters through the 20th century, these were fueling electric power plants and atomic submarines.

However, back in 1951 or so the government hungered for uranous extracts for one purpose—to feed to the A-bomb and H-bomb race with the Soviets.

"In other words a uranium mine was better than a gold mine," Toad surmised. The U.S. was thought to possess more than a third of the world's known reserves of a mineral called carnotite from which high-grade uranium could be produced. Another mineral, coffinite, would be found even more potent for uranium mining. The minerals primarily would be found in Utah, New Mexico, Wyoming, Colorado and Arizona with coffinite restricted mainly to Wyoming and Arizona.

But back in the mid-twentieth century overnight prospectors figured they could stumble onto a rich lode anywhere.

"Over cocktails one night in Dallas, the topic of the uranium craze was explored. My good friend Wayne Freeman said. 'Toad, your ranch in New Mexico might hold some promise.' So it was decided. We loaded up a Geiger counter and headed west for a little prospecting."

Upon their arrival at Pendaries Ranch the party contacted Celestino Martinez, whom Toad called "a native of that part of the country, a good guide and wrangler who knew every trail in the high mountains." The intrepid prospectors headed up to Toad's small cabin on the Valdez River. The area was in a lush national forest to which Pendaries Ranch held grazing rights. Toad used the cabin each summer as a line camp for his cowboys.

"Dawn saw the three of us on horseback and on the trail to great riches," Leon said. "A packhorse with our bedrolls and provisions followed along. Wayne carried his Geiger counter and a sack of small samples of uranium ore—one of which I had pilfered the night before.

"We rested our horses at an old mica/copper mine and explored the slack on foot. As Wayne poked around at the rocks, I slipped the small ore sample inside my glove."

He picked up a rock and held it in his gloved hand. "Hey, Wayne, try this one," Toad suggested. The Geiger counter went wild with "click-click-click-clickety-click."

"My god, Toad, look at the meter!" Wayne yelled.

"I was able to pull this little ruse a time or two before Wayne got wise," Toad recalled.

"We reached the cabin at dusk. The walls were rough-hewn pine logs, the roof was tin and the floor was dirt. The single room, about 10 x 12-feet, held two aspen-pole bunk beds. a wooden table, a couple chairs, and a wood-burning cook stove. After a long day in the saddle it was more than adequate.

"Following supper we stored our food supplies under a large dishpan on the table. We were bone tired and ready for bed. Celestino chose a lower bunk. Across the room Wayne had staked his claim to a top bunk. I took the bunk below him.

"Sometime during the night I heard a scratching, shuffling sound. In my flashlight beam I saw a large rat rooting around the dishpan. He wasn't in the least intimidated by our presence. Even Wayne's snoring didn't bother him.

"Celestino, are you awake?" Toad whispered.

"Sí."

"Hold the flashlight on him."

Toad fumbled around for his 30.06 rifle. "When I saw him through the scope, only a few feet away, he looked big as a warthog. I squeezed the trigger. The sound that reverberated off the tin roof and around that little cabin could have knocked a mule down."

Wayne, startled out of a deep sleep, shot straight up in terror. "What the hell...?" he screamed.

"The explosion also spooked the horses in the corral behind the cabin. When one nickered, it flashed through my mind, 'Damn! Did I hit a horse too?'" At least, the thieving rat paid a permanent price for his pilfering.

After two days of prospecting the party headed down the trail for home. If the Pendaries area contained a uranium vein they hadn't found it.

Back in Texas the idea still had merit. Everybody wanted a piece of the action and Jack Stroube was no exception. He was an oil man who lived in Abilene and was a close friend and golfing buddy of Toad's.

"Jack had heard that there was a little uranium action in Dickens County," Toad said. "We drove up there one afternoon. As I motored down the highway Jack held his mineral detector out the car window. Between Spur and Dickens the detector went crazy. This just had to be a hot spot." Toad's niece, Mildred Leon Blackshear, and her husband, Bob, lived in Spur. Since Bob knew all the local residents Toad and Stroube enlisted his help.

"The next week Jack, Moose Stovall (a former NFL lineman with the Detroit Lions who lived in Abilene), and I drove up to meet the owner of the land closest to where the detector had gone crazy. Bob introduced us to Mr. Burnett. He was a wily old farmer who, during the conversation, let us know right quick that he wasn't going to sign a lease contract. However, he did mention that he needed to drill another irrigation well, if only he had the money."

"How much would a well cost?" Stroube inquired.

"Aw, 'round $1,500, I reckon," Burnett drawled.

"Why don't you let us drill your well, in exchange for the use of your land?" Stroube offered.

"W-e-l-l, I'll hafta ask the wife," the farmer replied, obviously content that he had just out-traded these high-rollers from the big city.

"Anyway," Toad continued, "a deal was made. In the middle of one pasture was a low mound of likely-looking rocks. We scrabbled around on it and collected some promising looking samples. Now, my job was to take them back to Dallas and have them assayed.

"We were all anxious for the results. When I returned to the assay office, the man in charge asked me, 'Mr. Leon, where did you get these samples?' Thoughts of claim jumpers crossed my mind.

"Oh, I'm not real sure," I hemmed and hawed.

"Well, you can put them back where you found them. They're worthless," Leon was told.

Toad would never know why Stroube's mineral detector went crazy along the road near Farmer Burnet's place. Surely the old guy hadn't sweetened the roadway with the uranium-filled glove as Toad himself had done in New Mexico!

At any rate the mother lode had eluded the three prospectors who went back to their primary callings in life.

"Our Arizona desert sourdoughs know
prospecting is the pits," Wyatt chided.

To Burger...To Burger Not

Among Toad Leon's many investment adventures were two decisions on backing hamburgers. One, Woody's Hamburgers of Distinction, was a fast food try Toad readily admits he should have passed on. This was in the mid-1950s. Toad had built the Town and Country Drive-In Theater in Abilene, patterned after his highly successful Twin Drive-In in Fort Worth. He had admired an upscale fast food establishment there named Goff's Burgers of Distinction. He particularly liked the name.

"We were always looking to make a dollar." he said. "I'd never heard of McDonald's. Back then, it was still in San Diego, California. I wanted this to be a really high class place."

He took in some partners and built a distinctive looking place near Abilene High School. From the start it was destined to fail for a number of reasons. Mainly a railroad underpass was built right at his front door and suddenly his prime location deteriorated considerably. Also, Abilene just didn't seem ready for distinctive burgers.

Maybe that's why, twenty years later he had another chance to sell hamburgers but couldn't make the commitment. "I owned 300 feet fronting North First and Leggett," he said. This was only a block from where he would put in Square's Barbecue a couple years later.

A Burger King regional executive based in Houston contacted Toad, and asked if he would be interested in selling the property. The franchise was moving into Abilene, and it sure wanted this piece of real estate upon which to build its flagship restaurant there. At this time, about 1975, Toad had a car wash and "Gas 'n' Go" on the property that was doing fairly well, even though it had some of built-in problems. Not the least were teen-age boys who would empty quarters from coin drops every week or two by using a hammer.

"N-o-o, don't believe I'd be interested in selling just now," Toad responded, figuring if Burger King was really wanting the property that was located just two blocks from the city's first McDonald's, they would sweeten the deal.

The Burger King man's next pitch caught Toad off-guard.
"Well, if you won't sell, would you like to go into partners with us? You furnish the site, we do the rest, and we'll split the profits fifty-fifty."

Toad considered the two offers and decided maybe selling was better than taking another chance on fast food. The price the soon-to-be hamburger giant wanted to pay for his land was inviting and if he didn't take the deal, Burger King would buy somewhere else. So the sale was completed, Toad's convenience store/car wash was razed and Burger King built an impressive fast food restaurant.

Toad couldn't help but keep up with the place. "I found out they grossed a million dollars the first year. That got me to thinking. Even conservatively, you could figure on a twenty percent profit, or $200,000. You've got to figure they did at least that well from then on. My share, then, would've been around $100,000 yearly, without lifting a finger. Let's see; $100,000 a year for twenty-seven years plus...hell, you do the math."

The New Mexico Caper—1955

Sometimes close friends and family knew they were about to be had by Toad Leon who just loved to watch them wriggle. Sometimes they knew. They just couldn't do anything about it. Such was the fix Wilbur Leon found himself in. Even his young wife knew Uncle Toad was up to no good. "But to no avail," said Virginia Leon Barnhart. This is the way Wilbur's cousin remembers hearing about the New Mexico Caper:

When his father, Carroll Leon, died in 1952 Wilbur Leon was already married and had three children including a new baby girl. Wilbur was the only son among five brothers. Clarence and Toad Leon, the oldest and youngest, respectively, of Carroll's brothers probably felt a real duty and sincere desire to inaugurate the only carrier of the Leon name in the younger generation into the camaraderie of the Leon men.

On this occasion in 1955 Toad and Clarence were en route to Toad's Pendaries Ranch in northern new Mexico. When they arrived at Wilbur's isolated West Texas farmhouse, 300 or so miles from Pendaries, they found Wilbur home for lunch. The uncles were welcomed with gracious hospitality and served a hearty meal. But when they responded by asking Wilbur to join them for "a couple or three days" at Pendaries young Mary Leon became a bit concerned.

"I guess it'll be OK, Wilbur," she told her husband, "but remember your uncles sometimes conveniently lose track of time."

The six-hour trip to Pendaries according to Virginia was filled with stories of business deals, cattle breeding, recent hunting trips, and, as always, encounters with traffic cops on the long Texas highways. Day one of the caper ended soon after they pulled through the ranch gate at dusk.

At breakfast the next morning Toad mentioned that there were a few steers that needed vaccinating. Wilbur had been hoping to take a leisurely horseback ride around the ranch and maybe deeper into the spectacular Sangre de Cristo Mountains that surrounded it. However, darkness caught the three still working cattle. End of day two.

By noon the next day Wilbur swore they had inoculated eight or nine hundred steers. However, before packing to leave, Wilbur got his horseback ride into the mountains.

By the time he had been away from home for the negotiated three days, they were back on the road, Wilbur behind the wheel and heading east. But then Clarence said, "Since we're this close, let's run down to Escabosa and see Bob Sullins. His ranch is just a few miles out of Albuquerque."

Wilbur obligingly headed the car in that direction, more southerly than east. Bob was glad to see them and insisted they spend the night. The conversation carried on far into the evening. End of day three.

Next morning they got a late start. Again Wilbur tried to head for home only Toad said, "You know, Jack Reynolds has a ranch near Socorro. It's only about a hundred miles out of the way We ought to go by and see him since we're this close.

"Listen, I need to get home," Wilbur said

"Oh, Mary won't mind and we really need to see Jack," Toad replied. "He's getting pretty old."

They found Jack in poor health. But discussions of past hunting trips helped ease the pain for a while. And before long, it was dark. Jack urged them to spend the night. End of day four.

Next morning, they had scarcely reached the city limits of Socorro when Clarence and Toad had convinced themselves that they needed to motor on down to see Tom Shortly He lived in Truth or Consequences, "not too much out of the way," the uncles promised. Wilbur, still driving, gritted his teeth and headed south. He didn t know any of these people he was visiting. He was at least a generation younger. And not only was he feeling awkward he was absorbing guilt for being away from home. They found Tom hale and hearty and very glad to have some company. Two neighbors were called to join them for cards. Wilbur was relieved his Texas Tech brand of poker held up. They played well into the night. End of day five.

It was close to noon when they dragged out of bed and late afternoon by the time all the good-byes were said. They stopped in Truth or Consequences for supper, during which Toad and Clarence speculated about going to visit Ben Clark in Silverton. After all it was less than an hour away and the countryside was scenic. Wilbur was too tired to argue, but when they reached the cut-off to Silverton, much to Clarence's and Toad's surprise, Wilbur pulled the car over.

"Men," he announced as he got out of the vehicle, "you go where ever you like and stay as long as you want. But I'm going home. I'll hitchhike if I have to. Mary is going to kill me."

"OK. Get back in the car, Wilbur," Toad said. "It's probably time for all of us to get home. Besides you're our driver." Very little conversation was exchanged until Clarence finally asked, "Wilbur, will Mary really be mad?"

"Listen, we have three little kids at home and I told her I would be home three days ago. What do you think?"

Silence returned, as Wilbur contemplated the fact that he hadn't even called his wife since he'd been gone. It was after midnight when they arrived at Wilbur's house. "It's late and we've got plenty of room. You all come on in and spend the night," he asked, half hopefully and half pleadingly.

"No, guess we better get on down the road to Rotan," Clarence replied.

"Yeah, we had better move on along," Toad seconded. "Well, good luck."

"You cowards!" Wilbur sneered. "I'll know better next time." He turned resignedly and walked up to the house to face the music.

End of day six.

And Wyatt found a soul mate in Wilbur Leon.

Donna's Surprise—1956

Donna Leon loved going places and having fun. Her husband enjoyed pulling fast ones on people. With a little help from their friends, the two situations once came together to provide Donna with one of her happiest times.

"Donna and I had driven from Abilene to Dallas the day before," Toad Leon recalled. "Our plans were to catch a flight to New York at 4:30 in the afternoon. We were going to a theater convention and I anticipated getting a dose of culture while there since she was along. Maybe the Metropolitan Museum and a Broadway play or two."

He was having lunch with his good friends Hugh Briggs and Johnny Black at the Baker Hotel when the specifics of the trip came up. "Y'know, I'm not very busy and I haven't been to New York City lately," Hugh said, "maybe my wife and I should go with you all."

"I'm not very busy either," Black added. "Let's call our wives and see if they'd like to go. This afternoon, right Toad?"

"I knew this was now a done deal," Toad recalled. "Jane Black and Cris Briggs were always ready to go anywhere at any time. Of course a little last-minute shopping at Lou Lattimer's would be in order first. Soon enough the plot was hatched. I wanted it to be a surprise for Donna. But that would take some cunning."

Behind the scenes, the Blacks and Briggses had reserved seats in the coach section since, for once, Donna and Toad were flying first class. They had booked rooms at the Plaza, where Toad and Donna were staying and had hurriedly packed their bags. The two couples drove Donna and Toad to Love Field airport and convincingly said their goodbyes. "Have a great time! See you when you get back!" they shouted and waved. Then, while Toad and Donna boarded the plane in the front, the Blacks and Briggses were getting on through the rear into the coach section.

Toad began to wonder if maybe he had outsmarted himself when, about midway through the flight, Donna said, "I'm really looking forward to this trip. It will be the first time we've been to New York alone...just the two of us."

"When the plane landed at La Guardia Donna made the move to disembark with the first-class passengers," Toad said. "I fumbled around with my seat belt and stalled by suggesting we let some more people get off in order to avoid the crush. She was looking back through the aircraft toward the tail section when she spotted her close friends in their big hats coming up the aisle."

The good times couldn't have been much better than during this party scene in 1956 that included (from left) John Black, Snooky Hubbard, Donna Leon, Betty Freeman, Ruben Knight, Toad Leon, Jackie Hubbard, Jane Black, Wayne Freeman, Florence Knight, Dodge Hubbard, and Morgan Hubbard.

"My gosh! Here come Jane and Cris! And there's Johnny and Hugh!" Donna squealed. "How in the world did they get here?"

"It was a wonderful moment," Toad said. "Donna was truly surprised."

The six spent the evening at Double Six Dominoes Supper Club in Harlem. "Many cocktails later, Johnny abruptly got up and left the table. A little later Hugh did the same. There I was with the three girls and the check," Toad said. Good joke guys Toad thought as he escorted the three ladies back to the Plaza Hotel.

They all went to Toad's and Donna's room for a nightcap. Then Jane Black bade them goodnight and headed for her room. She was back in an instant. "Johnny isn't in our room! Where could he be?" she asked.

"I wouldn't worry," Cris said. "You know how that husband of yours is. He'll be back soon. Well, goodnight all. I'm going to bed." She too was back in no time. "Hugh isn't in our room, either!" she cried.

"There we all sat in the hotel room wondering whether or not to be concerned when the phone rang," Toad said. "It was Johnny calling for Jane."

"Hello," she spoke into the handset. "Where are you? You're where!? Back in Dallas?"

It seemed Johnny Black had left the supper club feeling no pain. He hailed a taxi and then, having to come up with a destination, said, "La Guardia." When he got to the airport, he just sort of felt obligated to buy a ticket. To where? Home, naturally. "He explained that the weather had been stormy and the flight turbulent," Toad said, adding that Black had lamented, 'I think I flew all over the sky!'"

"Hugh showed up at the hotel later," Toad said. "We never did get the full story on his tardiness."

Jane and the Briggses would join Johnny soon since both couples were due to attend a big wedding party in Dallas the next night. Their flight schedules would barely get them back in time so the ladies dressed in their long evening dresses in New York. "What an elegant sight they made for their fellow passengers!" Toad said.

"Donna and I did spend the next couple of days as previously planned—museums and such with just the two of us. But the highlight of the trip was Donna's big surprise sprung on her by her dear friends."

And that wild ride Johnny Black gave his wife? The couple was good at it. "We used to party in Dallas at a place called the Cipango," Toad said, "Sip 'n Go, to us. One night, Johnny kinda acted up,' Toad explained. Jane was so steamed at Johnny she told Donna she was 'going to Mexico City, all by myself. Right now!'"

Jane Black did leave. And it would be three hours before she returned to the table looking a little sheepish. It seemed she had actually tried to fulfill her plan. She caught a taxi to Love Field and immediately boarded a plane heading south. "She got to San Antonio, changed her mind and caught a plane back," Toad said, laughing until tears welled up in his eyes.

And Johnny Black? "He thought his wife had been in the ladies room the whole time," Toad said.

Ah, friends! Don't you just love 'em? Wyatt asked.

How to Break a Haberdasher's Heart—1956

This is one of those Toad Leon stories that just won't go away. Toad was planning an elk hunt to Meeker, Colorado. He was to be accompanied by his brother, Clarence, and two of Toad's close friends in Abilene— Jack Yonge and Horace Holly.

"Cold weather was predicted. Maybe a chance of snow. So plenty of warm clothes were needed," Toad recalled. "We were leaving at dawn on the following Monday morning. As I packed my bags Saturday night, it became apparent that I was lacking in the long underwear department. My friend, Jack Tucker, owned S & Q Clothiers in downtown Abilene and I knew he could help". Toad picked up the phone and dialed the home of the owner of S & Q, the most popular clothier in town and lovingly referred to as "Skin 'Em Quick" by some locals. "Jack, this is Toad. I'm leaving on a trip early Monday and I need two new suits. I hate to ask but would you mind opening your store Sunday morning?"

"Of course, Toad. I'll meet you there at 10 a.m."

Now when Toad had lived in Dallas he had been a regular shopper at the S & Q there. Mr. Quicksilver, the owner, and Toad had shared some good times at the Variety Club. When Toad moved to Abilene, Quicksilver advised Tucker that Toad would be a good customer. Jack and his brother, Howard Tucker - owner of Tucker's Cleaners, had become good golfing buddies of Toad's.

"Anyway, we met at the store as scheduled. 'C'mon in, Toad,' Jack invited. 'I know you like the Hollywood branc so I've laid out some nice suits, with shirts, ties, and socks to coordinate. Hope you like the colors,'" Howard said, telling the story.

Toad let him run with his sales pitch for a while before he calmly deadpanned, "Jack, I think you misunderstood. I'm going on a hunting trip. I need a couple of union suits."

"I don't know about Wyatt but this sure made Jack Tucker want to urp!" Toad concluded with a laugh.

Jack Tucker died many years ago. but the story still circulates around Abilene, thanks to Howard Tucker.

Surprise, Surprise Charlie!—1956

Riding along the highway one early December day, Toad cooked up yet another of his patented practical jokes.

"It was 1956," Toad recalled with a smile. "We lived in Abilene at the time and were active at Abilene Country Club. Abilene High was enjoying its third straight state championship football season under Coach Chuck Moser.

"This year Abilene High was playing at another perennial powerhouse, Wichita Falls, in the semifinal game. About fifty club members chartered two buses, with a bar in each, and set out the 150 miles to see the big game.

"Now, Charlie and Glenna Featherstone lived in Wichita Falls. They were very close friends of Donna's and mine. We had visited them several times and they us. Charlie was one of the country's most successful feedlot cattle buyers. Anyway, our buses stopped in Haskell, almost midway to Wichita Falls and I thought I'd call Charlie. I told him we were coming up there to see the big game and he said great, come on by the house when you get here and we'll have a drink and then go out to the stadium together."

Poor Charlie. He had played into Toad's hands—again.

"Now Charlie, there are several of us along on this trip."

"Doesn't matter. You all come on by."

"Several people on both buses knew the Featherstones. They liked what was transpiring," said Toad as he continued the story. "I directed the drivers on how to get to Charlie's. They had this big circular drive in front. Our two buses drove in there and honked their horns. Here came Charlie and Glenna and their housekeeper outside and, my gosh, did they look shocked! I said, 'Well, here we are!' Charlie then smiled and invited us to 'C'mon in and have a drink.'"

Another time Charlie and I were in the Texas Hotel in Fort Worth. It was 1948. Former Governor Coke Stevenson was running for the U.S. Senate against Lyndon Johnson. Charlie and I differed on one thing and that was politics. He was a big Democrat and backed Johnson. I happened to be kind of a Republican although I never was active in party politics. My brother, Server, always said that politics was bad for our theater business. If we were active in politics, we would make half the people—our customers—mad at us.

"Anyway, I was for Coke Stevenson. Pretty soon someone asked Charlie if he'd like to meet Stevenson. 'Sure,' he replied. So this guy took us over and said, 'Coke, this is Charlie Featherstone.' Now at that time

Coke smoked a pipe. If you've ever been around a pipe smoker you know he's always doing one of three things: either lighting it, smoking it or packing it. Well, he was lighting his when he shook hands with Charlie."

"Glad to know you, Mr. Featherstone," the candidate said.

Later, Featherstone said, "Here I was, about to meet maybe the next senator from Texas but all he could do before shaking my hand was try to light his pipe."

"Show me a man who smokes a pipe and I'll show you one lazy son of a gun," Charlie observed.

Wyatt? He doesn't smoke. Like Toad, he chews.

The Appaloosa Coat—Mid-1950s

One had to know wheeler-dealer, high-roller businessman Jack McQueen of Abilene to really appreciate this excerpt from "The Toad Files." Regardless, it's priceless. But we're getting ahead of ourselves.

The mid-1950s were the early years of the West Texas Rehabilitation Center in Abilene, soon to expand to San Angelo, almost 100 miles to the southwest. WTRC provided much-needed services. Valid insurance or other means with which to pay were not considered when one became a client. Only his or her need for those services.

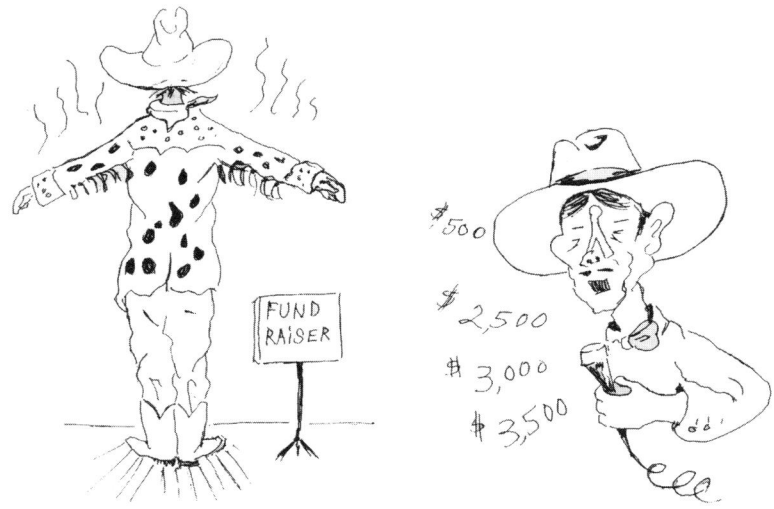

To help pay for those who couldn't the center's founder and executive director, Shelley Smith, inaugurated the Rehab Telethon. Entertainment and other celebrities would come to town once a year to run the show and draw in the crowds and TV viewers. Items to be auctioned were donated. At this particular time, Abilene had only one TV station. KRBC was an NBC affiliate.

Native Oklahoman and real-live cowboy, Dale Robertson, star of the hit western series, "Tales of Wells Fargo," was a natural to emcee the show.

"Along about then I was deeply involved in the Appaloosa horse business," Toad Leon recalled. "Earlier that year a colorful mare of mine had broken a leg and had to be destroyed. Her hide was sent to Jonas Brothers in Denver and tanned with the 'hair on.' Then it came to Abilene, where the Galloways tailored a western jacket out of the skin. It was beautiful!"

Ah, but sometimes beauty is deceiving.

"Later that summer, I wore the jacket to an Appaloosa convention in Denver," Toad continued. "It was quite a conversation piece. However, the convention center wasn't air-conditioned and as the evening wore on I detected a rather unpleasant odor. It was the jacket! I smelled like a hot horse!"

That fall Toad was approached by Frank Sheffield, then a fellow picture show man who was becoming a close friend. "Toad, do you have something you could donate to Rehab for our TV auction?" asked Sheffield.

Hummmm! Do you do this to a friend? Maybe it was just a fluke of the atmosphere or something in Denver. Maybe the thing wouldn't stink anymore. "Uh, well, Frank, I do have this Appaloosa coat..."

"Great, Toad! That sounds like a winner," Sheffield exclaimed.

The night of the auction was exciting. Entertainment abounded. Dale Robertson was doing a bang-up job. The auction was bringing in more money than had been anticipated. "The whole town was in a party mode," Toad said. At last Toad's Appaloosa coat became the center of attention.

Robertson, a horse man of no small stature himself, put on a real sales pitch. But there was no bidding war. It was over in no time. Jack McQueen had come up early—before the coat was flashed on TV, actually—with an offer of $3,500. No one would touch it.

Sheffield went around next day delivering the items purchased at the auction. "Coat! COAT?!" I thought I was buying an Appaloosa COLT!" McQueen exclaimed.

Toad, who knew McQueen as "an all-around nice guy," couldn't help but laugh at the high-roller businessman who thought he was stealing a high-dollar horse for peanuts, relatively speaking.

"Jack took it in stride," Toad said. "After all, it was for charity, and a very good one at that.

The next year, he donated the coat back to Rehab to be auctioned again." This time Dr. Wayne Ramsey, a noted local physician, purchased the coat, and he was not disappointed. He really wanted it.

"As far as I know, his widow, Marie, still has the coat," Toad said.

The colorful Jack McQueen died early in 2001. He always smiled when someone asked him if he was the Appaloosa Coat Man.

McQueen would have been the first to admit that he knew exactly what Toad Leon meant when he asked, "What made Wyatt urp?"

Throwing Bull in the '50s

Those who have hung around Toad Leon for any length of time quickly develop an appreciation of his sense of humor. If, that is, they particularly enjoy an extra helping of corn. Toad loves a good story, and it can't get too corny.

Ben Davis, Toad's CPA at the time, and Ben's wife, Bonnie, had driven from Abilene to Pendaries Ranch for a visit. One morning Toad took them on a drive through the mountains toward Taos. It is a road that contains many tight "S" curves with remnants of rockslides in evidence.

"Ben said the road reminded him of the legend of old Throwing Bull," Toad recalled, with his patented chuckle. "It seemed Throwing Bull was chief of a small band of Indians. He was getting a little long in tooth and was worried about the future of his tribe. So he called his two sons to his teepee."

"Come, sit at my feet, Running Deer and Falling Rock," Davis said the old chief commanded of the young braves. "I have devised a plan whereby I will choose my successor before I am called to the Happy Hunting Grounds. Running Deer, you run east and bring back all the game you can find and lay the game at my feet. Falling Rock, you go west and do the same. The son who brings back the most game will be named chief."

A week passed and Running Deer returned. "See, my father, O Great Throwing Bull, I have brought you the deer, the elk, the bear, and the buffalo and have laid them at your feet. Surely you will appoint me to take your place."

"My son, you have done well, but we must wait for Falling Rock to return," replied the old chief. So they waited. And waited. And waited.

"See, Toad," Ben Davis concluded, "even today, as you drive the roads of the western states, you will notice signs: WATCH FOR FALLING ROCK!"

It might not be a bad idea to keep an eye out for Wyatt, too.

Drive-In Picture Shows—1950s and 60s

You name the problem, and once-robust Hollywood had it, as the motion picture business emerged from the flush forties to face uncertain times in the fearsome fifties. The major studios' holds on movie distribution were folding. Screenwriters and actors were being run to the ground by Sen. Joe McCarthy's commie witch hunts. And that ugly thing with rabbit ears

Grand opening night at the Fort Worth Twin is a sold out gala.

called a television set was beginning to keep families home—and away from theater box offices. Nobody knew where these changes in the business of exhibiting films were going to stop. Leon Theaters was looking for ways to either make the changes benefit their operations or perhaps cut their losses.

"Before Server's death we had discussed the prospects of drive-in theaters," Toad Leon recalled. "We had even gone to Corpus Christi to check out the first one built in Texas. It was a new frontier and we were intrigued.

"In 1946 I bought an unfinished single-screen drive-in in Tyler, Texas. Our capacity was 500 cars. Our sound system consisted of one loudspeaker that flooded the entire parking area and our concession area was a little popcorn stand just down from the ticket booth. It was primitive by later standards but very popular at this time. We upgraded as soon as material and new equipment became available. Copper was so scarce after the war that when we built our next single-screen drive-in in Sherman, Texas, we had a devil of a time finding enough wire to run the individual speakers for our 650-car capacity."

It was about this time that a major player in theater investing by the name of Major Childress approached Leon and asked if he would be inter-

Toad Leon helped pioneer a new market for movie-goers. Here, some of the opening night crowd find watching the silver screen from outside their car to be just the ticket.

ested in selling some of his small-town theaters. Childress was being backed by the deep pockets of financier H.J. Griffith. This got Toad's attention. If it worked out properly, the timing of the proposal couldn't have been more advantageous to Leon Theaters.

"By now," Toad continued, "a few drive-ins had begun to spring up. I thought I could see the handwriting on the wall. My gut feeling was that drive-ins were not just novelties but the coming thing. I figured they would be stiff competition for downtown movie houses especially in small towns.

"At any rate, the deal was made. We sold 10 theaters in six of the smaller towns - Crowell, Haskell, Albany, Graham, Slaton and Baird. The proceeds from the sale freed me up to begin expansion. Now it became a matter of finding locations. A single screen drive-in required at least 15 acres and this meant finding sites at the edges of towns. This turned out to be an advantage, since real estate usually was less expensive in the fringe areas."

Thus armed for expansion, Leon began simultaneous construction on three drive-ins in the Dallas area: the Hampton Road, Garland Road, and Denton Road. Toad had noted a unique concept in Philadelphia a year earlier, one that went against original designs by building the screens not in front of the complex, but in the rear.

"By placing our screen towers in the back, we were able to save on building costs. If you built a front-screen drive-in, it wound up being more expensive. The towers had to be dressed up.

"My good friend, Harvey Jordan, was of invaluable help during these drive-in construction years. He was a very savvy builder/architect/engineer who also had a pioneering mind. We had begun our association years before, when we were in the midst of remodeling newly acquired conventional movie houses.

"In the beginning, we were feeling our way along. But it was such a new concept, the only limit was our imagination.

Fast food dining service at the Fort Worth Twin.

"Of course, we weren't the only ones building drive-in theaters. One enterprising man, probably a lawyer, even tried to get a U.S. patent on 'ramping,' though the courts decided that you couldn't patent Mother Earth," Toad explained. Ramps were curved rows of terraces that faced the screen. They gave the parked cars the correct angle to see the screens over the cars in front. The closer to the screen the steeper the berm, or ramp.

"The rule of thumb for accounting purposes was that there were two and a half persons per car. Reasonably, we began to construct larger drive-ins to accommodate more cars. Then came the 'twins,' featuring two screens instead of one. In 1953 we built the Twin Drive-In Theater in East Lancaster, five minutes from downtown Fort Worth. It had a capacity of 1,600 cars."

The Fort Worth Twin Drive-In opened on July fifteenth as the largest such theater in Texas and second largest in the U.S. The opening bill was the Fort Worth premiere of "Cow Country," a western starring Edmund O'Brien. The second feature was "Jalopy" starring the Bowery Boys.

Leon is often credited with upgrading the drive-in theater concept to all-in-one family fun. Something special. He did this mostly through vastly improved concession stands. "We now found ourselves in the restaurant business as well as showing movies," Toad con-

The huge Tower Twin Drive-In screen is shown here under construction in Abilene in the mid-1950s.

tinued. "It became critical that our patrons be served promptly, because intermissions were only 15 minutes long."

He was the first to initiate the idea of hot and cold serving lines. The cold, or fast, lines were for drinks, ice cream, candies, and such. The hot lines were for fried chicken, hot dogs, hamburgers, pizza, and the like. His concession outlets at the twins contained identical lines for each screen. He staggered the intermissions in order not to create human traffic jams. This allowed the same staff to take care of both sides.

He also was the first to see the need for large, clean, well-lit restrooms—and I do mean large. This might seem to have been a minor innovation, however, up until then, as drive-in capacities grew, the importance of adequate restroom facilities had not.

"Our main focus was family entertainment. Back then Hollywood was producing good, wholesome pictures. Parents brought their children to play on the swings, merry-go-rounds, and slides. The family would eat supper at the snack bar and then sit in the comfort of their own car to enjoy the double feature. It was an exceptional era."

By the mid-1950s Leon Theaters had sold all its more than twenty single-screen indoor theaters located in the mostly decaying downtown areas, particularly in small cities. Drive-ins, such as the sprawling Town and Country in Abilene that more than duplicated the Fort Worth Twin, were the focus of the operation.

The Abilene drive-in was the best in a highly competitive market. It even made a quiet run at rebounding in the summer of 2000 more than thirty years after it had seen its heyday.

This resurrection of sorts brought Henry Wolff Jr. of Victoria, Texas, to Abilene to write a nostalgic piece about drive-ins for the Victoria Advocate. Wolff had grown up in Ballinger, about sixty miles south of Abilene. He was introduced to outdoor movies at the Horseshoe Drive-In there by his parents. Later, when he began dating, he and friends would take the girls to larger venues in San Angelo and Abilene. Wolff became a photographer at the Abilene Reporter-News in the early 1960s, when, he noted with sadness in his Advocate piece, one could sense the beginning of the end of outdoor theaters.

Several of the lesser Abilene drive-ins tried to stay in business with controversial fare such as "Never on Sunday," a film about a prostitute. There were even some early "nudie flicks" at drive-ins such as the Crescent south of town. These prompted several owners to make court appearances thanks to Abilene's strict "censorship board."

"When C.D. (Toad) Leon opened the Town and Country two-screen drive-in in 1956 it was billed as the largest in the Southwest," including 475 in Texas and just eclipsing its sister complex in Fort Worth, "and was (rated as one of the best) among 5,000 in the U.S.'," Wolff wrote.

"Times were changing in 1963 but better drive-ins like the Town and Country were still showing family films as a way to get Mom, Dad and the kids out of the house."

So why didn't the height of drive-in theater popularity last longer than a couple of decades? Television was the main culprit though not the only one.

"First it was Daylight Savings Time and then, finally, television, that rang the death knell for us," Leon said. Daylight Savings Time returned to force many drive-ins to wait until 9:00 p.m. or later in the prime summer time to start their double features. This necessitated that working families either skip the second feature or not head home with sleepy kids until perhaps 1:00 a.m. It was too much to ask of them, especially on weeknights.

"Hollywood film releases also began to change," Leon said. "More and more sex and violence movies were being released, and less family films were in the offing."

Still, it was the one-eyed monster that stared back at families in their own homes that caused drive-ins the most woe. "I often said, television sets should be treated like slot machines," Leon said. "It should be against the law to own one or to transport one across state lines. My friends seemed to think I made this statement because I was in the picture show business," Toad said with a chuckle. "But it wasn't only drive-ins that television affected adversely. When the public stayed home evenings to watch their TVs instead of gathering downtown to visit, catch up on the news, and browse the local shop windows, small town merchants also felt the pinch."

That is not to say Leon Theaters didn't enjoy a profitable twenty or so year run in outdoor film exhibition. And once it was over what was to become Leon Enterprises that had hundreds of acres of prime real estate.

"That was the safety feature of the drive-in theater, because in the beginning you were always on the edge of town. You paid maybe $100 an acre for drive-in property. By the time the drive-in was passe in twenty or so years, the city had grown up around your property and the land could be worth $5 a foot, and even more in places like Fort Worth, Dallas, and Houston."

Toad was still selling land from his drive-in operations in the 1990s, twenty or thirty years after the lights on the double screens had gone dark. And at the writing of this book, Toad still owned former drive-in acreage, waiting patiently for the right bidder. "Drive-in theaters wound up being an excellent way to warehouse land," he said with a knowing smile. "I was raised with the idea that they weren't making any more land. As long as they don't, the value should be there."

Overhearing her father's observation, his daughter, Sandra, added with a smile, "Daddy likes to invest in things he can feel, touch, see, and walk on."

It was a money-making equation Wyatt,
the Tombstone entrepreneur, could appreciate.

Psst! Want a Magic Bullet, Toad?

Toad Leon is always on the lookout for a sure thing, be it a business deal, a game of robins or skins on a golf course, a swap of ranch land, or whatever it is that has come down the pike recently. He also has proved to be a sucker for the "sure thing" that might be couched, "Psst! Hey buddy. You wanna try something that can't miss?" Toad has been there. Often.

One of the best "sure things" foisted on Toad was by Bob Springer, a businessman and scratch golfer who ran with the same 19th Hole crowd as Toad. Now Springer was this handsome, soft-spoken, no-nonsense ex-New Yorker whose brief career as an outfielder with the old American League St. Louis Browns was interrupted by World War II. He trained at Camp Barkeley near Abilene. He and his wife, Bev, fell in love with the town and returned to make it their home following the war. One would just not suspect Springer capable of crafting a practical joke. Ah, but Toad Leon was too neat a prey to turn down.

"This was back in 1955, more or less," Springer said. In other words back when many men only dreamed there would be something like Viagra just around the corner. "Toad was playing gin rummy with the boys at Abilene Country Club. I was an onlooker. In a voice easily heard by the players, I mentioned that I was going to the car to take an aphrodisiac pill. Toad bowed out of the game and followed me. Then he watched me take what really were allergy pills."

"Are you really taking an aphrodisiac? And does it really work?" Toad wanted to know.

"I assured him that they worked at which point Toad said that he'd like to try some. So I gave him a few of the pills. A week later, Toad asked for more pills. He told me that those pills were really great. That they worked like a charm."

One can only imagine Toad's reaction when Springer felt the need to confess—in front of Toad's gin rummy buddies, of course.

"End of story," the suave Springer said with a twinkle in his eye. "As far as I know, he may still be on that pill."

If it works who cares what the guys in the card room think?

Golf is the Name of Toad's Game

Early in the year 2001, Toad Leon proved what he had preached for seventy years—that the game of golf he held in such high esteem was one for all ages in a man's or woman's life.

On a business trip from Abilene to Houston, he and his longtime friend, Frank Sheffield, stopped off at famed Horseshoe Bay and teed it up at the Robert Trent Jones' three-course complex's Slick Rock layout. In this first year of the new millennium Toad was checking in at almost ninety-one years of age, complete with two relatively new artificial knees. "I was real proud of him," said Sheffield, nearly twenty years Toad's junior. "He played every hole and hit every shot."

Whether it was at Dallas' revered Brook Hollow, Harlingen Country Club and the annual Life Begins at 40 tournament in which Toad played more than forty times, at the Abilene Country Club, on the Pendaries Ranch layout which Toad designed himself, or Fairway Oaks Country Club in Abilene where his home overlooked

Toad sought professional help with his game during the 1970s at the Toski Golf School in Florida. Toad (third from right) is assisted by Bob Toski (on Toad's left), CBS golf analyst, Peter Kostas (on Toad's right) and John Lumpkin (right).

the second fairway, the game has always enriched Toad's life.

"Golf is very unique in that it is up to the individual on how proficient he becomes," said Toad, who in his prime carried a 6.0 handicap. Toad particularly likes the way the game spotlights the individual—both in competing and adhering to the rules."

Even though he had long since given up playing regularly, Toad kept his name on the Brook Hollow membership rolls right up to the turn of the century. "Being a member there and at Abilene Country Club, back when I did play a lot, allowed me to reciprocally play at other clubs in other towns," Toad said. "I would introduce myself to the pro and he would work me up a game with some of his members whose handicaps were similar to mind. Some of my good friends were met in this manner."

If you played one time with Toad Leon, you never would probably never forget it. How many golfers do you know who, before the advent of soft spikes, had cowboy boots with steel spikes in them? I've seen two, and one was Toad. In fact, he rarely wore any footwear except boots. World-famous bootmaker James Leddy of Abilene kept them coming Toad's way.

"Toad Leon and Pee Wee Flowers (an Aspermont, Texas cattleman) are the only two men I know who belong to the Boot of the Month Club," Abilene attorney Malcolm Schulz once wisecracked to a group in the 19th Hole at Abilene Country Club.

Toad also went through new clubs with startling regularity.

"What? Another set of irons, Toad?" a member of his foursome exclaimed years ago watching Leon take a box of clubs from the back of his car. "What are they this time? Wilsons? Hogans? MacGregors?"

"These are Wurlitzers," Toad deadpanned without missing a beat.

"Wurlitzers?"

"Um-hum. You know. Self-playing."

Although making a hole-in-one does not necessarily reflect the true capability of a player, Toad has done all right in aces. He has had six—

Donna and Toad Leon enjoy the party at the 12th annual Tournament of Seniors in March, 1970.

one in Graham, two at Abilene Country Club, two at Santa Fe (New Mexico) Country Club and one at Fairway Oaks.

"When we changed Pendaries from a ranch into a golf and country club, our main goal was to develop a small community for golf lovers and their families," he said. "One way to advertise the fact that we now had home sites available was to attend golf tournaments, as well as put on some of our own. But that's another story.

1967 Brook Hollow Country Club Peppermint Stick Invitational. Clockwise from left: Toad, Barbara Varel, Wilbur Leon, Mary Leon, Carol Ann Leon, John R. Black, Donna Leon, Jane Black, Dan Varel, Cris Briggs, and Hugh Briggs.

"My friend, Bob Ring, was the general manager of Harrah's at Reno and Lake Tahoe. Donna and I were invited to his first 'celebrity' tournament in Reno. There were Hollywood stars, big league baseball players, football stars and, of course, those who played golf and could afford to play Ring's casino games. Once you were included on the invitation list of such a tournament, your name quickly became included on those of other tourneys in places such as Las Vegas, San Diego, Lake Tahoe and San Francisco."

Sonoma Sibley, wife of Dr. Dub Sibley, recalled attending the tournament with Toad and Donna. "We went to San Francisco first," she said. "When it was time for the men to play golf, Harrah's sent their plane to San Francisco to pick us up. There were several Rolls Royces waiting at the airport in Nevada to take us to the club." It was quite impressive to the West Texans.

"It was golf during the day and gambling and partying at night," Dr. Sibley recalled. "We played black-jack one night until the sun came up. James Garner (the actor) and (Fort Worth businessman and civic leader) Amon Carter Jr. were at our table."

"I remember Donna was getting real tired and sleepy toward dawn," Sonoma said. "One time the dealer waited for her to say something. She just sat there like she was in a trance. Finally, he asked Donna, 'Ma'am, do you want a hit?' Donna looked up and said 'Sí...That's Spanish for 'Yes." The dealer smiled at her and replied, 'Yes. I know.'"

For Toad, these party golf out-ings were priceless. "I had the pleas-ure of playing with many of the celebrities but I believe my favorites were Baseball Hall of Famers Dizzy Dean, Joe DiMaggio and Mickey Mantle, cowboy TV star Dale Robertson, and former NFL great, Ted Kwalick. All were down-to-earth, good-humored men. Once,

Donna Leon and Rancher Pee Wee Flowers ham it up at the 1970 Life Begins at 40 golf tournament in Harlingen, Texas.

while at the Andy Williams Invitational in San Diego, our foursome includ-ed DiMaggio. After the third and final round, our team was tied for first place. We were asked to cut cards with the other team to break the tie.

"Toad, as lucky as you are, you cut for us," Joe said.

"First place was a small version of an Oldsmobile convertible," Toad recalled. "Second place won a quadraphonic sound system. To make a short story even shorter, the four of us went home with, albeit pretty expensive and novel for the early '70s, music equipment," Toad concluded.

He looked over his shoulder to see if a green-gilled
cowpoke named Wyatt was hanging around.

Finding Friendship Through Party Golf

Toad's love affair with golf has included a long relationship with "Life Begins at 40," a social tournament in Harlingen begun in 1953 that stresses wives' having fun too. Toad has established many friendships through various phases of his life, none more than through golf. And none of those more than through "LBA 40." Toad goes back almost to its beginning and at ninety-one still retained his cherished position among the 254 players.

Friendship included Frank Underwood of Bowie, Texas, who with his wife June used to drive to Abilene then make the final 525 miles in tandem, two cars going down the highway, was an example.

Back when fifty-five was the speed limit and CB radios were the rage, Underwood prided himself in beating the lawdogs, driving seventy-five or eighty and keeping an ear tuned to the CB. "His handle was Kilroy," Toad recalled with a chuckle. "One year, he insisted we drive right behind him. He'd protect us from radar-bearing DPS vehicles. But I said no, we'd just bring up the rear." On that trip Toad and Donna waved at Frank as they went around him and a state highway patrolman who was writing up a ticket. Two hours later, the same scene was repeated. *Underwood looked like he intimately knew Wyatt (as in urp) this time.* All Toad could do was wave again, with a big smile.

Another "40" buddy pair was Irvin and Dorothy St. Clair of Muleshoe, Texas. "When the sun would go down at our golf tournaments the parties would begin, always as couples," Irv recounted during a 2001 interview. Credit Underwood, Toad, Irv, and his brother, Bill, with dreaming up a way to spread the fun of Life Begins at Forty. They were sitting around one day back in the 1980s wondering how to accomplish that. The object was to copy LBA 40 in miniature, making golf the focal point but keeping the wives and significant others involved primarily with parties each night. The men would play handicap medal rounds for three days.

"What would we call our tournament?" Irv asked the formulating foursome.

"W-e-l-l," Toad drawled, "why not name it after ourselves? And the kind of people we would want to invite to this first one? Let's call our group the International Horse's Ass Association."

The name stuck. Several regulars to the Harlingen tournament came aboard immediately. Directors were elected. Sites were picked, intended to be on a rotating basis. Toad brought the tournament to Fairway Oaks in Abilene. They also played at Tapatio Springs just outside San Antonio as the late-April fun tourney entered the 1990s.

Popular Mills Creek course in Salado finally became more or less the official home of the H.A. Invitational. Due to the maximum space the course could afford to block off, competition was limited to 40 men.

All dressed up and ready to party at Harrah's in Lake Tahoe are, from left: Bob Ring, Betty Slaughter, Donna Leon, Jeff Browning, and Toad Leon.

Membership quickly became coveted. A new member would be "sworn in" during a party night. He would stand before the regulars, place his right hand on a roll of toilet paper, and take the I.H.A.A. oath while being serenaded by the membership.

> "Hooray for Wyatt,
> "Hooray at last...
> "Hooray for Wyatt,
> "Now he's a Horse's Ass.

For Toad and Donna, the game would give way to Texas Panhandle pheasant hunting each fall when the Irv St. Clairs and Irv's brother, Bill, and his wife Marlene, opened their spacious homes to about seven other couples besides the Leons. Most were connected to at least one of these golf tournaments.

"It was always fun the first day when everybody wanted to walk in and kill a bird but it wouldn't be long before Toad would be a blocker," Irv recalled. "He and Bill always had a bet going on one thing or another. I never could figure out who won."

Actually, bets abounded all around. The Chamber of Commerce sold raffle tickets for an expensive shotgun one year. The whole group was downtown having breakfast the first day of the hunt when Toad bought several tickets. The hunters then went out and about noon were returning to the St. Clairs' residences.

"Tommy Singleton met us coming out of the fields," Toad recalled. "He was all excited. 'Toad! They just announced on the radio that you won the shotgun!'"

"Nah. Not me."

"You sure did! I'll bet you a hundred dollars you won," Singleton said.

"W-e-l-l-l…"

"OK. Then I'll bet you a hundred you didn't win! Take your pick, Toad."

This intrigued Leon. He thought it over, and talked himself into betting he did win the shotgun. He promptly wagered himself out of $100.

Tommy laughed and Wyatt urped.

Bad Day at Broadmoor—1955

With all the good times Toad Leon has enjoyed on golf courses around the U.S. and elsewhere one might wonder if it has always been this way. Oh no. Take Broadmoor, Colorado for instance. Please! Toad might add.

It was 1955. Ed Hopkins, former University of Texas varsity golfer and the hottest thing in spikes at Abilene Country Club, had become a good friend of Toad's. So had long-hitting Dan Winters. Both won numerous tournaments in and out of West Texas, back when amateur golf was in its heyday. Hopkins was famous for having shot a 58 on his home club's par 71 layout. It wasn't in a tournament but the round was a hole-'em-all weekend money match none the less. The card hung on the A.C.C. pro shop wall for many years. Hopkins was a U.S. Amateur quarterfinalist who later moved to Houston, where he hooked up with Sweetwater, Texas, native John Paul Cain, a fixture on the Senior Tour in the late 1980s-'90s. The two made a formidable two-man team that was practically unbeatable in four-ball matches during the '60s. They played out of Jack Burke, Jr. and Jimmy Demaret's Champions Golf Club.

"Ed told me he was going up to Broadmoor, Colorado, for the big amateur tournament they held at the resort that bore the same name," Toad recalled in the summer of 2001. "He told me he could get me an invitation if I was interested so I said sure. Dan Winters was going to play, too."

Toad and Donna decided to drive up to Broadmoor and arrived a day ahead of the other two Abilenians. "I figured I'd get in a practice round so I checked in at the pro shop and asked if they could arrange it for me. The pro asked me my handicap and I told him I was a six." The pro was glad to oblige, and in no time Toad was standing on Broadmoor's first tee looking around the beautiful, mountainous layout and down the imposing first fairway. In his company was Eddie Creel, the reigning left-handed champion of Colorado, "and two Air Force generals who were scratch golfers."

It soon began to dawn on Toad that catastrophe was just a swing or two away, if he didn't watch his step. "Here I had gained my handicap from flat, wide-open ol' Abilene Country Club where drought had left our fairways hard as a rock. You could hit it a mile counting the roll you'd get." It came Toad's turn to tee off. "I took a mighty swing and hit the ball maybe 150 yards. I finally got on the green and four-putted! The rest of the round went pretty well the same way and I was really embarrassed. I never was so happy as when we holed out on 18 and I could get the hell out of there."

It wasn't to be Hopkins' year but Winters found himself playing for the championship. He had been in brilliant form throughout the qualifying round, the four-day match play format, and was rolling early in the 36-hole final. Toad was among the gallery. Winters may have had the fastest backswing of any scratch player in the world. He was a student of the golf swing and decades later would be credited with helping successful touring pro, Bob Estes, develop his own smoother, much slower swing.

But the crowd loved Dan's huge drives and many in the gallery were openly pulling for the tobacco-chewing Texan.

"Early in the round, maybe number five or six, Dan hit a solid tee shot that made the green on the three-par," Toad recounted. "His opponent caught a trap, blasted poorly, and would eventually two-putt for a bogey.

"Dan got ready to address his putt and his ball moved a fraction. He stooped down, moved the ball back the quarter-inch to its original position, and proceeded to two-putt for what seemed like a winning par.

"What'd you take?" his opponent asked.

"Three," Dan replied, puzzled.

"No, my friend, you took five. You moved your ball."

"Now, Dan was really hot," Toad continued. "He asked for a referee to assess the situation and here comes old man Maytag, the washing machine guy. 'Tell me the situation, fellows,' he said, then listened, and finally looked at the Abilenian. 'Mr. Winters, your opponent is right. You are assessed a two-shot penalty. So you lose the hole.'"

Toad said Winters all but erupted. "You want to play that way? Then you're fixing to see a lot of birdies from here to the house!" Toad recalled Winters saying. "Boy, you talk about fast! Dan would take a swing, and you could almost see his cap turn on his head."

Alas, the bit of gamesmanship aimed Winters' way worked. He eventually had to settle for second place.

And Wyatt carded a double-urp at Broadmoor.

The Toad Leon Get-Even Hole

"Thinking about Denver reminds me of a wonderful trip I've never forgotten all these years," Toad Leon said while this book was in the process of being born. The Mile High Colorado city had been a favorite family vacation for the Leons when the girls were growing up.

"It was 1938. We were still living in Graham. My good friend, Mack Williams, suggested that since the temperature was about 100 degrees every day we ought to take a trip up to Colorado. So he got Claude Kennedy and his wife, and another couple—four golfers and four wives in two cars. I asked Mack how much it would cost me for a week. I didn't have a lot to spend on something like this. He said we'd be staying in Evergreen, near Denver, and didn't think it would be very expensive."

"How much are you taking, Mack?"

"Oh, thirty or forty dollars."

"OK. I'll take forty then," Toad decided.

Everybody was on a budget. They stopped at a nice hotel in Pueblo for dinner but the cheapest items on the menu started at two dollars. They took a sip of water and quietly slipped away without ordering, intent on finding a "blue plate special" somewhere else in town.

"In Evergreen, we rented a large house with four bedrooms. It had everything. They even left their silverware. I think we might have paid fifteen dollars for the week. We played golf every day even Cherry Hills (site of the U.S. Open won by Arnold Palmer) in Denver once. Every night we went to Elitches Garden, an outdoor club that always had a big band style dance. We had a ball.

"To save money we drove all the way back to Graham, 740 miles in a day and most of the night.

"I played the others for maybe twenty-five cents each round of golf, and I may have won a little. I don't remember. But when I got back to Graham, I still had ten dollars left. It was the best, cheapest vacation trip ever. What could you get for thirty dollars today? Maybe a good steak, if you were lucky."

When Toad began converting part of Pendaries Ranch into an upscale vacation resort village and after he had put in the first nine holes of the 12-hole golf course he designed (Twelve holes? That's another story), he invited the three Graham couples to spend a few days in the Leons' beautiful mountain retreat. He warned the men to bring extra change. The price of golf competition had gone up since they toiled for twenty-five cents a bet in Colorado thirty-five years before.

The Graham guys were leery playing Toad on Toad's very own course, particularly number nine, which they had heard about. The major press hole, an uphill par four, had a blind second shot. Once on the green the putting surface had a deceiving undulation clouded considerably by the mountainous terrain in the background. To miss the green, especially to the left, was disastrous.

The visitors were up at daybreak the morning of their first round. After making sure with resident pro, Jack Free, that pin placements had been set for the day they took putters and chipping irons to the ninth green. Now Free was an old pal of Toad's from their 1950s Abilene Country Club days and a drummer. Free fronted his own combo as resident musicians at the club for at least two decades. Toad had played many games of golf with him and when Free retired, only to find he didn't care for having nothing but playing golf to do, Toad asked him to come to Pendaries and be his unofficial pro.

Free got word to Toad that his pigeons for the day were scouting the treacherous ninth, known far and wide as "Toad's Get-Even Hole."

"Now everybody knows that it is against the rules to practice on a course the day of play," Toad recalled with a smile. "So I told Jack to let us get our round under way, and when we got out of sight to re-set the pin at nine clear across the other side of the large green."

Sure enough the Graham golfers were struggling against their host and came to the ninth well down. Presses were applied. Drives were hit with Toad's the longest.

One by one, the visitors hit their second shots toward the blind pin, confident they had guided their efforts to the "fat" side of the green out of harm's way. If you missed to the left, you went straight downhill into a shallow ravine. It would leave an impossible up-and-down shot to save par. They could scarcely hide their glee when Toad approached to the left of the top of the flagstick, apparently putting his ball in jail since they all knew the pin had been set on that side of the green.

Imagine their surprise when they drove their carts up the hill and found the pin now on the right side of the green. Toad had hit his approach to the fat side just off the surface and they had stroked perfect shots not to safety but to an incline that carried their balls into hellish graves. To add insult to injury, Toad chipped in for a birdie.

"I was tending bar in Moosehead Saloon when they came in," Carol Ann, Toad's daughter, recalled. "You never heard so much griping in your life! And Daddy just sat their smiling in that annoying way only he can do."

Incidentally, the saloon got its name from the gigantic mounted trophy head that hung over the bar. Remember the huge moose Toad shot in Canada on his 1946 hunting trip? The same.

The trophy moose brought down by Toad during a 1946 Canadian hunt has followed its conqueror ever since. Here it hangs as a namesake at the Moosehead Saloon at the Pendaries golf course.

So what about that twelve hole golf course? Toad, the neophyte course architect, started on the road to building one of northern New Mexico's premier resorts by designing three holes on his ranch. "It started out because I liked to play golf," he recalled. "Here was this fantastic piece of real estate that we owned and had grown to love, and I thought, 'By gosh, what a beautiful place this would be for a golf course.'"

"I built three holes. People would come out there and say, 'Oh, what a beautiful place. How about if you sell me five acres so I can build a house on it and share this beauty with you?' Well, I didn't want to do that, so finally I said to myself, why don't I just start a development over here?"

"I began with twenty-nine lots, put in a water and utility system, and people started buying them. So I said to myself, 'Whoa! This thing is gonna work.' I decided to put in a full nine holes of golf. Lots on the golf course sold real fast. In no time, I was out of golf course lots. I decided to build three more holes. So I plowed up these trees—my God, trees fifty, sixty feet high—and bulldozed them out of there for fairways.

"Looking back, I was premature. If I had been at this a little later than the 1960s, I'd still be there. I took 750 acres from the ranch for the development of the golf course."

From the golf course and the first lot sales, followed by impressive summer homes being built, the Pendaries Ranch development exploded into a full line of resort services. Ranch hands found that they had to learn other duties. And the four Leons ran the whole thing. Toad said, "It was like a game." But fun and excitement became high profile fatigue along about early August each summer. Before, somebody who popped off about buying into the resort would get ignored, now the family listened.

"I'm going to tell you something. it's a hell of a job running a lodge, a golf course, a restaurant, a tavern, a swimming pool, and doing this and that," Toad said. "It finally wears on you. I think we were very successful. I don't think anyone has done anything quite like it, before or since. We extended our season more and more until we were up there in the dead of winter having New Year's Eve parties. We had our own snow mobile dealership. Skiing was only fifteen miles away.

"But we had no corporation behind us. We had a directors' meeting every night. Between Donna and me, Carol Ann and Sandra, we'd look at each other and ask, 'What are we gonna do tomorrow? How are we going to publicize this?'

"We had a fellow, Bob Neff, who came in there as general manager. He was very good. Word got around. Bob had people coming in to see Pendaries for themselves. Then we began hearing from different individuals and groups. Would you sell? Well, I might, I'd reply. But this would have to be a big deal for us to consider, and it would be quite a decision that would have to be made if we were to leave Pendaries.

"Anytime you have a private club, everybody is trying to tell the owner how to run it. Should do this, should do that. I only had forty home owners at that time, most of them wealthy people from Dallas and mostly friends of mine. But the criticism and suggestions kind of work on you. Finally, I said, 'I'll tell you what, fellas. Why don't you just buy controlling interest in this thing and then you can run it anyway you want to?' They said, 'Well, we might be interested in doing just that. Let's have a meeting.'

"The Dallas contingent chartered a plane and flew to northern New Mexico. They had a lawyer with them who was drunk when he got there and drunker when he left. They came on a Friday. By Sunday morning, they were ready to meet."

Toad, no lover of lawyers, smiled as he remembered what transpired. The visiting attorney pointed up to the mountains surrounding the ranch and asked, "Toad, what do you think that land way up there on the side of that mountain is worth?"

In a flash, Toad knew where this was going. "Oh, if you're talking about ranching, which we do a lot of around here, I think it might be worth five dollars and acre."

The lawyer smiled and nodded. "That's about what I figured. Well, we've given this a lot of thought, Mr. Leon. We'll buy fifty-one percent and take control. Here's what we'll pay you."

Toad took the piece of paper and looked at it for a moment. Eyes were on him. Then he spoke to the tipsy attorney. "I'll tell you what. That's the best proposition I've had today. And I want to take it under consideration."

Another pregnant pause, then Toad continued, "But I'd go on down there if I were you and see if I could get that ol' airplane cranked up. And if I could get it started, I'd just head on back to Dallas. This meeting has come to a sliding halt."

The deep pockets from Dallas never tried to purchase Pendaries again.

"There were other developers who we knew would come in and groom a place like ours, sell it, and move on. I really didn't want that. I wanted somebody who would be permanent to run this thing." Shastina, an offshoot of an outfit in California that had a development on Lake Shasta, finally talked the Leons into selling the ranch and resort.

"They showed up with finance men, their vice-president, president, and about ten lawyers. On our side were Joe Sommers, my attorney from Santa Fe, and me. I guess they thought they were gonna outman me. But this thing took six to eight months and about fourteen propositions to finalize. I sure got tired of the figures and facts, facts and figures."

The Leon family had bought a smaller adjacent ranch a few years earlier and stayed within walking distance of the blood, sweat, and tears they had left while building a really unique resort and historically significant working ranch. "Today there are about 250 houses and Pendaries and they're still building them. The golf course is a full eighteen holes. It's beautiful," said Toad, wistfully.

Part of the Pendaries purchase included a 5,500 acre ranch in remote southeastern Oklahoma for Toad. "There was the most beautiful lake on the property which could have been developed into a resort, maybe. But by then I was a little worn out on development, I kept the ranch for three or four years, did absolutely nothing with it, and then sold it to Bunker Hunt."

The Pendaries proceeds also enabled the Leons to go into widespread farming ventures in the South Plains of Texas. One might remember the vow Toad made in 1931, when the disgruntled young man "promised the Good Lord I'd never hit Mother Earth another lick!"

"I guess I lied to the Lord," said Toad.

And Wyatt wagged a finger at his pal.

Toad's Little Bit of Golf Heaven

There is a beautiful bit of acreage in Dallas few people know about, and that's just the way its owners want it. Brook Hollow Golf Club raised exclusivity to a new, upper rung when it came on the scene several decades ago. Normally, starting times aren't necessary. That's because the limited membership pays for the privilege. And they and their guests are the only ones who can take advantage of this pristine layout by noted course architect, A.W. Tillinghast. That the Texas Golf Association's prestigious 2001 Senior Amateur Medal Play Championship was allowed to compete there was a rarity for outsiders.

Toad Leon belonged to Brook Hollow when he was a Dallas resident. When the Leons moved to Abilene in the early 1950s Toad retained his membership and kept it for many years—even after the family had set up residence at their Pendaries Ranch in New Mexico. His close friend, Abilene businessman Bob Springer (yes, the same Bob Springer who sprang the famous "aphrodisiac pill" practical joke on Toad), devised a way he could give his Abilene Country Club friends a chance to enjoy Brook Hollow.

Abilene stock broker, Donald McDonald Jr., like Springer, a low-handicapper, tells how it worked: "I only got to play Brook Hollow once, but it was like being in golf heaven," he said. They had a foursome discussing the famously well-hidden course one day following their round at water-starved A.C.C. None but Springer had played it. "OK. Let's go down next week," Springer offered. "Pick a day."

Sure! Just walk on? No way!

To which Springer responded by picking up the phone, checking his wallet for the number, and dialing. "Brook Hollow Pro Shop?" McDonald recalled Springer saying. "This is C...D... Leon. I have this group of Abilene Country Club friends coming down to join me next Wednesday. Only thing, I have a meeting when they want to tee off, so I'll be late. I'll join them after they've started. They will charge their rounds back to their own club with which we have reciprocal privileges for our guests. OK? Good. We'll see you next week."

Of course, "Mr. Leon," who was 700 miles away didn't join his guests during their round. And it worked like a charm, McDonald said.

But a membership chairman named Wyatt urped.

Sale Day—1960

If anyone ever knew Pendaries Ranch anywhere near as well as Toad Leon it was Joe Lacy. Perhaps not quite as well overall but at least he knew the public relations end. He quickly learned about horses. And horses—specifically the beautiful Appaloosa—are an integral part of the northern New Mexico ranch's modern history,

Lacy and his wife, Fran, moved to Pendaries Village in 1968 and assumed overall management of the facilities. "He came to us with a great deal of experience in public relations," Toad said. "Joe loved to see people enjoy themselves.

"Sale Day," when Leon offered colts, mares, and stallions to the highest bidder was to Lacy the epitome of Pendaries Ranch. These are his observations of one of the most colorful of such events along with a short course on how Toad Leon became known as a valid candidate for the unofficial title of Mr. Appaloosa:

One thing about raising Appaloosa horses: if they are properly handled and cared for after a while you will have lots of Appaloosa horses. This happened to Toad Leon. Finding himself with about 300 head he decided to have a sale. And not just any sale. Never one to do things halfway Toad and his wife, Donna, spent more than six weeks planning and getting ready for the event. The dates July 4-6, 1960, were selected and an elaborate sales catalogue was printed. Seventy head would be offered.

With an uncanny feeling for the future Toad decided that the golden

Toad's tack room office at the Pendaries Ranch

New Mexico Governor Jack M. Campbell and 1963 National Appaloosa Queen, Sandra Leon, with Appaloosa Horse of the Year, Quanah.

days of the restoration of this particular breed were about over. The time had come to begin withdrawal.

Cecil Dobbin, well-known auctioneer from Colorado Springs, Colorado, was contracted. Arrangements were made for "ringmen" from among the leading horse magazines. More than 1,200 invitations went out and the advance indications were that most of the recipients would be accepting.

Many things had to be considered. These people had to have a place to stay. The accommodations in nearby Rociada were virtually non-existent, so guests were advised that if they didn't want to stay in Las Vegas, New Mexico, they should bring their trailers, tents, or bedrolls and camp on the ranch grounds.

Arrangements were made with Mack Eplen's Caterers of Abilene and Mack himself arrived to supervise the feeding, especially the free barbecue hosted by the Leons. In discussing the menu Toad said that in order to hold costs down maybe just one meat—beef—should be served.

"Toad, you may know a little about the theater business and a little about the horse business," Eplen replied, "but you don't know a damn thing about the restaurant business. We'll serve beef, ham and sausage. And every time they choose sausage or ham, you've saved money."

Families began arriving. They caught fish from the lakes, warmed themselves by a huge camp fire, feasted at a chuck wagon, and listened to the sounds of western music. The ball started rolling when Ethelyn, Donna's cousin, and her daughter, Carol Lynn McGowen, led singing around the campfire. A high-fashion western wear style show, a sunrise trail ride, and, for the competitive horse people, jackpot cuttings, reinings, and stake races were all part of the occasion.

Toad leads a Pendaries Ranch mountain trail drive. (Life Magazine photo).

Life Magazine sent a crew to take photos. Toad's comment on shep-herding this operation was that it had to be some of the most difficult work he had ever done. One industrious photographer, not content with his first shot, asked that a certain horse be taken back for another drink of water. Apparently this photographer had never heard the cliché, "You can lead a horse to water…"

The sale was a huge success. Records indicate that it produced the highest sale average and highest selling pair—Apache Princess and her foal—for any Appaloosa sale up to that date. Actress Greer Garson and her husband, Buddy Fogelson, bought Golden Sandstorm and three other horses for their Forked Lightning Ranch near Pecos, New Mexico. Later, when commenting on her purchases for national TV, she said, "They make an ordinary entrance followed by a beautiful exit."

Everything went well and Toad says the only mistake he made was that he didn't sell all his horses. The sale drew prominent families from nearly all the western states with one buyer coming from Fairbanks, Alaska. The entire deal was planned as an "old-fashioned, western-style get-together."

Celestino Martinez, prominent citizen of Rociada, attended all the functions. He owned the Martinez Bar there which opened occasionally as it suited his fancy. Toward the conclusion of the festivities Martinez announced that he intended to open the bar and everyone was invited. Many accepted, including the Leons, and a never-to-be-forgotten day would soon come to a close.

Celestino's was where political deals often were made in those parts. A local resident came up to Toad and reminded him, "You know, my wife is running for county tax assessor," he said in a hush-hush tone. "She—we—would like your and Pendaries Ranch's support. All those beautiful horses you keep out there? I'm sure my wife would not consider them expensive so far as the tax rolls are concerned. *Qué pasó!?*"

A first for Toad and Donna occurred at the dance. He was used to his wife being singled out for the celebrated "first dance," but Toad did a double take when not Celestino, but his wife requested she be allowed to open the festivities by dancing with Donna. Apparently in the Old Country this celebratory act to open a dance was not so much customary but a special honor. Donna never missed a beat, either dancing or accepting Señora Martinez' offer to be her partner. As usual, Donna was the belle of the ball.

And Wyatt yelled, "Ai-ai-ai-ai-eeee!!"

Chief of Fourmile—1961

While many of Toad Leon's many, many business ventures would've made Wyatt urp his foray into the registered horse breeding business was one that could've made ol Wyatt smile.

Toad got in at just the right time in the mid-1950s when the Appaloosa breed, known for its wildly colorful coats, was languishing on past glory. Almost twenty years later, he had amassed a superb herd of the original Southwest Indian ponies, had held three major, nationally heralded sales, and would now bow out at the top of the market he helped develop.

Toad sits atop Quanah, his Appaloosa champion stallion.

"Carl Miles introduced me to Appaloosas," Toad said. The Abilene oilman knew of the Leons' beautiful Pendaries Ranch in the mountains of northern New Mexico. Appaloosa horses were bred to do particularly well at higher altitudes.

Miles owned Joker B, one of three top Appaloosa stallions in the world. One day he invited Toad to visit his ranch south of Abilene. "I want to show you something," Miles said.

When the Appaloosa was trotted out for inspection, all Toad could do was to gush admiringly, "What kind of horse is that?" Miles explained the nature of the breed and Toad was hooked. Quanah, considered on a par with Joker B as a stud, and standing second only to the renowned Chief of Fourmile, could be purchased.

Getting in on the Appaloosa business at its re-entry stage appealed to Toad's investment instincts. "The Appaloosa Association out of Idaho was brand new," he said. There were not many members and those who were in it had only five or six horses. 'My gosh, Toad,' Carl said, 'I can have Texas and you can do the same in New Mexico.'"

Toad and his trainer, Jim Trammell, took off on a buying spree through Nebraska and the Dakotas. They pulled a big horse trailer and when Trammell saw an Appaloosa he liked, they bought it on the spot. "Carl Miles was right. Between the two of us, we wound up with more horses than the rest of the association's members put together."

In 1958, Toad was ready to make his move. He accompanied Miles to the annual Appaloosa National Show in Hutchinson, Kansas, and bought not only Quanah sight unseen but another highly regarded stallion named Warrior. It was at Hutchinson that Toad saw a horse he really wanted. Chief of Fourmile, owned by Mr. And Mrs. Gus Oetterman of the Indian Lakes Ranch near Boerne, Texas. By performance and reputation Chief of Fourmile was the world's No. 1 Appaloosa. The Oettermans showed no inclination to sell him, however.

"I could only admire Chief, along with everyone else," Toad told *Abilene Reporter-News* writer B.G. Hughes. "I never expected in my wildest dreams to get the chance to own him."

Toad took his two stallions to Pendaries and then began talking to breeders and attending shows seeking to purchase top mares. "In 1959 Quanah was placed in cutting training," Hughes wrote. "Twelve years old, he was well past the usual training age when trainer Gayle Bourland took him over. But after three months in the ring Toad entered Quanah in the National Appaloosa Show at Santa Barbara, California, where he placed second in cutting and first in stake races. Additional training paid off. He took Grand Champion in several Texas shows, including at Plainview, Amarillo, and Fort Worth."

"Open Cutting was the next test," Hughes' article continued. "Since Quanah was the only Appaloosa in the show at Albuquerque, I hoped he would make a good showing." Toad said, "but I never expected him to take Grand Champion, which he did, handily."

About this time, Toad heard that Sam and Mabel Woodard of

Buckeye, Arizona, were considering disposing of their herd, which included Quanah's half-brother, Lucky Dot. Toad made the trip hoping to purchase the stallion. He returned to Pendaries with not only Lucky Dot but also fifteen mares and foals to boot.

Then, early in 1960, following the death of her husband, Mrs. Oetterman announced that she would hold a dispersal sale of their herd—including the coveted Chief of Fourmile.

"I was not optimistic about my chances for the Chief," Toad told Hughes. "He had been named the All-Performance Horse at two national and international shows and his racing had received so much publicity I knew breeders throughout the U.S. would be bidding for him. I was surprised and delighted when I got him."

Toad with Chief of Fourmile, his top Appaloosa stallion.

As the buying turned to selling, Toad learned quickly to spot the seasoned horse trader and someone like he had been just a few years earlier.

"People would come to me at Pendaries when I had these fine horses," he said. "If an ol' boy with a floppy hat, worn-out britches, and manure on his boots came by to take a look, I'd say, 'Help yourself,' and point in the direction he should go. I figure he knew more about horses that I ever would. But if a feller came by all dressed up in city clothes, I was pretty sure I could tell him all about our horses."

Due to considerable interest in the horse from legitimate breeders, Toad hatched upon the plan to syndicate Chief's services. "Syndication will add distinction to Chief's fine reputation as a performance horse with only the best mares in the country proving him as a sire," Toad told Hughes in 1961. "Benefits are not to the syndicate alone. Chief will add prestige to the Appaloosa breed and ensure a foal crop that will upgrade blood lines."

One aspect to Toad's life as a breeder that didn't pan out was the idea of syndicating Chief of Fourmile. The success that syndication in Thoroughbred and Quarter Horse circles enjoyed never materialized. "I thought it was a brilliant idea at the time," Toad said, in later years," but it didn't set the world on fire."

Still, his overall experiences with Appaloosas were rewarding. and in ways additional to financial. "It was fun, a very enjoyable time in our lives," he recalled, including Donna and his daughters. "It was a challenge. And you got very close to your horses. My gosh! They got to be almost like our children."

High-Tailing It to the High Country

Their beloved Pendaries Ranch meant much to the Leon clan. Strongest memories from the many parties, golf tournaments, hard work, challenges, successes, sad times—even catastrophes—probably depend upon their mood at that instant.

For Carol Ann Midkiff, her magic moment began one crisp summer morning in 1961 when she was twenty-five and her sister, Sandra, was seventeen. They would turn an errand into what their parents and the ranch's hands later would perceive to have been one or more potential life-threatening situations.

"The cattle had been driven to the grazing lease in Santa Fe National Forest a month earlier," Midkiff recalled. "Daddy, Jack Roberts, the ranch foreman, and a couple of friends packed a string of horses with their provisions and headed out. Sandra and I had asked to go along but Daddy said, 'No, not this time. This is a man's trip.' Not even a few tears would budge him.

"Mother received a phone call about noon from Dub Hayter, an Abilene businessman (and close friend of Toad's), regarding some property that had been in negotiation."

"Go catch your father and tell him to come home," Donna said.

"Now, 'Go catch him' is the operable phrase here," Carol Ann said.. "They already had a six-hour head start.

"Daddy was raising Appaloosa horses at the time. Even though we had more than 300 brood mares and several stallions standing at stud between the cowboys already working in the high country as well as Daddy's group, we were out of saddle horses."

She began calling around for a pair of horses to borrow. Finally, she located mounts for loan at Gascon Ranch, ten miles away. More delay but it wouldn't deter the Leon sisters.

Now Toad and his group had gone up the Lower Rociada Canyon

trail. Gascon Ranch was in the Upper Rociada Canyon. The two young horsewomen had decided that they could save time by simply cutting across a mountain ridge or two and intersect the trail her father's group had taken.

After a while, in the distance they saw a giant cross above the pine trees. Then someone blew a whistle. Men came out of the trees from all directions. "Can you tell us if this trail meets the Sparks Canyon Trail?" one of the men was asked.

Silence. Finally, one of the men explained that this was a monastery and all the men were monks presently "on silence." They weren't allowed to speak.

Carol Ann and Sandra realized they had lost precious

OCTOBER 1961
NOVEMBER 1961

35¢

HORSE LOVER'S MAGAZINE

NEWS · PICTURES · STORIES
ABOUT HORSES & HORSE OWNERS

Pendaries Ranch—Sapello, New Mexico. From a painting by Cecil Smith

In This Issue:
- SADDLES IN THE NEW WORLD
- SHETLAND PONY EXTRAVAGANZA ● PLANS FOR A TRAIL RIDE
- TRAINING A BLIND HORSE ● QUARTER HORSE RACING
- TEXAS NEWS NOTES ● WESTERN WEAR STYLES

Cecil Smith painting of Toad Leon and his two daughters, Sandra and Carol Ann (kneeling). Chief of Fourmile is being ridden by Toad, Quanah is in background. The painting was commissioned by the magazine.

time. But they plunged on anyway. "As we rode we climbed higher and higher. We experienced all kinds of weather phenomena. It was hot. Then cold. The wind blew. Then it sleeted. Hungry and running short of time they continued their trek. Soon, chopping sounds were heard. A forest ranger was out marking trees for a trail.

"Understandably we startled him when we rode up. He wanted to know what we were doing up here. We told him we were looking for the trail to the Border de Medio where our cattle were pastured. He gave us some vague directions, terse instructions to stay in camp once we found it, and for certain, not to come back off the mountain until morning.

"Keep your matches dry, ladies," he called after them. "You've got a long way to go."

"We crossed one ridge after another until we finally stumbled onto familiar territory," Carol Ann continued. "It was late afternoon by the time we topped out on the big clearing at 11,000 feet. Now all we had to do was find the Valdez River and the campsite somewhere on it." Their luck had changed. They rode straight to it. No one was there. Good! Since they had begged to go on the trip in the first place, they feared their father would figure they hatched up this wild plan to come along anyway.

"We found some bacon wrappers and got pieces of charcoal from the fire. We wrote on two wrappers, 'Daddy, Mother said come home. You've got an important phone call.' We signed them 'Guess Who?' One message was put under the coffee pot lid, and the other we hung from a wire on their tent. Just as we finished, a dog came into camp. We knew the men weren't far behind so we mounted up and galloped away before they saw us.

Ignoring the ranger's warnings, they began the trek home. They had to find the trail quickly, though. It would be dark soon. More bad weather luck. A heavy fog set in, so thick they couldn't see their horses' heads from the saddle. "And keep in mind these borrowed horses had never been on this trail," Carol Ann said.

"All of a sudden, we heard the most awful noise! Something rushed toward us, thrashing through the undergrowth. Even the horses got nervous. But it turned out to be Cherokee Clown a pack horse that had been lost earlier that summer. He still had his halter and I grabbed the lead rope. But it dawned on us that we had enough problems, so we set him loose."

One problem had been solved, however. The fog was gone. Enter an even greater problem though. "Now it was pitch-black dark. No moon and not one star. We had to negotiate each fork in the trail on horses that didn't know their way home. At last, we saw a light through the trees, then came to a road. One of the old abandoned copper mines was back in production. The light came from a trailer house that stood at a fork in the road.

"We didn't know which fork to take, so we called out to the house. Through the window we could see a man lying on his bed. He jumped up like he was shot. We saw him hit his head on the bunk above." The man came warily to the door.

"What're you doin' here?" he demanded to know. "Where did you come from? This is posted country!"

"Since we had scared him out of his wits, he wasn't friendly at all," Carol Ann said. "We were too tired for explanations. We asked which fork to take to get to Rociada. He said the one on the left—the one with the gate locked. For a minute or so he acted like he wasn't going to open it for us. But finally, he drove his pickup down to the entrance and let us ride through, reminding us with a bit of a grin that we were in bear country."

Great! The sisters knew this but it was no time to be reminded. Unless they stepped on a bear cub they probably wouldn't be bothered though.

"Finally, we hit the real Rociada road. But we weren't home free yet. At each house along the road dogs ran out, barking and nipping at our horses' heels. Even more bad luck. My horse went lame just above Rociada. The dogs became a real nuisance now that I was on foot and leading my horse. We finally got home around midnight."

Next day, Toad came down from camp. He eyed his daughters warily. "What were you two riding?" he wanted to know, first thing.

"No, Daddy we didn't ride Chief of Fourmile or Quanah," the prides of Pendaries and the numbers one and two Appaloosa stallions in the world. It turned out to be a win-win situation," Carol Ann Midkiff concluded. "Daddy's deal went through, and Sandra and I got our trip to the high country."

And somewhere, even though he had looked
pretty sickly there for a while, Wyatt smiled.

A Twist of Fate—1962

The timing for Toad Leon's tormenting toothache might have been worse back in March of 1962. But it could've been a whole lot better, that's for sure.

Here Toad cuts a rug with Sadie Monfree during the 1964
Life Begins at 40 Golf Tournament.

"Donna and I had planned a trip to Europe with Jack and Lois Yonge," Toad said. "The SS France was making its second crossing from New York to Southhampton, England. Since none of us had ever crossed the Atlantic Ocean by ship the trip sounded intriguing. "About a week before departure, I developed a nagging toothache. Henry McGowen, Donna's cousin and our dentist in Abilene, suggested a visit to a root-canal specialist in Fort Worth."

Upon arrival at the dentist's office, Donna asked the receptionist, "How long will this take?"

"Well, it will be at least two hours," was the reply. "This is painful, so we will put Mr. Leon under for the entire procedure."

She waved goodbye as they led her husband from the waiting room. "Good luck," she called out.

Now a block from the dentist's office Donna had seen an Arthur Murray Dance Studio sign. "The twist was the newest dance craze and she always wanted to be on the cutting edge of everything," Toad recalled. So what better way to kill a couple hours in Fort Worth? Donna Leon took a twist lesson.

She later remarked, "Toad says that while he was under the influence of ether and, according to him, without knowing whether he would wake up or not, I was out dancing."

"I have to admit the lessons did come in handy," Toad concluded. "She in turn schooled me on the finer points of the dance and aboard the SS France we took first place in the twist contest.

"I guess sometimes what you don't know won't hurt you."

Bon Voyage—1962

By the 1960s, Toad and Donna Leon were making more or less regular trips to Europe. One of their favorite trips was taken with two good and close friends from Abilene. As usual with Toad what made the trip memorable were the spontaneous antics that involved their group.

"Our good friends from Abilene, Jack and Lois Yonge, were going to Europe on the second crossing of the SS France," Toad recalled. They had said they'd like us to go with them.

Dining aboard the S.S. France in March, 1962. Clockwise from left: Donna Leon, Lois Yonge, Jack Yonge, Toad Leon.

"We drove to Dallas and stayed in the Statler Hilton," he said. "The date was March 11, 1962. I'm sure of it because I checked Donna's diary. We had dinner at Cipango Club and next day flew to New York City. John and Jane Black saw us off at the airport." The two couples stayed at the Astor Hotel in New York as final preparations for the sailing were made. This included some extensive shopping excursions by Donna and Lois.

"Donna bought an autumn haze fur and Lois purchased a stole," Toad said. "Jack and I didn't buy anything. We just wanted to get our wives out of those shops. That night we hired a limousine and drove around the city."

They boarded ship the next day and found their suites filled with flowers, fruit baskets, other bon voyage gifts from friends back in Dallas and Abilene. "It was fabulous," Toad said. "Everything was so nice, so wonderful."

As with luxury liners there was no shortage of sidelights to keep one busy during the six-day voyage to South Hampton, England, especially if he or she resided in first class. "Jack found himself on the top deck one day where they were skeet shooting over the water. Now you had to know Jack," Toad explained about the highly successful car dealer in Abilene who always stood high profile in a crowd and never got embarrassed when he made a faux pas—which happened rather frequently.

Jack was watching them shoot when he couldn't stand being on the sidelines any longer. "Gimmie that gun!" he ordered, barging up to the inner circle. "My son George and I used to do this back home." Yonge picked out a gun, took his stance and with all the authority of a veteran shooter yelled, "Pull!" The clay pigeon went sailing out over the Atlantic, and Jack pulled on it. The only trouble he had a double barrel shotgun and pulled both triggers at the same time. "It very nearly blew him off the deck and into the ocean," Toad said, seriously. "And that's no exaggeration."

That evening at a fancy formal dinner dance, one of the skeet kibitzers apparently was enjoying himself, going from table to table and telling of the rip-snorting Texan and his double-barreled debacle. "I heard him telling some other guy about it when he noticed Jack and the rest of us come in." In a loud voice amid laughter, he told his acquaintance, "See? There he is! It's a wonder he's still alive!" Yonge only smiled and took it in stride Toad said. "You just never saw Jack Yonge get embarrassed."

Later, during the dance, the topic of conversation among many of the passengers was the presence of royalty—"a real live prince and princess" held over from some long and forgotten European principality. "It wouldn't do for Yonge not to dance with the princess," Toad said. Jack strode to the royal table, bent over and whispered something to the beautiful lady, and stood at attention as she answered him and cast her eyes at the prince. To the horror of Lois and Donna and the delight of Toad, Yonge then stepped over in front of the prince, again stood at attention, spoke and, when the suave sovereign nodded with the hint of a smile, reached out and took the hand of the princess. He escorted her to the dance floor and led her to the Leon-Yonge table. After introducing her to his wife and companions, Yonge said, "Hey Toad. Did you know that over here you have to get permission from her husband before asking a princess to dance with you?" His partner seemed to be lost in a stare directed somewhere out in space.

The two couples spent time in Italy and the South of France as well as England. "We met Tuffy and Liz Goff on the ship, and ran into them in

London, Rome, Paris, and Venice," Toad said. "We had dinner with them several times." Tuffy was from Arkansas—Mena, he liked to say, a true-blue hillbilly community. When the conductor on the train from Fort Smith to Texarkana announced it as a stop, Tuffy said, he would holler, "Mena! Mena, Arkansas...Don't forget your shoes and your grapes."

"Tuffy was Abner on the 'Lum and Abner' radio show," Toad said. "He never told us, but I found that out when we got back to Abilene. We continued to be good friends and visited them often in their home at Palm Desert, California."

While in the heart of France's wine country, Yonge would invariably ask waiters at dinner for Pootenay Kootenay. It was his favorite French wine that was rarely found back in the wet areas of Texas. "You know, that

Donna and Toad (in background) and Lois and Jack Yonge are serenaded by musicians in Rome.

imported wine with the chicken wire around it," Yonge would tell the waiters who sometimes had trouble with his pronunciation. Of course, when he asked for "imported" French wine in France, they'd be lost again.

The couples' adventures continued through France and on to Switzerland, Italy, and Spain. They leased a car in Paris to motor to Switzerland but found out quickly that the main road was closed. So they put the car on a train flatbed and rode to Zurich inside, "bouncing along the tracks and going through tunnels. One must have been 100 miles long. It took us four hours to get through," Toad said.

Waiters along their tour route had their hands full with Jack Yonge. Once, at dinner after the four had taken the sky tram up Mount Presanella, Yonge drank the kirsch meant for the fondue. "Whew! Not sure I care too much for this wine," he said, thumping his mid-chest area with a clinched fist as if to make the kirsch go down quickly.

In Milan, Italy, Lois and Donna insisted on seeing an opera at the famous La Scala but Jack and Toad would have none of it. They went to a follies-style nightclub patterned and named after Maxim's in Paris. "Jack told them we were from West Texas and we wanted the best table in the house. They put us right next to the dance floor and we had young ladies coming by for drinks all evening long. They didn't worry too much as the evening wore on. Donna and Lois were committed to almost five hours at La Scala. "Finally," Toad continued, "well after midnight we decided to call it an evening."

"La cuenta," Toad asked the Italian, in his best attempt at Spanish. The bill amounted to almost $500.

"This is robbery! I won't pay it!" he told the headwaiter.

"Yes, you must," the man replied.

"No, I won't, but you can accompany us to our hotel and maybe the concierge can work this out.

"Now, this big guy, about six-two and real muscular went with us and he didn't seem all too pleased. We told the concierge our problem and he said, 'Mr. Leon, this is not out of line; but maybe I can get $40 knocked off.' Fine, I said. I'll pay." He went upstairs and sought consolation plus perhaps a change of the subject from his wife, who with Lois had stayed for only half of the opera and then returned to the hotel to wonder what the guys were doing all this time.

"Donna, we've been robbed!"

"Oh, shut up, Toad, and go to bed!" she replied.

"Meanwhile," Toad said, "Jack told Lois the same thing and she was very concerned, very interested. "You poor dear! We'll go to the police tomorrow," Lois said, prompting Toad later to opine on the differing levels of devotion and understanding between their two wives.

Then Lois found a woman's name and number written on a match cover on the dresser and confronted her husband.

"Oh, that," Yonge replied. "It's a lady I met last night at this club, and she wants to meet you." Through Jack's efforts the matter was quickly forgotten.

While in Milan, their rental car threw off its license plate, and the party was stopped on a "citizen's arrest." There would be an investigation, a hearing, and a probable fine at the neighborhood precinct house next day.

"You handle it, Toad. I'll watch the girls," a gracious Jack Yonge said.

Next day, Toad settled in for a long stay at precinct headquarters, battling language barriers and red tape. It seemed forever before the desk sergeant got around to filling out the paper work. Only, he was out of typing paper! No one seemed to move to solve the problem. Finally, Toad asked, "Where can we find some paper and get this thing settled?" There was a drug store in the next block. Would he mind...? So Toad walked to the place, bought typing paper, took it back to the police station, and waited until the complaint against him was completed.

The couples by now were more than two weeks into their European trip. They turned in the car and headed via train to Madrid. It was there that Toad hollered "calf rope"—it had been fun but he had had enough. He and Donna boarded a plane for home. The Yonges stayed on for another week or so.

"It was a great trip, one I'll always remember," Toad concluded. "It was made all the better because Jack and Lois were with us."

Who Needs Pheasants? We've Got Lots of Ducks

George Slaughter likes to tell about a pheasant-hunting trip to North Dakota that turned into one weird kind of outing, in the center of which his pal Toad Leon stood tall. Which is an oxymoron, of course. Toad standing tall.

Anyway, four hunting acquaintances from Dallas and New Mexico who went north to hunt were Toad's close friend Slaughter, his cousin Jeff Browning, Leroy Lowrey from Albuquerque, and Toad. Leroy and Toad drove up from New Mexico in Leroy's pickup with a camper. Slaughter and Browning flew to Iowa, then rented a car, and met up with their companions in Hamilton, North Dakota, "the home town of Lawrence Welk," as Slaughter put it.

They had leased a farm south of town for hunting purposes but were disappointed to find that cornstalks were head-high. Or more. "We'd go down the rows, and three of us could barely see above the stalks," Slaughter said. "Toad? We couldn't even see him! He was out of it and pretty disgruntled, too."

The farmer could only apologize, Slaughter said. Then Toad spied a tractor with a front-end loader near the barn. "Let me get in the loader, and you hike it up high as it'll go," Toad said, offering the farmer $50. "Then I can see over the corn. These other guys can walk the birds up for us."

Slaughter said the hunting didn't improve much but Toad was the only one who had any luck at all, of course. "I think we maybe shot five or six pheasants all told," Slaughter said.

But that didn't mean they went back without a full camper. The farmer sold produce "at wholesale prices, and Toad didn't like to pass up making a buck. They filled the back of the camper with dozens of eggs," Slaughter said.

"You interested in some ducks?" the farmer added. "Got some mallards with clipped wings out back we've been feeding corn. They're up to four, maybe five pounds apiece. They make fine eating. Sell 'em to you wholesale." Toad couldn't resist, and Leroy was all for his idea of taking twenty-five full-grown mallards back to Toad's ranch in New Mexico. They put them in the back of the camper with the eggs, and George and Jeff suddenly were extra glad they were flying back.

Toad and Leroy got near Omaha on the first night of an expected two, maybe three nights on the road. They got a motel room and after supper became worried about what the ducks were up to. Toad spied the motel swimming pool which had water left over from summer. Along toward midnight he and Leroy slipped the twenty-five mallards into the pool for a refresher and cleanup swim.

"Man, the ducks just loved it!" Slaughter said he had learned. "Pretty soon they were quacking up a storm. All the motel guests were awakened. So was the manager who told those two crazy Texans to get those damn ducks out of his pool and don't bother ever stopping there again."

The mallards did get to Pendaries Ranch, where Toad soon lost track of them.

The Colleyville Blues—1962

One of Toad Leon's financial misadventures is referred to within the family simply as "Colleyville." It was a strip of real estate between Dallas and Fort Worth that was largely farmland or small ranches. "It was 1962. I was in the Appaloosa horse business in northern New Mexico," Leon recalled. "I ran into a friend from Dallas, Joe Humphries, at a horse show."

After a while, Humphries mentioned that he had a nice place for sale over at Colleyville. It had a little lake and stables for about twelve horses.

"I got to thinking that this might be a good investment," Toad said. More to the point, it appealed to him when a light bulb flashed brightly in his ever on the go mind. Toad for some reason had been dreaming of what he thought would be a sure-fire way to sell pricey horseflesh. He figured he'd bring a few horses down from Pendaries Ranch and get them close to Dallas. Each year at Christmas Neiman Marcus published a posh catalog that included conversational items for deep pocketbooks—especially those in Texas during the early 1960s.

"I'd make a deal with Neiman's to feature some of my horses—maybe pitch them as 'His and Hers Appaloosas,.'" Toad explained. "I'd have a $25,000 horse or two, some $15,000 horses and some $10,000 horses. Sure looked like a better deal than a Chinese junk," which Neiman's had featured as its drop-dead deal in the previous Christmas catalog.

So Toad bought the 160 acre parcel of land from Humphries and shipped some of his prize horses to the Colleyville ranch in plenty of time to make the catalog, he figured. Right away his high-falutin' fantasy started going south. "I believe to my soul that every fly in Texas came to our stables that July," Toad said. Neiman's wasn't interested and the horses were miserable.

"Then along came this guy who said he might like to buy the place." It was difficult for Toad to contain his joy. Here he just might make a dollar or two. "I dunno if I really want to sell...but gosh, if you really want it, well OK.

No sooner had the funds been transferred than here came Joe Humphries. "Toad, my wife and my daughter are madder'n blazes at me for selling the ranch. I'd like to buy it back."

"I appreciate that, Joe, but I just sold it."

What Toad hadn't known, it seems—probably the only investor or businessman in a hundred miles of Dallas and Fort Worth—was the poorly kept secret that the real estate would be big time prime land in no time. It was next to what would become DFW Airport. "Last time I was at the place, it had a twenty-story bank on it. My little old ranch was bringing $6 to $8 a square foot."

"Now there was something that truly made Wyatt urp," Toad grumbled.

Election Year—1964

It was a booming summer at Pendaries. All the rooms at the lodge were booked with the majority of the visitors hailing from Texas. The national election to be held the coming November seemed to be on everybody's mind. President Lyndon Baines Johnson was being challenged by Arizona Senator Barry Goldwater. When the topic crept into a conversation, a lively discussion would ensue. Usually Toad Leon refrained from voicing his mostly Republican political persuasion. Furthermore, he had long ago been advised by his mentor, partner, and brother, Server Leon, not to run for or discuss a school board, city council or for that matter, never even judge a baby contest. "Controversy is bad for the theater business," Server had said. But in 1964, Toad just couldn't keep quiet.

"Someone had given me this book, *A Texan Looks at Lyndon* by J. Evetts Haley, and I was so taken by it I ordered a case of them," Toad said, grinning. "In fact I thought so much of the book, I put a copy in each lodge guest room right next to the Gideon Bible." *A Texan Looks at Lyndon* was a mind-boggling, in-depth exposé of LBJ's rise to political power including his controversial razor-thin senatorial victory over Coke Stevenson in 1948. "Landslide Lyndon," as he was often called was not, to say the least, held in very high regard by noted Southwest historian Haley.

"I viewed putting the book in the rooms as practically my civic duty and it was a little more subtle than a soapbox," Toad said. A note was attached to each copy that read, "If you like this book take it with you and pass it along to a friend."

Donna, half-kidding but perhaps not, warned Toad that if he wasn't careful he might be getting a midnight visit from the Internal Revenue Service. LBJ of course won the fall election in what was a true landslide.

And Wyatt groaned.

"In the past few years I've had the pleasure of visiting the Haley Library and Museum in Midland on several occasions, and also meeting J. Evetts Haley Jr. and his wife, Frances. I'm happy to report that he's a chip off the old block and a noted historian and author in his own right."

A Wild Bear Does What in the Woods?—1964

"Donna and I were at Harrah's in Reno at a golf tournament," Toad Leon recalled. "I phoned our Pendaries Ranch home to see how things were going since it was mid-summer and Pendaries was in full swing."

"Daddy, guess what?" his daughter, Carol Ann, announced excitedly. "We caught a black bear in one of the bobcat traps!"

"Ask Bill Gwinn to build a nice big pen for him," Toad responded, figuring it would be interesting to guests staying at the lodge as well as his property owners to "safely see a wild bear up close."

Gwinn, a top hand at the ranch, built an elaborate shelter that included all the necessities—water, a tree, and plenty of play room all with a concrete floor that could be washed down and kept clean.

"Our bear seemed happy and content in his new home," Toad said. "What bear wouldn't, with all the berries, watermelon, and honey he could eat?" Word got around about the Pendaries' star attraction—including to the local game warden. "It seemed it was against every law ever written, statewide and nationwide, to hold a bear in captivity. It would not be tolerated!" Toad said. "Everyone involved was given a stiff fine and the bear was summarily hauled off and released."

Just as he and Donna returned to Pendaries, another bear got himself caught. No more publicity. Please! Those wardens were on a tear...

Then Toad got an idea on how to make bear-catching publicity an asset. "Joe Lacy had brought officials of the Santa Fe Chamber of Commerce to the ranch that weekend for a series of meetings. So it was planned. We would have a 'bear releasing party.'" Early that evening with a sizeable group in attendance and everyone in position Toad's son-in-law, Square Roberts, carefully opened the trap door.

"The bear peeked out then stepped out and high-tailed it to the hills. It was difficult to judge which ran the fastest. the bear or the Santa Fe Chamber of Commerce. "In opposite directions, of course." This was the nice bear encounter. There had been another, early in marriage of Toad and Donna Leon. And it had not been so nice.

The first-ever Toad-and-Clarence family trip that included Donna was in 1937. Carol Ann was just a baby. Toad and his older brother and their families, including Donna's mother, Johnnie McGowen, headed in two cars for Yellowstone National Park. "We had had a great time," Toad recalled. "We had heeded all those signs to 'Don't Feed the Bears,' and we had kept our distance. But it was our last day, and we came up on this really beautiful grizzly, the biggest bear we had seen since we arrived.."

Several cars were stopped, admiring the bear which didn't seem too concerned that she was the center of attention."

"I've just got to get a picture of that grizzly!" said Donna, who jumped from the car.

"You be careful now," Toad called after her rolling down the car window. Clarence and his family also watched with some concern from the safety of their auto.

The bear was munching on something, centered in a sort of natural horseshoe. Donna looked through the viewfinder on her trusty Kodak Brownie camera and didn't care for the pose. The sun was coming up from the east and she was down sun. So she slowly maneuvered herself 180 degrees to get the light over her shoulder not paying attention to the fact that she had placed herself directly in the grizzly's path of retreat. The road filled with cars was in the opposite direction. Suddenly the animal rushed Donna, grabbed her in a classic bear hug, raked a claw across her back, and then on her arm. Cars began honking. The grizzly took note, saw that her escape route where Donna had been was now clear, and promptly dropped Donna in a heap before ambling off into the woods.

Donna emerged in relatively good shape considering what could have

Yellowstone Park, 1937. Donna and Bear.

happened. But she did leave Yellowstone with a scar on her upper back and another on her left shoulder that she could show and tell about the rest of her life.

You can rest assured she also spent the rest of her life telling about her two familial would-be heroes and where they were in her time of terror.

"Get out of the way, Nora! Let me out! I've got to help her!" Clarence is documented as having ordered his wife. A confusing edict to say the least since Clarence Leon spent the rest of his life at family gatherings trying to explain why he was wanting to exit his car from the passenger side, occupied by his wife, instead of his own driver's side.

Toad? He would always have some explaining to do, too. The athletic if not sort of short husband of the damsel in distress bolted from his car. Only en route to saving his wife's life from that monster she-bear, Toad kept slipping and falling down on Yellowstone rocks. When he finally gained solid footing the grizzly had loped off, leaving her human interloper in a heap.

Oh well, as Wyatt may have said, with no apologies
to Shakespeare that morning in Tombstone
while the dust settled at the OK Corral:
"All's well that ends well."

A Chat With H. L. Hunt—1965

H. L. Hunt would become one of the world's most interesting—if not secretive—figures of the 1950s and '60s. Perhaps the richest man of his time, there was a bit of Hunt in J.R. Ewing of "Dallas"—by design of the popular prime time TV soap's writers, of course. Hunt was the patriarch of a wealthy family that had expanded in several directions from the base of oil wildcatting established by H. L. His only public exposure was as a political newspaper columnist whose wildly far-right conservatism had few peers. Hunt's foes even tried to link him to the assassination of JFK.

A noteworthy party in 1965 was attended by (clockwise from left): Donna Leon, Barbara Varel, Toad Leon, and Dan Varel.

Toad never met the famous billionaire when they both shared Dallas as a base of operations. But he finally got his chance when Barbara Varel, then wife of his good friend Dan Varel, phoned Donna in Abilene and asked that she and Toad be their guests at their table for a charity ball being held at the Fairmont Hotel. Dan was founder of one of the world's leading diamond oil drilling bit companies.

"Donna had to have a new evening gown with the proper accessories and I had to have my tuxedo altered, cleaned, and pressed," Toad said. "After much anticipation and many hard-earned dollars, we chartered a limousine and made the trip to Dallas. Thank God we were also house guests of the Varels. But we were dressed to the teeth. It was a festive evening. The people from Baird and Rule wouldn't have known us."

At intermission on their way to the bar Dan asked Toad if he'd like to meet H. L. Hunt. "Naturally, I said I'd be delighted."

"I'd like you to meet a friend of mine from Abilene, C.D, Leon—better known as Toad," Varel said, in making the introductions.

"How are you, Mr. Leon?"

"Fine and it is a pleasure to meet you, Mr. Hunt," Toad responded immediately seeking a way to be at ease and make conversation. He knew Hunt, like himself, was a gin player. Unlike Toad, Hunt was known to have played for as much as five dollars a point.

"From reputation, I understand you are possibly the best gin rummy player in the country."

"No, not really. But I used to think I was one of the best poker players around. We would go to New Orleans, get a suite of rooms, and play $50,000 freeze-out. Winner take all. They never beat me," Hunt said.

"How wonderful. Do you still play poker?"

"No, not for some time now."

"Why did you stop playing?" Toad asked.

"Well, about that time I got into the oil business."

"Oh? And were you successful?" Toad asked with a smile.

"Moderately. Moderately," Hunt replied, returning the smile.

"I thought Dan would fall through the floor," Toad said, looking back on the evening. "Mr. Hunt got a kick out of it. He knew exactly what I was doing and evidently possessed a great sense of humor many people didn't know about."

The Easiest Money Toad Ever Made

Toad Leon, by his own admission or perhaps claim, has had to hustle for the money he has made. Not much has come easy, sometimes in part due to the financial holes he has dug for himself whether it be sweating hogs, dying sheep, or the USDA riding an apparent phantom brucellosis scare against his cattle. Back in his early movie days, Toad knocked on doors to sell tickets, drove panel trucks hawking the current film in town, opened the theater at noon, and closed it at midnight, "seven days a week, 365 days a year." he recalls.

"I was always trying to figure out how to make a dollar," he continued. He even led a brigade of kids onto T&P passenger trains in the mid-1930s, selling sandwiches, bananas, and soft drinks while the train took on water at a service stop in Baird. But there was one day he relishes to recall, a day when he made several thousand dollars without lifting a finger.

"I had just sold Pendaries ranch and I had to find a way to make some money," he said. He had some cash from the sale so he decided to buy irrigated farm land in the South Plains of Texas and partner with his nephew, Wilbur Leon, a hands-on working farmer, which Toad definitely was not. The acreage he bought was near the towns of Cotton Center, Bovina, and Lorenzo. The partnership ultimately did not live up to Toad's expectations mainly because the farms were too far apart to make his plan of sharing equipment and personnel work properly.

He sold one farm but had to take it back when the buyer couldn't make a go of it. So Toad opted for a foreclosure sale. That meant the parcel would be advertised as such, then sold to the highest bidder "on the county courthouse steps, on the date specified." That day turned out to be bitter cold. A north wind howled. And the law specified that the sale had to be conducted outdoors on the courthouse steps.

"It was so bad, only ten or twelve people showed up," Toad recalled.

The man handling the sale explained that if no bids exceeded $100,000, "Mr. Leon would put in that bid himself."

Well, nobody bid, so the man said, "The land is going back to Mr. Leon." One potential buyer apparently was hiding out in back, trying to snatch the land cheaply. "Wait a minute!" he cried out. "Didn't you see me hold up my finger?"

"Then do you now want to make a bid? I have one for $100,000 from Mr. Leon."

"Yes! I'll bid $105,000!" the hideout hollered. And that's what he paid. No one else bid again. Certainly not Toad Leon!

"It was kinda interesting," Toad said with a chuckle. "He could've had the farm for $100,001. I made $4,999 before a gnat could swim a dipper."

The Plane Truth About Flying

What is it about people, particularly men? They get a little money in their pockets, think about how maybe they could save more of it on travel expenses, and suddenly decide to learn to fly. With the FFA waiting to bust their chops over the least little thing and heavy aircraft crowding the skies while possessing no notion of sharing it with Cessna 152 or Cherokee 180 drivers not a whole lot of potential pilots get past their student ticket. That first session under the hood introducing them to instrument flying also chases quite a few. Toad Leon had his fling with the wild blue yonder. In two different doses, actually.

"It was 1942 when I decided to take flying lessons," he recalled. "Driving by car to check on the different theaters consumed a lot of time. So it only seemed logical that flying back and forth was the answer. We were living then in Amarillo and Donna's cousin, Juanita Fincher, was in Canyon, Texas. Her husband, Kenneth, was a flight instructor, so I began a series of lessons.

"Back then you were required to stall the aircraft, put it in a downward spin and then pull out of it. Having successfully accomplished that maneuver, plus a few others such as learning how to land, qualified you to fly solo."

The stall-and-spin was enough to convince Toad that highways weren't all that bad. "It was a hair-raising lesson," he said.

"Kenneth, how much do I owe you for your trouble?" he asked, as he bade the airfield good-bye.

Fast forward to 1967. The memory of that one and only exposure to the feel of the yoke and the power of the pedals had faded from his memory. He began another set of flying lessons at Abilene Regional Airport.

"John and Jane Black had a beautiful ranch outside Granbury, Texas," roughly between Abilene and Fort Worth, Toad said. "Their ranch house was tremendous. It was large enough to comfortably accommodate the more than twelve couples they invited to a dove hunt that September. Among the guests was Jody Tompkins of Abilene. He was a good pilot and had been teaching me some of the finer points of excelling at aviation. In fact, we had flown to Dallas just the week before in his Bonanza—with me at the controls.

"Anyway, he landed on the Blacks' private strip that hot September morning. On arrival he asked the group at the ranch if anyone wanted to go up and fly around the considerable acreage.

" 'No, thanks,' was my reply. 'I'm in the middle of a story in *Police Gazette*.' I went up to my room to take a nap. John Black, Snooky Hubbard, and the ranch foreman took him up on his offer. Tom Jarman drove them to the strip. As Tom sat in the jeep and looked on the four got into the four-place Bonanza."

Looking back the luggage from his flight from Abilene was still on board so they might have been somewhat overloaded. Also, since the warm morning had turned into a hot afternoon the lessening of lift potential of the air was also a factor.

"They sped down the fairly short strip and took off," Toad said. "They weren't going quite fast enough, however, so the plane settled back down. Up ahead the end of the runway was at hand. They proceeded to ricochet off down the hill, through a barbed wire fence and onto a tree, where the plane burst into flames.

"It was one hell of a wreck! Thank God, Tom quickly drove down, jerked the door open, and pulled them out. To this day I believe he saved all their lives.

"Back at the ranch house my nap was interrupted by the commotion. Downstairs were John, Jody, and the ranch foreman. They were thoroughly shaken up and bloody. Everybody was talking at once, reliving the crash, and trying to decide whether or not to go to the hospital.

"In the midst of tending to the wounded, I saw Hubbard standing across the room. I didn't see any blood on him so I asked, 'My God, Snooky, where have you been?"

"Well, Toad, I have just been on my last plane ride."

Toad's flying days, for the second time in almost three decades, also ended that hot September day near Granbury. "I cancelled my remaining private pilot's lessons when we got back to Abilene," he said.

Food Stamps Make the Woman—1968

Government agencies usually are not among Toad Leon's favorite entities. He likes to cite as a case in point the Mora County, New Mexico, food stamp program—or is it food stamp worship?

"That summer Bill and Amber Cree of Abilene leased a house for a month at Pendaries Village. They decided to give a small dinner party one evening. Amber had heard of a man in Mora who had a garden and grew

Sherman Hotel, Chicago. From left: Bill Cree, Donna Leon, Amber Cree, Toad Leon.

wonderful vegetables. She and Donna drove the ten miles to Mora early that morning. They promptly found the man and bought an assortment of fresh produce. Just a few more items would be needed.

"On the main street was a small grocery store with the customary large front window. Amber drove her long, black Cadillac up to the curb in plain view of the people inside. She and Donna jumped out ran a few short steps to the door and entered the store. Hurriedly they made their selections."

In the checkout line, the cashier looked at Amber and asked, "Will you be using your stamps?"

"Pardon?"

"Will you be using your food stamps?"

"Uh, no. I'll just pay cash."

"Evidently, people driving Cadillacs are eligible for food stamps in

174

Mora, New Mexico," Toad continued, ready to cite some figures he had come up with. "It has been told that when the food stamp program was initiated, only 600 people in Mora County qualified. But in just six months, with a little juggling the local woman in charge had recruited 2,500 more. Another case of your government at work."

That wasn't all. Amber Cree, recalling the incident thirty years later, said what really blew her away was walking outside the store and being greeted by young "hippie-like" street entrepreneurs selling fresh strawberries they had just purchased in the store at a fifty percent discount. "With food stamps, of course," she said as she and Donna learned later.

"These people could have been poster children for DEA bulletins. So you had to figure they used food stamps to buy the strawberries, undercut the store (which didn't care that much, since it had already rung up a full retail sale with the stamps) and pocketed the proceeds, and probably then go out and buy some dope."

Like Toad had said—your government funds hard at work. But nothing—NOTHING—to compare with the nightmare he endured at the hands of the United States Department of Agriculture along about this time.

"When I was in the ranching business at Pendaries, twenty-five miles northwest of Las Vegas, New Mexico, I ran several hundred head of commercial cattle," Toad said. "I also had some registered Simmental, which were kept separate.

"Well, one day we sent an old cow from the commercial herd to auction. They were testing for brucellosis and said she came up positive." So the cow had the ultimate scarlet letter for her species—a big "B"—painted on her jaw. She was sold for a cut-rate, sure-loss price.

"That meant they had to test my whole herd. Some USDA guys—they always wore hard-hats, so you could tell 'em a mile away—they came to Pendaries and tested the commercial cattle and found nothing. 'Is this all?' they asked me. Well, I said, I had some registered Simmental cows and calves in a separate pasture, but they were all vaccinated at birth. They decided they had to test them anyway."

You guessed it. Three or four Simmentals tested positive for brucellosis. Toad was ordered to sell the beautiful creatures for $200 apiece "when I could have gotten $2500 with a simple phone call, had it not been for the ugly "B" plastered on their jaw," Toad recounted with disgust.

The USDA decided it should test the Pendaries stock every thirty days. Sometimes the cattle would be clear. Sometimes one or two would test positive. Toad figures it was a "reactor" syndrome from the animals' inoculations. Instead of cutting his losses, Toad kept them. The USDA would come back in thirty days and at Toad's insistence the government boys had to test the animals again.

Um-hum. They'd be negative.

"This went on for about six months," Toad said. "Finally, I decided to get these cattle down to Texas, even it had to be under quarantine. I knew a lot of people down there who would listen to me. These animals had been vaccinated.

He trucked his Simmental herd to Lorenzo, Texas, and here came the USDA people from Lubbock. The same thing happened. One month positive; the next month negative. "Finally, I got so mad I said, 'Okay, you're going to come back one more time and test 'em. If they don't show positive, I'm gonna build a ten foot high fence and you're not going to test these cows or calves again.'

"Sure enough, they were all clear. 'We're lifting the quarantine,' the USDA hard-hat said. This ended about four years hassling with these people and it cost me $200,000. So you can imagine what I think of the USDA."

How Does Your Garden Grow in Lorenzo?

Forgive Toad Leon's daughters, Carol Ann Midkiff and Sandra Roberts, if their mouths do a little sour pickle pucker when the name Lorenzo comes up. The small Texas community near Lubbock became headquarters for the Toad Leon family for a few years. It was a short time after they answered the bids of big-time real estate developers and sold their beloved Pendaries Ranch. Toad bought three South Plains irrigated farms and entered into a partnership with his nephew, Wilbur Leon. An ongoing battle with the U.S. Department of Agriculture over the definition of brucellosis, as it pertained to Toad's prize herd of registered, well-inoculated Simmental cattle pressed some of the farmland into acreage where his New Mexico raised beeves could wait out the feud.

The move soon became designed to make farmers out of his daughters and their families, long accustomed to the luxury and good times at Pendaries. Curiously enough Toad, the moneyman behind the operation and his wife, Donna, were not often found in the bleak farmland, opting to run things from either Santa Fe or Dallas with occasional stops in Abilene.

"The year we moved to Lorenzo, Daddy told us we needed a vegetable garden," Carol Ann recalled. Wilbur made sure it would keep Sandra and her occupied. A ten acre plot in growing season might as well be a section and a half of cotton worked with a mule. "We'd be out there early every morning. It was hot that summer but we wore sleeves because we had mosquitoes as big as bombers"

She confessed to "wishing something would happen to our garden—something that would kill it dead. We had okra, peas, squash, tomatoes, some corn, green beans—the works." Wilbur came by often enough with his tractor to make sure the tract didn't go to seed and give his cousins reason to rejoice. The one garden area that thrived was the cucumber patch. It was a bumper crop. Carol Ann's next door neighbor, Merle Morrison, suggested that the sisters take to pickling the cucumbers.

"Merle and her husband, Lewis, were two of the nicest people we ever knew," Toad Leon would say years later. To get them started Merle had a recipe that her mother once used to win first place in the Texas State Fair and the girls rounded up all the canning paraphernalia they could find.

"That was the biggest bunch of crap I've ever seen," Carol Ann said, of the first large batch. "It had this real thick layer of scum right on top."

"Carol Ann's kitchen smelled something awful!" Sandra said. "If you lifted the lid on that bubbling stuff it would knock you over."

Carol Ann's pantry soon outgrew the bumper pickle crop. One day she noticed an article in the Lubbock Avalanche-Journal about how to enter various competitions in the upcoming annual South Plains Fair. Included were pickles.

Several ladies around Lorenzo were pros at pickling. Toad's girls figured they had two chances to even make the finals— slim and none. But make them they did. Carol Ann eventually won first place with her sweet pickles and Sandra won second in the gherkin competition.

The girls had done it! Carol Ann was so proud she tracked her father's whereabouts to a posh yard party in Dallas. It was at the home of Jeff and Susie Browning. Susie answered the phone call from Carol Ann who could hear a full orchestra playing in the background. "I need to talk to my Daddy!"

"Good or bad news?" Susie asked.

"You won't understand," Carol Ann said, but she told her anyway.

"You're right. I don't understand. I'll get your father."

Toad took the phone when he heard it was from Lorenzo.

"Daddy, I have some news!"

"Is anything wrong with Dexter?" an apprehensive Toad blurted, immediately concerned about his prize Simmental bull. When his excited daughter told him the story of how she and Sandra had shamed all the ace picklers of the South Plains of Texas, Toad cheered for them.

"I never had boys who could score touchdowns," he told friends at the party. "But when Sandra was crowned National Appaloosa Queen a few years back, and our stallion, Quanah, was horse of the year, I'd tell people with tongue in cheek that I didn't know who I was prouder of— my daughter, who won for beauty as well as horsemanship or Quanah.

"But this pickle queen thing is really something special!"

You know Toad. The success of his daughters' pickle garden got him to thinking. "Hell, if they can do this well in this garden they can do better on a larger scale. I had heard about this place near Hatch, New Mexico, where they grew chile peppers. A friend of mine in Santa Fe, Big Ed Brosseau, had an airplane so we flew over there to take a look at their operation."

What he didn't take into consideration was what do you do with something on such a grand scale, once it's harvested?

"We tried the highways—you know, the farmer's market approach. But everybody out there had a garden. We sold maybe three dollars' worth."

"Carol Ann and I strung chiles that no one wanted to buy," Sandra added. Finally Toad sent bell peppers to New York City by rail. He got $5,540 for the load, meaning he only lost $340, once the expenses were tallied.

Toad kept his eye on onions all the while. He noticed he could buy all he wanted around Lorenzo in September for five cents a pound. By late November, that crop would be worth one dollar a pound. He found out the Santa Fe Railroad was selling its refrigerator cars so Toad bought a couple and put them on his farm for onion storage. But to corner the world's onion market he needed more cars.

"Then, my friend, Windy Watkins, and O.J. Jones from Abilene found out the Santa Fe was selling dozens of refrigerator cars in Clovis, New Mexico, for $250 apiece. We formed a partnership but I had to go to California. Windy was going to buy them for us. But Windy drank on occasion. At the crucial time for the purchase he twisted off and forgot to buy them. All the cars were gone."

Wyatt urps again!

However, Toad did leave his mark in Lorenzo. Maudie's was the local café. He suggested that Maudie could sell gift certificates for the Christmas season, a marketing concept she couldn't comprehend at first.

"You mean, they'll pay me before they eat?' But she took the advice, and loved the results. So did someone else, probably, as he slapped his certificate on the counter.

> *"I'll have a chicken fry, Ma'am," Wyatt would say.*
> *"Easy on th' gravy though. Been a might queasy lately,*
> *for some reason."*

179

The Toad Leon Golf Classic

The history between Bob Lapham and Toad Leon goes farther back than the idea for this book which was conceived by his daughters. Back in the late 1950s, I regularly played golf Sunday afternoons at Abilene Country Club with Jim (Oscar's Boy) Rose and Tommy Estes. Twenty-five years later Estes would coach two future touring pros (his son, Bob, and Mike Standley), another who almost made it (Kyle Coody, Masters Champion and Senior Tour star Charles Coody's son), and other Abilene Cooper High golfers to three consecutive Texas state high school golf championships.

Donna Leon chats with an official at the first Toad Leon Golf Classic held at the Pendaries Ranch Golf Course in 1952.

"More often than not, it seemed, we'd play behind Toad's foursome that might include left-handed swinging C.E. (Sonny) Bentley, J.D. Perry, Coony Coulson, E.F. Smith, Paul Hodge, Moose Stovall and others. We were twenty-three year-olds facing military service obligations. They were these rich guys who were having so much fun, it seemed downright criminal. Except for the fact that all three of us hoped someday to get as much joy out of life as "those old phartes up ahead," laughed Lapham.

Old? In their fifties? At least one of them would be having as much fun on the course thirty-five years later.

"But Toad and I didn't personally connect until 1973, when he and Donna made their annual appearance at the great party-time, week-long wintertime tournament, Life Begins at 40. It was played at Harlingen Country Club.

"At the time, I was sports editor for the local paper, The Valley Morning Star. Toad and Donna were in town for golf and partying with 255 other couples. Due to the Abilene connection we shared, I tracked Toad down one day, between rounds. As we talked, the makings of a pretty good sports news story emerged. My paper ran it under the heading, 'The Toad Leon Classic.'

"I got a short course on the northern New Mexico mountains; how Toad converted part of his ranch into vacation home sites and a golf course he designed himself. How he spent one winter, plodding through the snow and stretching twine down prospective fairways on what would be an 8,000-foot high layout.

The prize for the first hole-in-one at the Toad Leon Golf Classic was a year's free pass to the Grande Theater in Brownsville, Texas—about 1,000 miles away.

A natural golf course architect? It would seem so. Only his frequent playing companion, Bill St. Clair, thought otherwise. "I know how Toad designed this course," he said, the first time he played Pendaries. "He'd hit his three wood, and where ever the ball stopped, that's where he'd put a dogleg."

"What intrigued me most was that Toad's course wasn't nine holes, which it started out to be; or eighteen, which it would become in a few years. In 1973, the Pendaries Golf and Country Club was a twelve-hole layout. Par forty-eight."

"That's what I advertise," a grinning Toad told me. "I have the world's finest 12-hole golf course even if it is the only one. Anyway, who decided a golf course had to be nine or eighteen? Somebody told me the only reason it was that way was that it took a couple of Scots nine holes to drink a fifth of whiskey."

"His wife, Donna, decided her husband needed his very own golf tournament to go with his very own golf course. So she gave him one as a surprise Christmas present. She told me that Bing Crosby had his own tournament and there were the Bob Hope, Glen Campbell, Andy Williams, and Dean Martin classics. Why not a Toad Leon Classic?"

"Donna gave him everything he needed—bag tags, prizes in the form of exceptional pieces of Indian art and crafts, nice souvenir decorator ash trays for the wives, and pre-paid entry fees for twenty couples of her husband's choosing that would include plenty of food and drink along with two evenings of live entertainment.

"Toad's first-ever concept would continue a few more years though without Donna's direct hands-on attention. He developed a format that included a minimum age limit (the golfer had to be at least forty-eight), and a maximum field (forty-eight, naturally) that would compete for forty-eight holes in forty-eight hours (twenty-four holes per day). The entry fee? Why, forty-eight dollars, of course.

"Toad had a great hole-in-one prize during the Classic, especially for the movie-going golfer and his significant other. "You get an ace during my tournament, and you get a year's free pass to the Grande Theater," Toad offered. The Grande was one of Leon Theater chain's best venues only it was in Brownsville, Texas. That's a good thousand miles from Pendaries Ranch and still hundreds of miles from anywhere in Texas except Corpus Christi and Laredo and a few smaller towns in between."

It sounded good, though Wyatt noted that
no one ever claimed the prize.

...and She Didn't Spill a Drop

Hugh and Cris Briggs, Jane and Johnny Black, and Toad and Donna Leon were couples' imitations of The Three Musketeers back in Dallas of the 1940s-50s. The three twosomes stayed close after Toad and Donna moved to Abilene and Santa Fe.

"We loved going on trips together," Cris said in the summer of 2001. "Not long ago, I was talking to Toad and told him, 'You know, we were the jet set before the jet set was invented.' We'd do things like go to Chicago for dinner and be back at midnight. And this was before there were jets or a DFW Airport."

The time they accompanied the Leons to New York for Donna's surprise trip was a high point but Cris remembered another jaunt that was just about as good. "We talked about going to California one summer and decided we'd drive on out, three cars in tandem," Cris Briggs recalled. "Our plan was to wind up in San Francisco. We decided to go by way of Lake Tahoe since Johnny said he knew the owner of a casino there and we could get some great accommodations."

As it turned out, Black's pal was not there when they arrived to check in. The desk was not accommodating. They seemed to enjoy telling the troupe that since they had not bothered to call ahead there was nothing available.

"Johnny had taken his mother's limousine on the trip," Cris said. "This was before the stretch limos, but Johnny's was still impressive. The guy at the hotel desk walked the six Texans to the door, took a look at

The infamous pier where Donna "didn't spill a drop."

that big black limo, and suddenly remembered three rooms set aside for high-rollers they could have for the night."

"It was a lovely evening so we took our drinks and went for a walk down by the lake," Cris said. "If you've been to Tahoe you know the water is deceptively clear. You might think you're looking down two or three feet, but it could be ten or twelve. There were stories of people who slipped in, panicked, and were never found again probably lodged in a crevice or something.

"Anyway, we were on the pier having our drinks and really enjoying ourselves. You know how you can have an intuition that something is about to happen but you're helpless to stop it? Well, Donna had on this beautiful evening dress and a light coat. She stepped back and I just knew she was going in."

That she did.

"She came up, teeth chattering and her glass held high. 'Look Cris! I didn't spill a drop!'" Toad was beside himself until we got her out.

"I miss Donna Leon terribly," Cris sighed.

And so does Wyatt.

Idea Men Often Leave the Details to Others

There are idea men in this world, and there are detail men. More often than not, the two remain separate. Idea men usually know what their calling in life is. They also recognize that if they have all the ideas and do all the details associated with their brainstorms then it's not fair to others who wouldn't have anything to do if idea men didn't leave the mop-up details. Or something like that.

Frank Sheffield, longtime movie business competitor, then associate, and, finally, close friend of Toad's, says that's a pretty good description of Toad Leon. In other words, ideas are a whole lot more fun. But the details Toad leaves lying around can be pretty taxing at times. Even Toad admits to that.

Morgan Hubbard could also attest to the description. Hubbard was an Abilenian by way of Dallas just like Toad. Both loved to play golf. They were naturals to become close friends during their West Texas days.

"It was about 1960 and I had the Pendaries Ranch," Toad recalled. "I had my two prize Appaloosa stallions, Chief of Four Mile and Quanah, out at Carl Miles' place near Abilene. I wanted to take them back to Pendaries. I asked Morgan if he'd like to ride out there with me and he said sure.

"It was winter time, and we made it to northern New Mexico fine. But while heading back to Abilene in an Oldsmobile convertible that was pulling an empty horse trailer the weather turned on us. We got as far as Santa Rosa when a big snow set in."

Toad decided they had better buy a set of chains and put them on his tires. Also it helped when they got behind a snow plow on the highway even though the going was pretty slow. Then, with little snow between the highway and their tires, coupled with the decrease of snowfall the chains began fighting against themselves.

"They were flopping around under there, making an awful racket. I told Morgan that we had to get those chains off," Toad said, smiling as the recollection began to take familiar shape. Morgan, being a helpful fellow, volunteered to get down under the car with pliers. He started working on those chains.

"Now, it was freezing. The wind was blowing something fierce. Then it started snowing again. Morgan was having a real hard time with those chains. Meanwhile, I stood by. Finally, he managed to get the last chains off.

"I liked to tell the story around our club in Abilene and there's a possibility it could be true about how I saved Morgan Hubbard's life," Toad said, laughing. "Why, if I hadn't stood out there to the side of my Olds, shielding him from that north wind while he was under the car taking those chains off he could've frozen to death!"

Toad and his wife, Donna, also would become close party pals with Morgan and his wife, Dodge, and Morgan's brother, Harold (Snooky) Hubbard, and his wife, Jackie, who later would buy a lot and build a vacation home at Pendaries.

"Their father was Ray Hubbard, a big, big oilman in Dallas who created the Three Brothers Oil Company that got in on the ground floor of the Snyder boom."

One day in Abilene Snooky confided to Toad that he hated to tell him but fun times in Abilene were coming to a close. He and Jackie were moving back to Dallas.

"Why, Snooky?" Toad asked.

"Well, my Daddy made me a proposition I just couldn't turn down."

"What was that?"

"He said to get my fanny back to the Dallas office or he was going to cut me off!"

Toad's Trip of Trips—1970

Toad and Donna Leon spent a considerable time during their nearly sixty-one years of marriage on the go to exotic places as well as exciting destinations. But nothing compared to spending a couple weeks in 1970, tooling around the Mediterranean and Aegean seas on an Aristotle Onassis-style Greek yacht.

"My friend, Dan W. Varel, bought the winning raffle ticket for a sailing trip on a large yacht." Toad said. "We flew to Athens, did some sightseeing, then boarded the yacht for what would be the greatest trip I was ever on." Varel, incidentally, had a separate direct connection to Toad some ten years earlier when he was introduced to the Pendaries Ranch's new horse trainer, Jim Trammel of Clyde, Texas.

Jim Trammel, November 1992.

"I remember him!" Dan told Toad with a laugh. It seems Trammel, long before he was in Toad's employ, had invented a bit to use in training horses. While in Dallas during the 1950s he saw a sign pointing to Varel's factory and its "world famous bits." Trammel managed to get in to see Varel at his office. Varel still recalled their conversation almost fifty years later during a phone interview from his home in Dallas.

"Do you make bits?" he said Trammel asked him.

"Why, yes…"

"I've invented a new bit," Trammel went on. "I'd like you to manufacture them for me."

"How many are we talking about making for you?"

"About a thousand."

By now, Varel said he figured there was a miscommunication. "You don't understand," Varel had to tell the West Texan while attempting to keep from laughing as Trammel told him of his invention. "We manufacture rock bits for oil drilling not horse's bits, Mr. Trammel. Sorry"

But back to Toad's trip of trips. The Aegean swing, in particular, was breathtaking, Toad said. "Dan and his wife, Barbara, asked two other couples to go along. Every day the yacht captain would come by our break-fast table and ask, 'Mr. Varel, where would you like to go today?' Sometimes they'd use the engines. On other days the crew would hoist sails and we'd drift through water so clear you could see twenty or thirty feet straight down. We were treated like royalty."

Dan and Barbara Varel, standing at left, relax with their guests aboard a Grecian yacht in 1970 during Toad's "trip of trips." Donna and Toad are seated on the left.

"Early each morning, the captain and I would meet and pick a desti-nation for a harbor that evening," Varel recalled. "This would include where we'd like to anchor at noon so we could have a pleasant setting for lunch. The islands we visited were so beautiful. So clean and wonderful. The people on them were very friendly. It was a great time."

During one stopover, at a picturesque island the name of which Dan had forgotten, he said he, Barbara, Toad and Donna ventured into an ancient little village. "Our wives were always looking for places to shop so we scouted around for an antique store," Dan said.

"Now, there's a great looking prospect," Toad announced, pointing to an ancient, if not a little too ornate, storefront. So the four entered. They were the only ones around, and the women were—well, Dan said they acted just like they were in heaven. Shopper's heaven. Even Toad seemed impressed with the paintings, frescoes, religious artifacts, gold and silver pieces, aged furniture and other such bona fide antiques. The women were ready to make some purchases. Now, if they could only find a sales person. Preferably one who spoke English (although Dan was of Greek descent he did not speak the language fluently). They stepped outside, and pretty soon a likely prospect came walking their way.

"Pardon me, sir," Toad asked, pointing inside. "We'd like to make some purchases. Do you know where the owner is?"
The villager smiled, opened his palms in a shrug, and looked heavenward. Then he walked away. After a couple more efforts the Americans finally got the word. They were trying to buy "antiques" from a church. It didn't work, of course.

After the cruise, the party spent time in Italy, where they were guests of the widow of world-famous landscape designer Joe Lambert, near Venice at the forty-one room villa she was remodeling.

Then they flew to Paris and an afternoon of cocktails hosted by operatic soprano Maria Callas. Her lavish apartment, reputed to have been provided the diva by her former lover, Onassis, was upstairs. It was serviced by a free-swinging elevator, "my first time to be on one of those," Toad said. Callas didn't just go through the motions. She seemed genuinely happy to be around the Texan Americans. The visitors were having so much fun, the time seemed to just speed by. Barbara looked with dismay at the living room clock and saw that their allotted time to spend with Callas had expired.

"We've got to go," she announced to the group.

"Oh no. Not yet. I'll fix that," Diva Callas said, with operatic flamboyance. She then took her clock and turned it back 30 minutes. Not knowing what to expect she had turned her clock forward before her guests arrived should she need an escape mechanism.

"While we were there, the phone rang," Toad said. "It was Onassis." This was when the Greek tycoon was still married to the former Jacqueline Kennedy. The two women had become world-class tabloid figures in the battle over Onassis. Callas, in particular, was outspoken.

Not only a great trip, but a juicy one too, Wyatt might say.

321 Hillside—Santa Fe, New Mexico

Actress Vivian Vance and her husband, publisher John Dodd, grew to love the northern New Mexico mountains—particularly Pendaries Ranch. That's where they were in the process of buying one of Toad and Donna Leon's vacation townhouses in the 700 acre development and golf course the Leons had established within their working ranch.

"But as fate would have it, they were called back to New York, indefinitely," Toad explained. Vivian, long a co-star to Lucille Ball on her "I Love Lucy" and spinoffs TV series had a stage role she wanted to pursue. Her husband's publishing business needed attention.

321 Hillside Avenue, Santa Fe, NM

"Imagine Donna's and my delight when they called and asked if we would be interested in leasing their home in Santa Fe," Toad recalled. They owned one of the most historic territorial style houses in the small city. The picturesque adobe home had been part of old Fort Marcy in the early 1800s. The wide entry hall suggested it had been built for use by a U.S. Cavalry officer.

"They loved the home so, they wanted someone who would love it just as much and take care of it," Toad said.

Historians say that a royal family named Hesse vacationed there and a German princess married to a Russian czar may have spent summers in the house. New Mexico Governor Seligman and his wife owned the house for thirty years prior to World War II. Mrs. Seligman said that a Russian duke had died in the house.

"Bill Lumpkins, a well-known Santa Fe architect, thought all this might very well be true for while refurbishing and restoring the old home he discovered several beautifully carved double eagles that were said to

Donna, Toad, and Sandra Leon get ready for a garden party at 321 Hillside Avenue, Santa Fe, NM.

be the insignias of the Russian czars," Toad said.

The two-foot thick adobe walls kept the house cool in the summer without air conditioning. "The location was perfect— one and a half blocks from the historic plaza,yet situated in a quiet neighborhood," Toad said. "Out back, several terraced gardens separated the main house from a cute guest house and small heated swimming pool. From there, a naturally landscaped area extended to the top of a hill."

All in all, it was an ideal home for the Leons. Vivian and her husband visited them two years after the lease was drawn. It seemed they would be in New York City to stay.

"We know you and Donna have come to love the house as much as we do," Vivian said to Toad. "We want you to buy it. We'll make you a deal you can't turn down."

"Donna and I spent the next seventeen years in this unique residence," Toad said. Toward the end they were not spending as much time as you'd expect—anywhere. They also had established a residence in Abilene, purchased The More or Less Ranch nearby, and still owned a home in Kerrville, Texas, at the River Hills Country Club.

"In the end, Santa Fe's 7,000-foot altitude became a hardship on Donna's health so we reluctantly gave up on the house at 321 Hillside. However," Toad added, "not the happy memories of visiting friends, parties, garden tours, and family holidays."

With one less "primary residence" to attend to, Donna would be able to keep up with her favorite skillet.

High Life at the Hyatt—1975

There was plenty of evidence, after doing an overview of Toad Leon's life at age 91, that the man had to have spent many mighty interesting mornings. Either he would wake up ready at the first rattle to find a way to make a buck or he'd arise wondering how he could get a rise out of his buddies.

One incident involved an ex-NFL star, a ritzy hotel in Tony Bennett's favorite town, a butler and a phone call back to Texas, and acupuncture.

"It was Harrah's 17th Invitational golf tournament in Reno, Nevada," Toad recalled. "I was paired with Ted Kwalick, who starred at tight end

The high life in Reno, Nevada, 1971 is enjoyed by (from left): Donna Leon, Bill Browning, Jane Browning, Toad Leon, Betty Slaughter, George Slaughter, Suzie Browning, and Jeff Browning.

for the San Francisco 49ers. He also was a representative for the Hyatt Hotel chain." After the tournament Kwalick asked Toad, "How would you and Donna like to be comped for three days at our downtown Hyatt in San Francisco?"

Naturally, Toad said he'd like that very much.

"Tell me. Do you have another name? I kinda hate to send a VIP for the penthouse named Toad."

"Well, you could use my initials, which are C.D. And did you say the penthouse? Betty and George Slaughter from Dallas are with us. Could they come?"

"That would be great. Now, Toad, a limousine will meet your party at the airport and take you to the Hyatt. On arrival, a hostess will escort you directly to the penthouse, bypassing check-in. There you will be introduced to Jacques, your French butler. I'm sure you will enjoy your stay."

"That was putting it mildly," Toad said. "Our lavish accommodations consisted of a six-room suite complete with kitchen, bar, huge living room, and all the accoutrements. Jacques waited on us hand and foot.

"One evening Ted treated us to a sumptuous wine-tasting party. We returned to our suite in such high spirits we asked Jacques to place a call to our good friends Suzy and Jeff Browning in Dallas"

When Jeff came on the line, Jacques cooed in a thick accent, "Hello, Mr. Browning. I am Jacques, Mr. Toad Leon's private butler. Mr. Leon would like to speak to you, please."

"A butler!? What the hell is a fellow who came from Rule, Texas, doing with a butler?" Jeff Browning growled into the phone.

The Slaughters and the Leons lit up the night life while in the City by the Bay. So much so Betty Slaughter felt the need for recuperative attention. Why not slip over to Chinatown and try acupuncture? Uh-uh, her companions said. Finally, Toad said he'd try it, so Betty wouldn't have to go alone.

"There we were lying in this room with more than 100 needles stuck in various places in our bodies," Betty recalled. "It got kind of weird, when they started lighting some of my needles on fire. But it didn't hurt much, that I can recall. In fact, it may have helped my hangover."

She laughed when she recalled Toad's reaction to George wanting to hit the club circuit one more time that evening, before bidding San Francisco, the Hyatt penthouse, and Jacques good-bye.

"Easy now," Toad moaned. "Some of us are recovering from surgery."

The Barbecue Business—1976

Having done quite well pioneering up-scale fast food at drive-in theaters only to strike out with "hamburgers of distinction," Toad turned his interest toward his, as well as a growing number of other West Texans, favorite food of choice in the mid-1970s. Barbecue!

Square's Bar-B-Q, shown as it opened in 1976. It was a Toad Leon food enterprise that worked.

As Toad's family knows all too well, he will detour fifty miles on a highway trip if he sees a sign that reads, "Real Pit." He built Square's Barbecue in northwest Abilene and tabbed his daughter, Sandra, and her husband, Square Roberts, to run the restaurant for him.

Al Callaway, Toad's grandson, now owns Square's Bar-B-Q.

"I had this friend of mine, Sonny Bryan, who had a top-notch barbecue place in Dallas," Toad recalled. "I called him up one day and said, 'Sonny, how would you like a pair of workers for about a month who'd work for free?' Well, Sonny was all for that. So Square and Sandra spent that time with one of the best, learning the business from the ground up.

"One of our specialties was smoking hams," Toad said. "We got real good at it. These were the best you ever saw and were absolutely delicious. We'd buy the hams from Gooch Packing Company in Abilene and smoke them for twenty-four hours."

Audrey Anders ran the office of Abilene oilman Buddy Williamson and like others who frequented Square's on Leggett, between North First and Second streets she loved the hams. She was working on Williamson's Christmas gift list one year and got an idea. Could Sandra and Square fill her order and ship 300 hams in time for the holiday season?

The small business made the deadline and a new enterprise under the Toad Leon flag was born.

"Here we had this little-bitty kitchen and this little-bitty smokehouse out back," Sandra said. Because of the smoked ham business on top of their regular barbecue business, the setup soon became overtaxed. They leased another building and added additional smokers in order to keep up with the demand.

Toad soon got into his favorite end of any enterprise—marketing. "I still did a good bit of business in Santa Fe," he explained where he sold a few hams to acquaintances. While up there late one summer his regular golfing partner, ex-Cowboys star quarterback Don Meredith, said, "Toad, tell you what I'll do. If you play me even today, I'll sell eighty-five hams for you."

"I'll do that, my friend," Toad replied. Meredith was buying them for another pal of his, Santa Fe Bank president Bill Bucholz. Soon two lumber yards and a roofing company in the town got into the act until Square's Barbecue was selling between 400 and 500 smoked hams a year, just in Santa Fe.

Donna Leon and football legend Don Meredith cut up at a party in El Rito, New Mexico.

This is a continuing good ol' American success story with Square's Barbecue still in its original location, though now owned by Al Callaway, one of Toad's grandsons.

And Wyatt took a bite off a rib before signaling,
"Two thumbs up, way up!"

The More or Less Ranch—1977

Unusual ranching interests became a Toad Leon trademark. Besides Pendaries and excluding farm purchases, he bought medium-size spreads in Oklahoma, west of Dallas and northeast of Abilene for various purposes.

The Oklahoma spread, back in the southeastern hills "where the natives would just as soon shoot a stranger as look at him," was a tax deal that came along following the sale of Pendaries. Bunker Hunt bought it off Toad. He was a member of the famous (or infamous, if you happened to get caught holding a lot of silver bullion or coins) Dallas brother team that cornered and pretty well ruined the world's silver market in the 1970s.

Perhaps the most intriguing of all of Toad's ranches turned out to be a spread about thirty miles south of Abilene. "Of course, it wasn't in the

An ariel view of the Hunting Lodge at the More or Less Ranch

Rocky Mountains, but it did have a house, barns, corrals, the Jim Ned Creek, stock tanks, beautiful dots of live oak trees, scenic canyons, and, best of all, it was close to Abilene," Toad explained. "Donna and I were still in Santa Fe, but we were spending more and more time back in West Texas.

"We were at Abilene Country Club one evening when my good friend and tax man, Ben Davis, remarked, 'Toad, I understand you bought a ranch near Lawn. How many acres are in it?'

"B-e-n!" I said, sounding shocked, "I can't believe you'd ask such a question! It is bad form to ask a rancher the size of his spread. It's akin to asking a man how much money he has in the bank. But since you were bold enough to ask, I'll be frank enough to tell you. It has 10,000 acres." Toad's daughter, Carol Ann Midkiff, was nearby and overheard the conversation. "DADDY!" she blurted.

Safari time at the More or Less Ranch

"Well, it's 10,000 acres—more or less," Toad amended.

The name caught on. It officially became the More or Less Ranch.

"We ran cattle and horses a few years. But, with such a varied terrain and having always been fascinated with wildlife it seemed an ideal site for adding some exotic game."

Toad and his wife, Donna, had recently spent parts of a couple years living in a home at River Hills Country Club in Kerrville, Texas. The famous and historic YO Ranch is located near the hill country town. Toad had become well acquainted with one of the YO's owners, Louis Schreiner. The YO had been a pioneer in importing exotic wildlife species from around the world. Toad visited his friend and further investigated his plan for the More or Less. Finally, it was a done deal. The YO would furnish seed stock for Toad's operation.

More or Less Ranch manager and safari guide, Square Roberts, with a harvested aoudad.

"But first major modifications had to be made. An eight-foot-high, game-proof fence was built around the perimeter, with special care taken at gates and water gaps.

"It was very exciting when the animals began arriving. We eventually had about fourteen species from four continents. Along with our native whitetail deer, we had aoudad sheep, mouflon sheep, ibex goats, eland antelope, blackbuck antelope, scimitar horned oryx, rocky mountain elk, fallow deer, axis deer, sika deer, watusi, llama, and zebra along with various birds."

All cross fences from the interior were removed, allowing each species to seek its own comfort zone. The wildlife thrived in their new home. There was a little anxiety among Toad's neighboring ranchers in the early 1990s when a flood washed out some fences at creeks. However, only twenty-five Rocky Mountain elk left the More or Less for new territory. The large animals were posing a major problem until Toad hired a father-son helicopter team from the hill country of Texas. The chopper would fly low over the elk and drop nets on them. Ground crews from the ranch would then tackle the task of loading the elk in trucks and returning them to More or Less. "It was a thing of beauty to watch the helicopter come right down on top of the elk and net them," Toad said.

After a while, the time came to harvest the trophy males from throughout the ranch's game population. "We advertised 'fair chase' hunts which were conducted safari style and believe me they were just that," Toad said. His son-in-law, Square Roberts, guided all hunts. "He exhausted the hunters, the jeep, and himself at the end of each day. The aoudads were especially difficult to get. They were our biggest challenge."

The Trophy Lodge is a popular hangout at the More or Less Ranch.

TV crews from various wildlife and hunting shows began arriving. There seemed to be no shortage of safari-goers—big time or small scale. An example of the latter was Jack Riley. The businessman from San Francisco had moved to Abilene several years earlier and had shared an office with Toad's flagship company, Leon Properties. Riley said that Toad chided him for his lack of outdoorsman skills. "I told Toad I had never shot a deer so he decided it was time that I did. He took me out to More or Less and we drove around the ranch one morning in his Suburban. We didn't see a whitetail."

This bobcat made the mistake of crossing the path of the More or Less Ranch owner, Toad Leon.

"Square can join us this afternoon, so we'll have the expert on board," Toad promised. Roberts guided the vehicle to a likely spot. Pretty soon he pointed to the right. "There's one," he said to Toad and Jack who were in the back seat.

"I got real excited even though Toad said, 'Nah. That's a tree stump!' But I couldn't get my window down at first. When I finally did I got a cramp in my leg. I had to hand the rifle to Toad who kept insisting it was a tree and not a deer. But I figured Square knew what he was talking about." Finally,

Ed Brosseau, left, Toad's granddaughter Noel and John Martin get ready for a trail ride at More or Less Ranch.

Riley got his act together and fired. And with just a single shot Riley reduced the ranch's whitetail deer population by one. "What's always puzzled me is, how did Toad Leon develop this big, successful game ranch if he couldn't tell a deer from a tree stump?" Riley concluded, with a smile.

Toad would keep adding to the outdoor ambience of More or Less Ranch. "Before long, we found the need to build a lodge to accommodate our hunters," Toad said. "Square, my grandsons, Al Callaway and Tim Roberts, and one carpenter built our Trophy Lodge from the ground up in only six weeks. It was constructed from old bridge timbers and was what we called 'comfortable rustic.' It had a large rock fireplace, high tin ceilings, a full kitchen, and two bunk rooms.

"Later we added a bunk house and a large outdoor pavilion, and leased the facilities for private parties during the off-season. In fact, my daughters threw my 88th birthday party there in 1998. But that's another story.

Square Roberts, left, and Ben Callaway, Toad's grandson, ended this five-foot diamondback rattlesnake's days at the More or Less Ranch.

"We sold the More or Less Ranch in 1999 to Abilenian Ron Clark who still operates it for hunting."

A Weekend at Vermejo Park—1977

Toad and Donna Leon's friends in Dallas and Abilene were aware of their "other" life on Pendaries Ranch. It took some doing for some of them to realize that during the late 1960s and '70s the Leons had yet another complete social existence in Santa Fe, New Mexico.

"I had this group of friends who gathered nearly every weekday for lunch at the Palace Restaurant in downtown Santa Fe," Toad recalled. "We were called the Round Table Group. After a martini or two on one of these occasions the topic of conversation moved to the auto show that was being held at Nash Hancock's De Vargas Shopping Mall."

"All the new models are on display," Nash told the Round Tablers.

"Come on down this afternoon. It's quite a show."

"It was impressive," Toad agreed, "but what really caught our eye was the two-tone blue Dodge van. It had all the bells and whistles. I mean, it was loaded—four captain's seats, a table and a couch in the back that could be let down into a bed. We decided it would be perfect for camping and fishing outings or our day trips to Albuquerque for golf. Before long, we didn't need a salesman. We had sold ourselves!"

Ralph Petty, president of the bank most frequented, suggested that he and Toad go partners. "We'll finance it through my bank and share the costs for upkeep. Go see what kind of deal you can make."

A week later, Ralph called Toad and said, "We're taking some of the bank's executives and a few of our special customers up to Vermejo Park for a weekend of fishing. We'll go in several cars. Levitt will take Jones and Price. And you and I will take Rvhikel!"

"Don't think I've met him," Toad replied. "Is he new at the bank?"

"Who?"

"R.V. Hikel."

"Toad, you dumb s.o.b.! Our vehicle. You know. The VAN!"

Thus the dashing Dodge was named. Its license plates read RVHIKEL.

"Our weekend destination, Vermejo Park, is a ranching empire," Toad explained. "It straddles the New Mexico and Colorado border and covers between 600,000 and 700,000 acres. It is heaven for elk, large blacktail deer and various other wildlife. The many lakes and streams abound with trout. It's truly a sportsman's paradise.

"Saturday we were up at dawn and off to the lake. The day was perfect. The weather was moderate and the rainbow trout were jumping. Phil Levitts, a vice president at the bank, Ralph Petty, and I shared a boat.

"We couldn't wait to get our lines in the water. Ralph drew back his rod and cast. But it wasn't a big trout he hooked. It was Phil's upper lip. This called for a halt to the fishing expedition of course. At least for our boat. We were obliged to work on poor Phil and his lip. We fiddled around with it for a while, long enough for Phil to finally suggest that we take him to the emergency room in Raton. Once there it took just minutes for a doctor to remove the hook and administer a tetanus shot.

As we arrived back at Vermejo Lodge some of the fellows who were unaware of the situation asked how the fishing was. "How many did you catch?"

"Just one," Ralph replied. "A jewfish. But he was the biggest on the lake."

The Speech—1979

Toad Leon likes a good story as if you haven't already found out by now. So it stands to reason that he admires a good story-teller too.

"Jack Stroube was one of the funniest men around," Toad said. "For many years he sent out a monthly bulletin to his friends. It was loaded with words of wisdom." In 1979 Jack's Christmas bulletin contained the following story:

Baseball legend Mickey Mantle, a native Oklahoman with a tiny bit of Indian blood, attended a banquet honoring Native Americans. He found himself seated at the speakers' table next to Chief Dan George. The Chief had been nominated for a supporting Oscar in Dustin Hoffman's period adventure drama, "Little Big Man." Both Mantle and the Chief were to speak.

"Although Mickey comes from bow and arrow country, he don't speak no real Indian," Stroube wrote. "Only what he had heard in movies. The Chief was dressed in full battle regalia. He stared straight ahead without so much as an 'Ugh!' to Mickey."

Mantle wanted to be polite. When the food was served, he addressed Chief Dan George with such utterances as, 'You likum butter? You wantum bread? You needum napkin?" No acknowledgement from Dan. Just a straight forward stare. Then the emcee invited the Chief to the speaker's podium. Mantle said Dan George spoke for 25 minutes, in perfect English, without using a note. When he finished, there was a standing ovation.

As Dan sat back down, he turned to Mickey and asked, "You likeum speech?"

"Mick said he never had a tougher act to follow," Stroube concluded.

Stroube was a colorful oilman whom you may remember from Toad's uranium-hunting days. He also was Toad's close friend and golfing partner.

Back in my days of helping stake drilling locations for the civil engineering firm for whom I worked during summers away from college, I heard about Stroube trying to save a buck and staking his own location amid a complex lease. He stepped it off, 330 feet by 330 feet—and promptly put his lathe into the ground, showing his driller where to set up the rig—on someone else's lease. It was drilled and would you believe it? The site made a well. Stroube, it was said, made a deal to recoup drilling expenses from profits the rightful owner gleefully took to the bank.

Toad carried a membership in Dallas' exclusive Preston Trails Country Club, a men's only club begun by Pollard Simons. Stroube also belonged there as did Mantle. Both men got to play with the great Hall of Famer on occasion which probably is how Stroube got his Chief Dan George story.

Mrs. Joe Lambert, widow of the world-famous landscape designer, had befriended the Leons—particularly Donna. One afternoon she asked where Toad was and Donna replied that he was at Preston Trails.

"I guess he's out there playing golf with the over-privileged group," Mrs. Lambert said with a laugh.

Another connection Stroube and Toad shared was helping a major PGA touring pro get his start on the play-for-pay tournament trail. Don January was this tall, lanky kid from Dallas who frequented the colorful West Texas amateur golf circuit each summer in the late 1940s and early '50s. He often played in the Abilene Country Club's annual Fourth of July amateur and teamed with U.S. Amateur champion (and later a PGA tour regular) Billy Maxwell, among others, Also included in the group was Maxwell's twin brother, Bobby. This group helped to bring North Texas State University into U.S. collegiate golf prominence. This included a national championship.

Foy Fanning, pro at Abilene's Maxwell Municipal Golf Course, sought to broker a pro sponsorship for January with local businessmen. He approached Toad and Stroube and they included Carl Miles and J.D. Perry in on the deal. The way it worked was that the four would pay January's expenses until he was able to pay his own way in return for a cut from January's winnings.

"We told Don that anytime he felt like he could make it on his own we'd be glad to get out of the picture," Toad said. "All we were interested in was helping him get started. Well he won $50,000 in Dallas later on so he told us he thought he could make it now and that was fine with us.

"Don January was one of the finest people I ever met through golf," Toad continued. "Every now and then, he'd come to Brook Hollow Country Club in Dallas, where I also had a membership, for the Peppermint Stick Partnership. He'd team with Dick Jennings of Lubbock. Don never failed to come over to my table or catch me in the club house and thank me profusely for us backing him."

January was a winner on the regular tour, including a major PGA Championship title. He was a mainstay in the early days of the Senior Tour and one of its frequent winners. When the seniors added a thirty-six-holer for established veterans sixty and over January seemed unbeatable.

"What a great swing he had," Toad recalled. "Especially in his hands. He was something to watch. Still is, I'll bet."

Meanwhile, Wyatt was trying to figure out how to
build a Preston Trails in Tombstone.

Hang By Your Heels Toad Leon...Oops!

Somewhere along about the mid-1960s, two basic principles of life became self-evident to our man Toad Leon. One, he was about to leave middle-age and undertake that dash through the shadows of the rest of his life. Two, he had not taken particularly good care of himself through the first two phases of his existence.

Walter Johnson, Toad Leon, and Bob Springer play gin rummy in Kerrville, Texas during a golf outing for his Abilene friends.

If he wanted to make the former as pleasant as possible then he had to take some crash courses in proper attention to the latter. This was a subject that came up during the 1970s in Kerrville, Texas. He had invited some pals from Abilene for a men's party at the Leons' vacation home. Mack Eplen, Bob Springer, Richard Johnson, Stormy Shelton, Buck Kent, Ken Murphy and Walter Johnson visited Toad for three days of golf at River Hills Country Club and good eating at Toad's house.

It's not to say Toad didn't do anything good for the body as a young man. He did try the famous sweat boxes at once-trendy Baker Hotel in Mineral Wells, Texas, in the 1920s and '30s. And there was that "miracle dirt" from Ivan, Texas, he frequently was on.

Taking care of himself past middle age—or more realistically seeking cures for not having done so before—included by the numbers: (1) a spa in Switzerland; (2) acupuncture in San Francisco; (3) Chelation in San

205

Dr. Dub Sibley and his wife, Sonoma in 1999.

Francisco; (4) Chelation in P h o e n i x , Arizona; (5) Chelation in Big Spring, Texas; (6) Chelation in Abilene, under the direction of his longtime personal physician and friend, Dr. Dub Sibley; (7) a spa in Romania; (8) c o p p e r bracelets; (9) elastic knee bands; (10) magnets; (11) 30 years of taking Nutri-Homo, Dr. Sibley's health concoction; and (12) the topsy turvy machine.

Come again on number twelve? "Topsy Turvy machine," Toad explained. "I think I ran across this contraption in a magazine. Or maybe it was on television. Anyway, I ordered one." He had it in Kerrville when he hosted his friends from Abilene and prepared to feed them.

"What are you doing, Toad?" demanded Eplen, Abilene's most famous restaurateur.

"I'm broiling steaks, Mack."

"Not inside! You'll smoke up your whole house. You mean to tell me you don't have a barbecue pit?"

With this Eplen rushed from the house, found an appliance store still open, bought an expensive outdoor broiler and donated it to the cause. All of which is interesting, but what about the Topsy-Turvy Machine?

"This thing looked like the rack from a torture chamber," Toad replied. "But the claim was it was beneficial in getting blood to your brain. Instructions called for you to back into it, strap your ankles down, and then with a mighty heave throw yourself over backwards. The machine would pivot, and you would be left hanging by your heels."

When the boys saw Toad's new gadget, they were curious. "What in the hell is it, what does it do, and how does it work?" one of them asked.

Toad said he would demonstrate, so they gathered around as he strapped himself in and tilted back. He hung there briefly before his feet slipped out of his boots. He suddenly dropped straight down close to a foot, landing on top of his head on the concrete garage floor.

"I believe it has affected my thinking ever since," Toad said. "But through this experience I can add a line to that wise old saying, 'Don't squat with your spurs on.' And 'don't wear your boots while on a Topsy Turvy Machine.'"

Amen to that, Wyatt would say.
The experience might have rung his bell, too.

The Ringers—1980s

Some of the most fun Toad Leon ever had was making people squirm. Particularly his friends. And the closer they were to him, the better. What made his day on the golf course was to slip in a ringer now and then and make his pals whine like whipped pups. A ringer is a low-handicapper disguised as just another hacker. He would be Toad's partner in four-ball bets.

Toad Leon loved to sneak low-handicapper, Bill St. Clair in as a ringer against his unsuspecting golf partners.

Some of the Santa Fe, New Mexico, contingent of Toad's pigeons included Houston Frith, Nash Hancock, Charlie Horne, Stu Harvey and Big Ed Brosseau. It was Brosseau who told on Toad, during a 2001 interview. "I got to the course late," Ed said. "We played fivesomes in those days. I don't think Houston and Charlie were there this particular day. Anyway, Toad shows up with this tall fellow he said was from Muleshoe, Texas, a farmer friend of his who, according to Toad, was breaking in a brand new set of clubs."

"Ed, I'd like you to meet Bill St. Clair," Toad said, when Brosseau joined the group on the third tee."

"Hello Bill. What game are you guys playing?"

"Aw Ed, I volunteered to take Bill against all combinations (Toad and Bill versus all other two-man combos in the fivesome), five dollars a hole with automatic presses (beginning a new bet each time one twosome lost a hole)."

Ed said he always kept his guard up when doing anything for money against Toad Leon. "Hummmm. What kind of player is Mr. St. Clair?"

"Aw, he plays about like me," Toad replied.

Brosseau was wary, knowing Toad, but he went along anyway. "This cowboy from West Texas was a true ringer," he recalled. "Bill was killing us. On number three he put his second shot right next to the pin for a pick-up birdie. But when he laced a drive more than 300 yards on the eighth, our hardest hole, and had only a fifty-yard pitch that he got up and down for another birdie, I had had enough. I walked off the golf course after the ninth. I owed $85. Those poor suckers who stayed with Sinclair and Leon on the back nine probably lost $200 apiece."

Toad Leon with "Dark Cloud" Rawlins, a scratch golfer and a ringer for Toad.

Another long-time pal and occasional ringer of Toad's was Bob (Dark Cloud) Rawlins of Dallas. Poor Toad didn't get to utilize Rawlins' partnership prowess for long since Dark Cloud's reputation preceded him real soon after he won the 1987 U.S. Senior Amateur title at the age of fifty-eight (this USGA championship is for scratch players fifty-five and over).

"I don't recall exactly where it was, but Toad invited me to join him for a little game against some friends of his," Rawlins recalled, during an interview. "Now, Dark Cloud, keep that big bag of yours in the car trunk until just before we get ready to play," Rawlins said Toad told him. "I don't want these old boys to, uh, get the wrong idea."

"I had this pro tour style bag given to me by Rives McBee, pro at Las Colinas (in Irving, Texas, site of the Byron Nelson Classic on the regular pro tour), right after I won the U.S. Senior Amateur. I mean, it was BIG.

Had 'Bob Rawlins' lettered on one side, and 'Dark Cloud' on the other," remembered Rawlins.

"Toad's friends were whipped from the start with never a chance. I had to ask about here in our interview—why do they call you Dark Cloud?" asked Brosseau.

"Well, that goes back to 1956. I was selling insurance for a living. I was working with these guys on the side trying to get a new country club and golf course going in South Dallas. And I was on the committee getting the Dallas Open regular pro tour stop up and running. It was a bit much. I'd meet with someone, and sometimes couldn't remember if I was trying to sell him an insurance policy, sell him an ad in our tournament program, or get him to buy a membership at the new club. Apparently I had this confused, lost look on my face a lot of the time," said Rawlins.

"Bob, you remind me of that little Indian feller in (Al Capp's comic strip) 'L'il Abner,'" one of his contacts said at their club. "You know. Dark Cloud."

"Next day, the caddies at our club were referring to me as Dark Cloud. Once a nickname catches on its sticks with a person. I'm kinda glad mine did."

Toad helped get Rawlins a one-time entry in the prestigious Life Begins at 40 Golf Tournament in Harlingen, Texas, along about this time. "I got beat in the finals by this old guy (Fred Rohde of San Antonio) who chipped in on the first hole of our playoff for the championship," Rawlins said. Shortly thereafter, "since I had won about all the pots and pans and trophies I'd ever need,"

Dark Cloud decided to give the Senior PGA Tour a whirl, even if at fifty-eight he was well past the recognized prime for contenders. Senior pros can join that circuit at fifty. He did OK, winning a couple of super seniors (sixty-plus) while having a lot of fun. Along the way, Dark Cloud kept up with Toad.

"We've played together all over—Dallas, Abilene, Pendaries Ranch, California, Old Mexico," he recalled. "I remember when Toad put on this big invitational partnership golf tournament for high-rollers at Pendaries. He invited me to team with him. First prize was a lot at his place.

"Well, I went out there and looked at that lot which was way up in the mountains. You'd have to have helicopters instead of trucks to build on it. The lot was so remote I was afraid we'd win. I told Toad, 'if we're in contention at the eighteenth, I'll twenty-seven putt it if I have to just to make sure we don't come in first."

Toad would buy a raffle ticket to anything. He won several times, including use of a mansion in Acapulco once owned by Frank Sinatra and used as a hideaway for him and actress Ava Gardner in the early 1950s.

"Toad thought it was for a week but actually it was for a month," Rawlins said. Toad wasn't about to give it up early so he and Donna invited Dallas, Abilene, and Santa Fe friends down, three couples at a time, for a week of golf, fishing, luxury and fun, with a use of a yacht by the owner of Frito Lay thrown in. Rawlins and his wife, Noni, accompanied the Dallas contingent.

"I couldn't believe where I was," Dark Cloud said dreamily. "I loved Ava Gardner. I got a semi-erection just walking around that place thinking I was walking in her footsteps.

"That Toad, he is a piece of work, all right,' Rawlins said in concluding the interview.

So are many of his friends from the fun years,
Wyatt might add.

My Friend George—1985

While Harlingen's Life Begins at 40 Golf Tournament produced dozens of close friendships for Toad and Donna Leon, they seemed to have struck out while trying to rekindle yet another. Only this one wasn't actually connected with the competition. The year was 1985.

"That particular year we leased a house on the golf course for the entire month of February," Toad said. "When the tournament was over, the Browning brothers from Dallas, Jeff and wife, Suzy, along with Bill and his wife, Jane, came down for a few days. Later, Nash and Libby Hancock and Ed and Roberta Brosseau from Santa Fe visited. So we utilized the accommodations almost to their fullest.

"Our friends had gone home and our lease was about to run out when I remembered that an old playmate of mine from Rule had moved to Harlingen many, many years ago. We had been childhood buddies. After his family moved, my mother even took me to Abilene once to visit him so we could ride the streetcar from Simmons College (now Hardin-Simmons University) located twenty-three blocks into the city's north side, all the way to South Seventh Street and back."

Toad looked him up in the phone book and called. "Hello, is this George Kirk? Are you the George Kirk who came from Rule, Texas?"

"I sure am."

"This is Toad Leon."

"Oh sure, Toad. I saw your name in the newspaper where you were playing in the tournament. I wondered if you were the same Toad I used to know."

"I'm one in the same, George. How about joining my wife and me for dinner tonight?"

"Well, I'll have to ask Ollie Faye. She's my wife, you know."

The Kirks accepted the invitation and were given directions to the Leons' leased house. Toad and Donna were having cocktails when the visitors knocked on the door. Introductions were made and the two couples sat down.

"Would you like a drink?" Toad asked.

"Oh n-o-o-o! You know, I'm in the selling game."

"Really?" Toad inquired. "What do you sell?"

"I sell Cyclone fences and I won a prize one time. A trip to Las Vegas...NEVADA! We went out there and when we checked into the motel they gave us a ticket good for two drinks. Of course Ollie Faye didn't drink and I didn't drink either. But since they were free, I tried it. Drank both drinks. I didn't like it. Haven't had a drink since."

212

The conversation lulled a bit. "Um, well, George, do you play golf?"

"Oh n-o-o-o! When I went to the War in '42, I sold my clubs. Haven't played since. I didn't like it."

Another lull. People in the Rio Grande Valley of Texas regularly hop the river and shop or party in Old Mexico. There are international bridges linking Matamoros, Progreso and Reynosa with Brownsville, the mid-Valley, and McAllen respectively. So Toad took another conversational tack he felt sure would find common ground.

"Let's see. George, do you and Ollie Faye go over to Mexico often?"

"Oh n-o-o-o! You know, Toad, we had some friends who went to Matamoros one time and got into all kinds of trouble. Ollie Faye and I went over there many years ago, but haven't been since. We didn't like it!"

By now Toad and Donna, who was trying to mask a growing smile, needed another drink. "I remember faintly that your father bought a farm down here," Toad said, mixing the two concoctions. "Do you still have the farm?"

"Oh n-o-o-o! I kept the farm for a while. But Toad you won't believe this. I was out there one Saturday and my hired hand was all dressed up to go to town and buy groceries. I asked him if he had looked in the west and seen all those clouds. It might come up a hail. I told him he needed to pick cotton before it got ruined. You know what? He went to town anyway. Dependable help is too difficult to find, so I sold that farm. I didn't like it!"

With that statement, Donna suggested they all go to dinner. A friend of Toad's who had played in the tournament each year owned a steak house nearby. As the four entered the restaurant the owner gave Toad a knowing grin. Evidently, George was well known in this middle part of the valley.

As the evening drew to a close, Toad decided to try meaningful conversation one more time.

"George, I nearly forgot to ask. Do you and Ollie Faye have any children?"

"Oh no-o-o!" Kirk replied.

Wyatt figured he already knew why.

The Smartest Man in Rule, Texas

Toad Leon, a man who loves a good story more than just about anybody, tells the following tale as the truth. Or, as he often says, when veracity is a part of the equation, "more or less." In 1988, Toad's Rule High School was having its 60th reunion. He wouldn't miss something like that, of course.

"I ran into my old friend, Buddy Lewis, who still lived in Rule and was by then retired from his lumber store business. His son, Jeff Lewis, is a prominent Abilene attorney, as well as avid golfer, as attested by his fellow Fairway Oaks Country Club pals."

Toad and Buddy discussed the events of the day, until Buddy said, "Toad, did you ever meet Joe Snodgrass? He is purported to be the smartest man ever to graduate from Rule High."

"No, Buddy, I guess I haven't. How smart is he?"

"Well, they tell me he can take any word in the dictionary and make a sentence out of it that you'll never forget." About that time, Buddy looked up and whispered excitedly, "Well, I'll be...! Toad! Here Joe comes now. I'll introduce you!"

In meeting the famous (except to Toad Leon) Mr. Snodgrass Toad said, "I understand you are the smartest man to ever graduate from Rule High School."

"Don't know about that," Snodgrass replied. "But I did attend Texas Technological College, Lubbock, Texas, where I studied very hard and made good grades."

"I've heard that you can take any word from the dictionary and make a truly unforgettable sentence with it. Is that right?"

"Well, I think I can. At least, I haven't been stumped yet. What word do you have in mind?"

Toad said he thought a minute, then replied, "I've got a long son-of-a-gun for you. How about trying the word...auditorium?"

Joe scratched his head. "Um, let me see...a-u-d-i-t-o-r-i-u-m...it is a

214

long word. But I think I can handle it. Back when I was in Texas Technological College, Lubbock, Texas, I was dating this little ol' girl from Muleshoe. Late one evening we drove in my roadster to a sandy lane just outside of Sudan, Texas. I began to make love to her. Toad, I believe she had on the tightest panties I ever saw. I tried to pull them up! And I tried to pull them down! Toad, I guess I or-ta-tor-e-um!"

Look out! Look out! Urp alert!
That one really got to Wyatt.

The Tax Man Cometh

Your doctor, your psychiatrist and your CPA know the real you. If someone wants to check up on Toad Leon, they have only two out of three with which to work. Toad hasn't required a shrink yet, though those with whom he has dealt, business wise, might have felt the need from time to time.

Bobby Melson is Toad's accountant, and the Abilene CPA figures he could write a book himself on his client's dealings. The two have become close friends down through the years.

"Toad is unusual, to say the least," Melson said, during an interview in the summer of 2001. "People find out he's my client, and they usually say something like, 'That Toad Leon! Everything he touches turns to gold.'" To which Melson replies, "I'm not at liberty to go into details, but trust me. Everything that Toad touches does not turn to gold."

But if you've read his story thus far you know that already. The bottom line, as any good CPA will tell you, is cutting to the skinny. Toad's far-flung business ventures are like the ebb and flow of a well-defined tide. He keeps flowing with ideas and brainstorms, and the ebbs just get outnumbered.

"The thing about Toad is his ability to talk to people, to convince them go along with him," Melson said. Back when Toad and Donna had Pendaries Ranch and its companion resort development, Toad was playing in celebrity golf tournaments and pro ams all over the country, as well as in Mexico.

"Bobby, I want to charge off all these golf tournament trips as business expenses," Toad said, as one tax season approached.

"I don't know if we can get away with that, Toad, but if this is what you want me to do, I'll do it." He did, and before long, the IRS was knocking on their door.

"Yeah, I remember," Toad replied, when asked his input. "That guy must've stayed with us for a whole week." Toad championed his own cause, with Melson at the head of the long table while the adversaries sat across from each other. Melson would nod occasionally and try not to look apprehensive while somewhere over there, *Wyatt was wiping his brow*.

"Sir, I want you to understand that everything I do in business is golf oriented - everything!" was the gist of Toad's argument. He told the tax man how he had this resort development on his ranch in New Mexico that was struggling to make a buck. "I have to go to these tournaments to promote our place to people who can afford to buy lots and build houses there," he said.

Bobby Melson

Melson could hardly believe it, but the IRS agent finally bought it. He gave Toad one-hundred percent of what he was asking in the way of tens of thousands of dollars in business expense deductions while wheeling and dealing on golf courses in some of the world's favorite watering holes. No one but Toad, "who can talk anyone into about anything, could've pulled that off," Melson said..

During the early 1990s Melson accompanied Toad to Fort Worth to look over the prospects of selling a property. "We got there in the early afternoon," Melson said. Toad was ready to unload the site of one of his great business ventures, the Southside Twin Drive-In in Fort Worth. Toad's property was not too appealing since it was in a low-lying area next to a creek," Melson said.

"There was this church on the adjoining land. Toad got the idea that the church might like to buy the acreage." So Melson and Toad met with the pastor and some of his elders and Toad made his pitch. Maybe the church could develop the land, use part as a recreational area, then subdivide the rest.

The pastor listened, nodded, then finally said to all in attendance, "OK. Let's stand, join hands and pray about this."

"Now, I have nothing against prayer, but I felt a little strange about this one," Melson said. But they bowed, joined hands, and listened to the pastor's lengthy prayer for guidance, one that included perhaps "Mr. Leon being led to the decision to donate this land to us, in the name of the Lord."

Afterwards Toad and Melson shook hands with the others and beat a hasty retreat.

"It was evening, and we stopped by Billy Bob's to have dinner and relax from our ordeal," Melson said. Billy Bob's was the bar and grill famous for its country music fare. "Before long, Toad told me he had to cut the evening short," Melson said. "He had to get back to the hotel before 10 p.m. It was Wednesday, lottery night. He said he had gone into partnership with his friend, Jimmy Roberts and some other guys on Jimmy's sure-fire formula for winning the Texas Lottery which was up to more than $20 million."

It turned out that Roberts had purchased about 500 one-dollar tickets with various select combinations covered. The six drawn numbers came on TV just before the local news and Toad—ever one to sucker workers into his schemes—halved his list of Roberts' numbers with Melson.

"We spent the better part of an hour, checking and re-checking the numbers," Melson said. He recalled Toad and Company getting $20 back from their investment."

"I got out of the lottery game right then and there," Toad said later.

This time, Wyatt forgot his furrowed brow.
This time he urped.

How to Squelch a Toad—1997

Toad Leon has spent much of his considerable lifetime making people laugh. Especially at themselves, as the butt-end of pranks and practical jokes he has set in motion sometimes with scarcely a split-second's

Toad knows he's been "squelched" so he joins Julie Price in her protection act.

notice. He also plays the game of what comes around, goes around quite well. Toad enjoys being the on the hot seat. Just allow him to place himself there if you don't mind. And let him be in charge of the sardonic circus that foists him into the center ring.

"It happened at Nickel Creek Ranch, a beautiful spread in the Guadalupe Mountains of far West Texas," related Carol Ann Midkiff, Toad's oldest daughter. "David Ligon hosts a marvelous music festival each year and my husband, T.O., and I had introduced Daddy to it."

However, you have to backtrack to the previous spring to set the perfect squelch on course. A number of the couples who partake of Ligon's hospitality at Nickel Creek Ranch got together for a weekend of houseboating on Utah's beautiful Lake Powell.

"As usual, Daddy was the life of the party, telling all those funny stories of his," Carol Ann recalled. "And also as usual he was everybody's pet. Particularly the women's." Many of the same couples would be showing up later in the year at Nickel Creek Ranch, including Bill and Ethel Mundy and Henry and Judy Coors of Chama, Jim and Evelyn Tune of San Antonio, New Mexico, Jasper and Sis Koontz and Cabot and Dorothy Dysart of Corrales, New Mexico along with Texans Omer D. and Julie Price of San Angelo and Bob and Kay Bennett of Midland. Noted psychiatrist Nat Winston and his wife, Martha, of Nashville, Tennessee, also were in attendance.

Cabot Dysart and Toad had become fast friends in a hurry, upon meeting for the first time at Lake Powell. They shared two especially important things in common. They both had the same birthday even though Toad's was ten or fifteen years earlier. And they both enjoyed chewing tobacco.

It stands to reason that it would be Dysart on that festive Saturday night at Nickel Creek who arranged to have Toad seated between two beautiful young ladies. Toad grinned broadly when he was introduced.

The ladies suddenly jumped up, crossed their arms over their chests and exclaimed in unison, "O-h-h, you're Toad Leon! I've heard about you!" Toad was taken completely aback. His face turned beet-red, Carol Ann said, and his mouth flew open. The rest of the guests roared. Toad knew he had been had, but good.

But did everyone else know it was only a gag?

David Ligon, "The Bard of Nickel Creek."

Regardless, it wasn't over. All through the evening, ladies made a point to come up to meet him. And as soon as he uttered his name in introductions they would quickly cross their arms defensively over their chests and say in mock dismay, "O-h-h, you're Toad Leon! I've heard about you!"

"This went on all night," Toad later recalled. "Everybody was having so much fun playing the game, I had trouble finding a partner to dance with. It really wasn't all that funny, if you want to know the truth of the matter."

Wyatt had his knee-slapping, side-grabbing disagreement.

A Tale of Two Bulls and a Pair of Ostriches

You think Toad Leon might have lost his deal-making touch as he neared age ninety? Don Vickery of Tuscola, Texas, doesn't think so. He tells Toad about it every chance he gets, too.

Vickery has a stock farm not far from the More or Less Ranch. A year or so before Toad sold the exotic animal spread he happened to run into Don at the Abilene Livestock Auction.

"What're you selling, neighbor?" Toad asked Vickery.

"Got a pair of Watusi bulls, Toad."

To which Toad perked up. It seems Vickery had purchased the bulls as calves at the Coleman, Texas Livestock Auction a few years earlier. These were direct offspring from the breed that the natives in Africa often are seen herding. Their hallmark is a rack of huge horns—particularly at

Toad with More or Less Ranch neighbors, Barbara and Don Vickery.

the base where the horns have an eight-inch diameter. How did they get to Coleman? Vickery believes they might have been donated as charity auction items probably at Abilene's West Texas Rehabilitation Center and the good heart who had bought them was now dumping the bulls.

Don wondered what kind of cross-breeding they might provide and decided to experiment. It was exciting around the Vickery place for a while. Don's wife, Barbara, is an artist. She painted the two once they had achieved their full and impressive bullhood. But the project never amounted to much, so the time had come for him to unload what had now grown from cute little calves to a couple thousand pounds of strange looking beeves.

"I might could use those critters at More or Less," Toad said. "You want to sell them to me and not put them through the auction?"

"Sure."

"Better yet, I have birds among my exotic animals at More or Less—rheas and ostriches, mostly. I have an extra pair of adult ostriches I would trade for those bulls." Vickery knew the emu boom had long passed. But people still bought ostrich eggs as well as the huge flightless bird's skin for tanning and crafting. He didn't expect to get much for his bulls. So he figured he soon would be one-up on the great wheeler-dealer, Toad Leon.

"Let's trade."

Tracking the bulls first, Toad managed to get some breeding from them but as intriguing as the foreigners might be, domestic-wise, the bulls did not fit in on an exotic animal ranch. Some yankee down for a safari might spot the beasts and blow them away before safari leader Square Roberts could stop him. So back to Abilene Livestock Auction they went. Their sale price made it moderately worth Toad's time, especially since they had replaced two big birds which had become excess baggage.

Now for the ostriches. Vickery put the pair of 400-pound birds on his farm and waited for breeding season while keeping his distance. "Them birds were mean let me tell you," he said. "They'd as soon take out after a man as look at him."

He still waited for breeding. And waited. Finally, about a year after they had begun eating their weight in grain every couple days or so, the ostriches started their dances of love.

The foreplay ended abruptly. This ostrich marriage was not made in heaven. "For some reason, the rooster killed the hen," Don said.

After several months more of feeding the fowl murderer, he gave the rooster to his farming son-in-law, Stan Marshall. In a few months the male ostrich got his just desserts. He keeled over dead, cause unknown—unless it might have been gluttony.

"We tried to get a guy with a wench line to come haul it off and he could keep the ostrich for its skin but we couldn't make a deal," Don said.

Two years later, in the summer of 2001, Vickery ran into Toad in Lawn. "I told him I'm still paying my banker $18.47 each month for those Watusi bulls, a note I was going to pay out from what I thought I would make on ostrich eggs and skin. Toad just smiled and nodded his head."

And so did Wyatt.

Birthday Party to End All Parties

The exotic wild game that populated Toad Leon's More or Less Ranch south of Abilene back in the late spring of 1998 probably figured the world was coming to an end. Amid fireworks, blasting shotguns, amplified live music, and the merry-making of almost 2,000 invited guests, the ranch was in a world of its own. The three-day party celebrated Toad's 88th birthday. His daughters and sons-in-law, Carol Ann and T.O. Midkiff, and Sandra and Square Roberts, hosted what many of those in attendance still call a party to end all parties.

Toad and daughters, Sandra Roberts (left) and Carol Ann Midkiff (right) who threw one whale of an 88th birthday party for their daddy.

A lavish invitation overseen by Sandra Roberts posed the question, "Ponce de Leon searched for the Fountain of Youth. Has Toad Leon found it?" The hosts promised "a Fountain of Youth (FOY) Seminar" and asked guests to "help us assess the rejuvenating merits of hearty feasting, restorative liquids, and invigorating exercise (dancing is indicated)."

Out-of-Abilene guests were booked into hotels in the southern part of the city some twenty-five miles to the north. Others were invited to take one of the RV camping and overnight sites at the ranch. Shotguns and shells were brought for clay competitions, wild game suppers, and various other chow line activities were provided.

Sandra "forced' her father to dress up as an Indian chief for the invitation, which was a little out of character since Toad suddenly had been linked by kinship to Ponce de Leon, the great sixteenth century Spanish explorer. Sandra tastefully set pre-festivities ground rules, such as:

"Confidentiality at the FOY Clinic (Your clinical records will be strictly private. No information will be given out to employers, friends or relatives without your written permission with our motto being, 'What you don't remember doesn't count—unless subpoenaed by a grand jury').

Also, insurance. "Most companies would laugh their asses off if asked to pay for diagnosis and treatment so in order to help us keep costs down don't bring any forms to fill out. And, "staff-client relations are strictly forbidden, but should they occur, it is best when based on mutual understanding. We make a special effort to explain everything to you. If you have any questions, or something is not clear, do not hesitate to ask. If we don't know, we'll guess."

Polly and Buck Denton were "official meeters and greeters" for the festivities which were photographed and videoed for posterity by Patsy and Marcus Bourland.

As guests drove through the main ranch gate and headed for the lodge they were greeted by a series of Burma Shave-style highway signs, popular in the 1940s-50s. A series of signs would tell a humorous four-line poem not unlike limericks and then would admonish the reader to try Burma

A takeoff on the old Burma Shave signs helped lead guests to the festivities.

Shave shaving lotion. The "Toad Leon Burma Shave signs," about seven series, picked out certain time periods of Toad's life. They were a hit and were composed at the invitation of Carol Ann by her close friend, Virginia Cox, a school teacher in Midland.

The first Burma Toader asked:

Feeling Nostalgic?
So is Toad.
Read the signs
and watch the road.

What makes Toad
look so trim?
The local draft board
is after him.

When the stork
delivered this boy
the town of Rule
jumped for joy.

Do these signs date you
'More or Less?'
They do Toad,
he will confess.

"We got a big kick out of doing these," Virginia said. "Older people knew what they were, of course. Younger adults didn't have a clue.

"I met Carol Ann in New Mexico," Virginia said. "My husband, John, and I got to know Toad through her." Cox said the size and scope of the birthday party was something to see. "I was impressed with Toad's family and how they came from as far away as California. Each one had his or her own job to do in putting on the party. They were very happy for Toad. It is a particularly close-knit family."

Sandra and Carol Ann had advised "hearty party-goers" that the FOY Seminar and related events "would not be suitable for children, dogs or gifts. However, horses are welcome to enhance therapeutics." In a way, leaving kids at home proved to be a bit sad when the professional fireworks team from New Mexico, overseen by Robert Oaks of Midland, Texas, set up shop for a 30-minute show that literally stopped traffic on U.S. 84 a mile away. Startled residents of tiny Lawn, a few miles further up the road, called in queries to the sheriff's department.

"Sunday morning, John and I started back to Midland and I wanted to stop at this antique store in Lawn," Virginia Cox said. "The lady who owned it asked where we were from and what we'd been doing and she gasped when we told her we had been to More or Less Ranch for Toad Leon's party.

"I heard this loud noise last night, I and ran outside," the lady said. "I thought it was rustlers after my livestock. Then I looked up yonder in the sky and I thought the Book of Revelations had come to life, that the world was coming to an end. When I found out it was fireworks, I sat in my yard and enjoyed the show."

Merle and Lewis Morrison, longtime friends of Toad, help celebrate the 88th. Merle drew the cartoon chapter introductions and cover for this book.

"Somebody at the party said they had been to Disney World, and the fireworks show there wasn't any better," Sandra said, adding that the "Wall of Fire" portion of the fireworks festivities "had people running for cover."

As invitee Frank Sheffield put it, "You had to be there to believe what this party was like. It was truly one of a kind."

Two party-goers made sure Toad's many friends in Santa Fe who hadn't made the long trip to More or Less Ranch got caught up. A banner headline inside the Lifestyle Section of The New Mexican under the byline of "Santa Fe Scene" columnist Kathy Flynn proclaimed, "A tribute to Toad draws friends from all over the U.S."

Jere Davidson and Gwen Rutledge, both widowed by 1998 but longtime friends of Toad's and Donna's, had answered the invitation and made the trip to near Lawn together. Like all of Toads and Donna's longtime friends, they had on occasion traveled with the Leons.

"Paul and I and Toad and Donna decided to go to Quebec one fall, to watch the leaves turn," Gwen recalled with a laugh. They flew to Canada, hired a chauffeur and limousine to escort them through the rural beauty of this special rite of fall.

"I'm in seventh heaven!" Toad sighs as Marge Baucum (left) and Claire Barnhart give him a birthday kiss.

Winter dipped into fall's annual show though and weather turned the green leaves of Quebec's trees directly into gray, bypassing brilliant golds, oranges, yellows and reds. "With nothing else to do, we flew to Cincinnati, caught the Delta Queen, and rode down the Ohio River to the Mississippi. Then we flew home, and finally got to watch the leaves turn - right outside our own windows in New Mexico."

Jere recalled the time she and her husband were visiting at Pendaries Ranch for the day when the men decided to hit the road to Las Vegas, Nevada. "I have to go home (to Santa Fe) to pack," she pleaded.

"Nah. If you do that you'll change your mind," Toad countered. "C'mon. Learn to travel light."

The first morning there she and Donna got up early to go shopping for Jere, "only stores didn't open in Vegas until almost noon. When the stores finally opened, I wound up buying the wildest wardrobe you can imagine," Jere said. "And I did learn how to travel light."

The birthday bash at More or Less Ranch Gwen and Jere had traveled hundreds of miles to attend was, to say the least, "quite a party," Jere said, noting that "even though there were hundreds who attended a thousand others would have come if they had not already been dead. That Toad is a survivor!"

Highlights for her were being chauffeured around the ranch in a horse and buggy or a large open wagon or individually on horseback and partaking of "cow pasture pool" on a hastily contrived golf course.

"Food abounded everywhere, and we simply could not believe the fireworks display," said Gwen Rutledge, a former band vocalist who sang "a special birthday song" for Toad.

Second generation kinfolks at Toad's birthday bash included (from left): Sandra Roberts, Leon Weaver, Linda Zachary, Virginia Barnhart, Polly Denton, and Carol Ann Midkiff. Seated are Madge Moore and Toad.

"I guess you could say I wrote the lyrics," she said with a laugh, during a phone interview in 2001 from her home in Santa Fe. Then she sang part of her vocal salute to Toad:

> Our good friend, this is your day,
> Full of sex and delight
> May you get some tonight.

> *Wyatt smiled broadly.*

Pointing the Southwind North—1998

About a month after Toad Leon's world-famous eighty-eighth birthday he decided that maybe his luxurious thirty-six foot-long motor home would be more useful in other hands. But not before one last trip. He asked his nephew, Leon Weaver, to pilot the huge, diesel-powered Southwind to Santa Fe, New Mexico, perhaps extended with stops at Pendaries Ranch and associated environs.

A nostalgic return to the Pendaries Ranch enabled Toad and his nephew/driver, Leon Weaver, to take in many other sights, such as the San Juan River below Navajo Dam.

The sojourn amounted to much more and many additional miles than that. Toad saw many of his friends along the way, most of whom you have met previously in this book. It was nostalgic, entertaining, and enough to try lesser men's souls had not Toad and his nephew, the son of Toad's sister, Mattie Lee, been very compatible.

"Leon is a young man of varied talents many of which he was called upon to utilize," Toad recalled. "Due to his very capable driving, mechanical knowledge, navigational skills, flexibility, and good humor our trip was a success."

"Typically, there is the risk of cabin fever" in such an extended moveable setting as their trip, Leon said, "but I never experienced that feeling. Uncle Toad set an example of maintaining an even temper that I can only aspire to emulate. Toad was invariably cheerful, energetic, interested, considerate, generous and entertaining.

"I met many interesting, friendly and beautiful people during our trip, mostly Toad's friends. But of them all Toad stands out. He has lived an interesting life during interesting times and is still doing it. He loves life and it shows."

The adventure began May 28, 1998, with the huge Southwind towing Toad's jeep while carrying Leon's bicycle on board. The following are excerpts from a trip diary kept by Leon Weaver:

5/28:
Abilene to Muleshoe, Texas—Once on the road, Toad called his friends, Irv and Dorothy St. Clair, by cell phone to advise them we were coming through Muleshoe. They insisted we stop by. They were such friendly and charming hosts, we wound up having dinner with them and spending the night.

5/29:
Muleshoe to Santa Fe—There is a lot of open road between Muleshoe and Santa Fe, 250 miles more or less, and I got more comfortable driving as the miles went by. We arrived in Santa Fe mid-afternoon and got set up in an RV park about five miles from the Plaza. Dinner with Gwen Rutledge and Jeri Davidson at the Palace restaurant followed.

5/30:
Santa Fe—Toad's friend, Big Ed Brosseau, entertained us with breakfast at the country club, a tour of an exclusive new residential area west of the city being developed by the Bass Brothers of Fort Worth, Texas, and Toad's former home in the old section of Santa Fe. That evening we had dinner at the Bullring Restaurant with Patricia Stillman, an accomplished artist I had met a month earlier at Toad's birthday party. Her home, near Toad's former home, is a Santa Fe-style showplace, both in architecture and décor. It is the most impressive one-bedroom home I have ever seen, not to mention the three-bedroom guesthouse. Patricia displayed several of her paintings and bronze sculptures in her home, as well as a wonderful bronze self-statue in her garden. I unpacked my bicycle and rode to downtown Santa Fe, then took an arroyo bike path. It was an enjoyable twenty-two-mile tour, following which Toad and I shopped, watched TV, and rested.

6/1:
Santa Fe to Chama, New Mexico—In the morning we went for a jeep drive up Bishop's Lodge Road to the pueblo of Tesuque and visited the Shidoni bronze foundry and art gallery. Later we re-hooked the jeep to

the motorhome and continued to our next destination—the Mundy Ranch south of Chama. We arrived just in time for happy hour and dinner with Toad's friends, Billy and Ethel Mundy. Billy is a story-teller in the best cowboy tradition with more than seventy years of venturesome New Mexico experience to draw on.

6/2:
Chama—Billy fixed us breakfast and took us on a long-ranging tour of his ranch. It would be hard to choose which was the most interesting—the beautiful ranch or Billy's colorful, nonstop commentary. That afternoon Toad and I jeeped over to the ranch of Henry and Judy Coors. Henry showed us around their place and local points of interest. The evening included drinks with the Coors, the Mundys, and some of their local friends, followed by a gourmet dinner by Judy and conversation and stories by all.

6/3:
Chama to Taos, New Mexico—That morning Toad and I boarded the scenic Cumbres & Toltec narrow gauge railroad from Chama, over Cumbres Pass to Antonito, Colorado, for lunch, then back. Late afternoon found us bidding farewell to the Mundys and heading to Taos, stopping long enough to photograph and marvel at the depth of the Rio Grande Gorge before arriving at dark.

6/4:
Taos to Pendaries, New Mexico—In the morning we headed to Pendaries over paved NM 18 which we both remembered as gravel in the 1970s. The route took us through Mora, Ledoux, and finally Pendaries, which now has its own post office. George Slaughter met us and took us for a guided tour of the newer developments of Pendaries. As an almost permanent resident and active member of the homeowners association, he filled us in on all the business and social news. He would make an engaging historian for the post-Leon Pendaries period. The lodge, motel, restaurant and Moosehead Saloon had changed remarkably little. But the swimming pool was filled in and the putting green, pro shop, and first two holes of the golf course were gone, as a result of local expansion to a full eighteen holes. There are new roads all over Bear Mountain, with new homes up to the ridgeline. There are also new roads in front of Goat Mountain that extend from the treeline to about a quarter mile into the open valley, where trees were first planted by Toad in the 1970s. Many new homes dotted this area as well. At the old ranch headquarters there

are townhouses along the now-paved road. We met George and Betty Slaughter in the Moosehead Saloon for before-dinner drinks and conversation. We concluded the day in a nostalgic mood with dinner at the lodge restaurant. (Incidentally, the saloon's namesake moose currently resides in Abilene, over Toad's fireplace. It was acquired by Toad during a hunting trip to British Columbia a year after World War II ended. But that is another story, told earlier within these pages by Toad).

6/5:

Pendaries, New Mexico—We rode around the golf course with the Slaughters and Nancy and Bruce McNaughton while they played. The course was in good condition, and still challenging because of the sloping fairways and greens. Toad and I jeeped the valley and more of Pendaries that afternoon. Toad is especially proud of the chapel that he had built with the help of donations from homeowners and friends; particularly the chapel bell which he wrangled from Al Packard, his friend in Santa Fe. (Al questioned Toad, hoping his donation would get him into heaven, but Toad had told him there were no guarantees, even if Al needed all the help he could get.) That evening Betty hosted a most enjoyable cocktail party for some twelve couples.

6/6:

Pendaries to Navajo Lake, New Mexico—After a late start occasioned by an attempt to look up some of the old-time ranch hands, we headed for Navajo Lake near the Colorado border. T.O. Midkiff, Toad's son-in-law, met us for three days of fishing in the lake and San Juan River.

6/7:

Navajo Lake—T.O. cooked us a huge breakfast, then we rented a boat. We fished nearly every inlet up one arm of the lake without a single bite. Trolling back toward the marina, we got a few strikes. After several passes over a promising area I finally landed the only catch of the day. It was a nice German brown trout, a 20-incher that weighed four pounds. The wind suddenly came up with gusts over forty m.p.h. that made for an exciting, bumpy, and tiring ride back to the marina.

6/8:

Navajo Lake—T.O. fished with a guide on the San Juan River while I drove to Aztec to get a tire repaired. I had visions of being back in the Baja because a whole family worked on fixing that one tire and it took them three tries to get it right. In the afternoon, T.O. and I fished the San Juan

A non-denominational chapel looks cut over Perdaries Ranch.

while Toad rested. We saw hundreds of nice-sized trout in the water, hooked two dozen or so using the smallest hooks and flies I've ever seen, then released them all. If it hadn't been for T.O.'s shouting professional fishing advice, I'm certain I would never have landed any at all. I think we had hot dogs for dinner.

6/9:
Navajo Lake to Durango, Colorado—The drive to Durango was easy. We got there in time for an afternoon tour in T.O.'s pickup. We made the 245-mile scenic loop through Purgatory, Silverton, Ouray, Ridgway, Pacerville, Telluride and Cortez, then returned. It was one of the highlights of our trip. The balance of the evening doesn't merit a report except to say that José Cuervo was there and I became the designated driver.

6/10:
Durango, Colorado—Some of us got off to a slow start. I won't name names. In the afternoon we went for a ride to and around Vallecito Reservoir, the site of a Leon family reunion some sixty years ago, more or less.

6/11:
Durango to Fun Valley, Colorado—This route took us through Pagosa Springs and over Wolf Creek Pass at an elevation of 10,550 feet. We arrived at Fun Valley in time for lunch and a tour of the Creede Mining

Toad Leon's Southwind motor home rests amid moss-draped trees at the St. John Plantation in St. Martinsville, Louisiana.

District in T.O.'s pickup. Creede was briefly a silver mining boomtown in the 1800s. Up one valley there seemed to be a jeep trail that climbed a pass over the Continental Divide, but T.O. didn't think it looked pickup friendly. Back at Fun Valley's dining hall, Toad introduced us to the owners—his friends, Mr. And Mrs. Mack Henson. They exchanged interesting stories about the resort business for the balance of the evening.

6/12:

Fun Valley to Basalt, Colorado—T.O. got an early start for home. Toad and I went north over Spring Creek Pass and the Continental Divide, over Slumgullion Pass (11,361 feet), down to Lake City, past the Powderhorn and into Gunnison for lunch. After lunch we headed east over Monarch Pass to the Arkansas River Valley and followed it north to Leadville. The Matchless Mine and Baby Doe's Cabin were closed for the day, so we backtracked some fifteen miles and, ignoring signs that prohibited vehicles more than thirty-five feet in length, headed west to Aspen, Colorado. Ascending Independence Pass (12,095 feet) was no problem and the view was awesome, but the highway descending into Aspen soon enlightened us concerning the prohibition of vehicles thirty-five or more feet in length. It became progressively more narrow and the curves became sharper. On Toad's passenger side there were jagged rock overhangs, and on my side a deep stream gorge without guard rails. Toad kept muttering,

"You're really giving me a thrill." I had to negotiate a fine line between rock faces and oncoming traffic, with clearances measured in inches, not feet. Fortunately, we arrived in Aspen without scratches or forcing anyone that I'm aware of into the gorge. It was probably very scenic, but neither Toad nor I really got a good look. Aspen considers itself too classy for RV parks, so we continued on to Basalt. It may not have been the most miles we covered in a single day, but it was the longest and most thrilling.

6/13-16:
More sightseeing in Colorado, including Grand Lake and Loveland, then Estes Park and across to Wyoming. This portion of the trip included Rocky Mountain National Park, the Medicine Bow Mountain Range, a drive down the Cache la Paudre River Canyon, Fort Collins, Colorado, and Torrington, Wyoming.

6/17:
Torrington to Hill City, South Dakota—A quick revision to our ever-flexible itinerary took us north with the Black Hills as our destination, then dodging heavy rains through a visit to Mount Rushmore.

6/18-20:
More sight-seeing through Hill City, South Dakota to Valentine, Nebraska to Liberal Kansas. Interesting and educational, although we have no reason ever to return to Liberal.

6/21:
It was back to Abilene, with an extended stop in Childress, Texas where we parked in an empty shopping center, turned on the auxiliary generator and the air-conditioner, raised the TV antenna and watched the finish of the U.S. Open golf tournament. Then it was on to the last leg of our journey, finding us parking in front of Toad's house at midnight.

We had accumulated 3,968 miles on the motorhome which did not include the thousand-plus we logged on side trips with T.O. and Toad's numerous friends. Obviously, I enjoyed the journey very much. I'd be ready to do another one anytime.

Call of the Open Road

A man's gotta have his toys, and just a few years shy of his ninetieth birthday, Toad Leon found he still had one he had wanted to own for years. A recreational vehicle.

"It just looked like something I would really enjoy," he said. His choice was a dandy. The Fleetwood Southwind measured thirty-six feet, bumper to bumper. It was diesel-powered, and if the manufacturer had left anything off, Toad, his family, and friends who inspected it didn't know what it could have been.

Toad used various drivers on his trips. Early-on his grandsons, Tim Roberts and Ben Callaway, piloted the behemoth of the highways and byways. The maiden trip was a family one, to see Frances Levert at her sugar cane plantation in St. Martinsville, Louisiana. It's an enterprise that has been in her late husband's family since before the Civil War. Toad's nephew, Leon

Tim Roberts heeded the "call of the open road" with his grandfather, Toad Leon.

Weaver, drove on a long and winding sojourn through the Rockies and Midwest, shortly after Toad's famous 88th birthday party at the More or Less Ranch.

And then there was the attempt to return to the Alcan Highway through Canada and Alaska. He persuaded B.C. Roberson and Tom Lewis, a couple of friends from his more active golfing days, to accompany him. He got Bill Allison, a retired Navy man, to steer the ship. And off they went.

They stopped for fuel at a self-serve near Fort St. John and one of the guys began filling the RV. "We looked up," Toad said, laughing. "He was putting diesel in our fresh water tank! Put in about ten gallons before we could stop him." They flushed the tank with soap, vinegar and several other concoctions. "We trailed foul-smelling water through most of Canada."

Toad found the new Alcan Highway nothing like the thirty-five-m.p.h. limit gravel road he and Donna had loved traveling, more than fifty years before. "Every now and then we'd see a sign pointing to 'The Original Alcan Highway '."

With each new excursion Toad learned more big truths about motorhoming. "I began to realize that having something this large. with this much stuff, was like putting your house on wheels. Something's always going wrong. The plumbing needs fixing. The jake brake needs repair. Then the air-conditioning or the leveling jacks. One time, the windshield even blew out.

Toad and his driver, Bill Allison, stumbled onto the aptly named rural cafe somewhere in Canada during a 1997 road trip.

"It takes a tinkerer, which I am not, to keep everything on board running up to snuff. Thank heavens, all my drivers were good at handling those details," Toad said.

Even so, he figured the RV had served its purpose. Having the Southwind had been an experience, and a fun one at that. "However, I believe owning a motorhome is a lot like owning a boat. It's a happy day when you buy it, but an even happier day when you sell it."

The Think Tank—1999

As Toad Leon neared his ninetieth birthday, coupled with the fact that he had traded his worn-out, arthritic knees for a brand new pair he was just getting used to, hanging around the home place seemed the smart thing to do. That place, as the close of the twentieth century loomed, was a home near the second tee at Fairway Oaks Country Club. If the golf that he had loved for seventy years was more for watching than playing, Toad still enjoyed being around people.

"Nearly every morning a group of us meet at Fairway Oaks for coffee," he said. "We delve into current events of the day. Now these are intelligent people. They know a lot about a myriad of topics.

"Though I studied engineering at Texas Technological College from 1930 to 1932 and took calculus and trigonometry, I still sometimes have trouble adding to the Think Tank conversation.

"The usual suspects include Irv Townsend, Harold Wicker, Jack Riley, Aubrey Roberts, Ron Knaus, Bob Karhan, Paul Ridgeway, Vince Swinney, Ken Curry, Pat Patterson, Jerry Gerard and Bill Hollowell. They run the gamut from petroleum engineers, pilots and school teachers, to a trucking contractor, a chemical engineer, an attorney, and even a pharmaceutical salesman." One morning, this mostly Republican group was complaining about the government and all the goings-on in Washington, D.C., as the second Bill Clinton presidency was drawing to a close.

"I told them about a conversation with Jerry Loper that had transpired a few days before," Toad told this grouping of the thinkers. "He owned a drug store in Baird for years and I have known him since 1935. We reminisced a while and then the subject turned to politics."

Jerry said, "Toad, the problem is that ten percent of the population holds ninety percent of the wealth. The government should divide up all the money. Take from the rich and give to the poor, as Robin Hood would say."

"But Jerry," Toad replied, "our government has been trying to do this for years. Eventually, the same ten percent wind up with ninety percent of the money."

"I appreciate what you're saying, Toad, but that's not what I have in mind," Loper replied. "In order for it to be a success, they should split up the money EVERY Saturday night."

"Well, hell," Toad shot back. "If they'd do that, I'd go for it in a New York Minute!"

Pure Toadese, all right. But while we're at it, what about that business at Texas Tech seventy years before? It includes more pure Toadese.

He was at Tech primarily because, back in 1927, his older brothers had promised their late mother that Toad would be educated. They had picked engineering for his degree plan. "I was studying things I'd never heard of," he said. After two years, a degree in engineering clearly wasn't going to happen. He wanted out despite his brothers' strong objections. Leave it to Toad to figure a grandiose way of exiting Tech's School of Engineering, one that would have students and faculty chuckling and scratching their heads for some time.

The Think Tank. Front row: Bob Karhan, Toad, Pat Patterson, Irv Townsend. Back row: Bob Rice, Jack Riley, Ken Curry, Bill Hollowell, Harold Wicker, Ron Knaus

"I don't want to know all this engineering stuff," he told school officials, as the reason for wanting to switch to business administration. "I just want to learn how to drive the locomotive."

A dour assistant dean looked up and drolly said, "Mr. Leon, you're going to the wrong school for that."

Toad stayed in character. "I said, 'Good God! Here I've wasted two years of my life!' And that's a true story."

Toad didn't find much enlightenment in BA either, and after a total of three years at the Lubbock school, he finally gave up on a college degree.

Toad's Tidbits

How many waitresses have heard this one from a smiling, well-served Toad? "Darlin', your service has been so good today, I'm going to put you in my will...Oh, but wait. That wouldn't work. It would be a dead give-away." Toad credits his friend, Dallas businessman Dan Varel, with this one.

And while in the restaurant service end of things, Toad on occasion has recited, "What will you have?" The waiter said, picking his nose, to which I replied, "I'll have two hard-boiled eggs, 'cause you can't stick your finger in those."

Likewise, while on the subject of nasal probing, "You can pick your friends and you can pick your nose, but you can't pick your own kinfolk."

"...before a gnat can swim a dipper." Toad says he picked this up as a child. "We had no running water, of course. We drank much of the time from a cistern bucket, using a dipper. It might be an old tin cup, or sometimes would be carved out of a dried gourd. Invariably, in the summertime, you'd have a gnat on top of your water, swimming like crazy while you drank."

Toad escorts his daughter, Carol Ann, to her 1955 Kappa Kappa Gamma presentation dance at Texas Tech.

Toad and Donna celebrate their 50th wedding anniversary in 1985.

"I can't talk to you now, 'cause I've got my horse tied in an ant bed." Another obvious early-Rule maxim that could be a little outdated today for anyone wishing a hasty exit line. But it is graphic.

"Fast pay makes fast friends." One could almost see this framed and hanging on Toad's office wall or maybe on a business card wherever Toad made deals. It has been heard many times in the 19th hole or around gin tables.

"Toadie, don't ever give up the ship," a Jewish friend once advised Leon. "Sell it!"

"A busy person is a happy person"…Sandra Roberts, Toad's younger of his two daughters, said her father was always roping her sister, Carol Ann, and her into "doing the hard work on his projects. Sometimes we were so busy that we weren't just happy, we were hysterical." Carol Ann had it embroidered on a set of towels she gave him." "I still use them," Toad added.

"Do you give ministerial discounts?" Toad will ask, putting on his best hurt hang-dog expression. This follows the answer to another question: "How much are you going to charge me?"

"I'll see you in the fall, if at all. I'll be ridin' ol' Paint and leadin' ol' Ball." One of Toad's favorite exit lines.

In 1990 Toad found his Dallas office door used fifty years earlier in an antique shop.

"If it's worth doing, it's worth doing now!" is Toad's ringing endorsement of anti-procrastination.

"Sorry. This is my busy time of the year." Sandra Leon Roberts has heard her father say this "a million times, down through the years," when he's approached to get in on a deal or donate time to a project that is not to his liking.

"Never look a gift horse in the mouth," some people say. Toad's rendition is, "Never look a dead horse in the ass."

"Show me a chewer and I'll show you a doer." Here, Toad tips his hat to fellow tobacco chewer Cabot Dysart for coming up with this one.

"I've got my ox in the ditch," presented as a plea by Toad when he needs help on a project.

"The old man said, 'Before I die there are five things I want to try: A tricycle, a bicycle, a snowmobile, a red-headed woman, and a ferris wheel.'" This was a common expression heard around Pendaries Ranch during its Leon era.

"Never ask a man the size of his spread," concerning ranch acreage, a maxim steadfastly held by Toad.

Toad's daughters, Sandra (left), and Carol Ann (center), attend their parent's fifty-eighth wedding anniversary in 1993. Gay Gerard is on right.

He claims to have coined the following when he was briefly in the grocery business in Baird, Texas, shortly after he and Donna married in 1935. An old hobo, Toad said, came into the store one day and said, "I'm in a big hurry. What time does the next train come in, and what time does it go out? How deep is that mud hole out front, and what is the price of your bananas?" "In at eight and out at nine; up to your ass and three for a dime."

"Wyatt, do you know the difference between humor and odor?" "No. Toad, don't believe we've heard that one in Tombstone yet." "Well, I'll tell you, Wyatt. One is a shift in wit..."

And Wyatt urped, before Toad Leon could finish.

Two Who Know Toad's Wit Well

Frank Sheffield and Jim Polk, both longtime Abilenians, have had half a century to view firsthand Toad Leon's wit and occasional wisdom. Both remain awed by Toad's legendary wisecracks.

"I think part of it comes from the way he enjoys life," Polk said, in an interview during the summer of 2001. "I don't believe Toad has ever been anywhere or been around anyone when he didn't enjoy himself." Polk even dated Toad's daughter, Carol Ann, when the Leons moved to Abilene. "Toad and Donna were good friends of my mother's and my

Toad and longtime friend and associate, Frank Sheffield (left), and Bob Lapham, author of this book.

Uncle Johnny Guitar, who lived in Baird (Donna's hometown)." Polk said when he would come to the door to get high-schooler Carol Ann, "Toad wouldn't say much. But he would sure cast a stern eye my way." That formality changed down through the years, when they would meet at functions with which they shared a mutual interest.

Polk still tells about the time when he and Toad were at a Ducks Unlimited meeting. "I walked over to Toad's table and spoke to him." He stood regally and addressed those sitting with him.

"Everybody, I want you to meet Jim Polk!" Toad announced loudly. "You know, I raised this boy!" Then, with a pause that would do justice to the best stand-up comic, he added, "Then he raised me back."

Sheffield laughed at this during his interview. He had heard hundreds of such quips and zingers down through the years from his longtime associate, competitor, and friend.

They first met fifty years ago as rivals of a sort, when Sheffield was manager of the Paramount Theatre, Interstate Theaters' local flagship movie house.

"As a young manager, I knew Toad by reputation when he moved to Abilene and built the Town and Country Drive-In. Of course he didn't know me. But we developed a lasting friendship I wouldn't trade.

"Toad and I have sort of an affectionate name for one another," Sheffield said. "We call each other Shorty. It goes back to this joke he told me a long time ago, one that still cracks me up today." Toad, Sheffield said, claimed to have had a friend in Rule High School named Shorty. "He had a sister named Virginia. Toad said everybody called her Virgin for short...but not for long!"

Sheffield accompanied Toad on an automobile trip to Houston early in 2001. "Once, when we were driving down the highway, I asked him to come clean—were all these legendary Toad Leon anecdotes original? Or did he borrow some?"

"Well, I have to say I have borrowed a few," Toad replied with a smile, then paused before issuing another certified original: "Then again, I have borrowed a few others back."

Wyatt had to smile at that, while nodding his head.

Get the License Number of That Truck!

"Oh...how...I...WISH...I hadn't...gone...back...for...that...chaw!" Toad Leon moaned through clenched teeth as he lay in extreme pain in a hospital bed in Kerrville, Texas. It was the second week in October, 2001. This book had already gone to the printer. Everything was set to publish *What Made Wyatt Urp* on schedule in time for Christmas.

Then something dreadful happened. An hour or so before midnight, Saturday, October 6, it looked as if there might not be a Toad Leon book, at least the one that had been planned. Toad tangled with a pickup while crossing a darkened street in Center Point, just outside the landmark original headquarters of the Texas Rangers. At ninety-one years of age, with a truck rambling along the street at about thirty m.p.h., odds are p-r-e-t-t-y good that you will miss your own literary autograph party.

But we get ahead of ourselves.

Saturday, October 6, included a festive occasion for the Leon clan. Toad's great-nephew, Chris Denton, was marrying Jennifer Welch in historic Boerne, a quaint village twenty or so miles north of San Antonio. The wedding was fantastic and so was the reception which moved on down the road to Center Point and the Rangers' landmark. A full jazz band played for the guests and young honorees. Toad, as usual, held court while dancing the night away. Finally around 10:30 p.m. it came time time to bid farewell to the bride and groom, head out, and turn in for the night. Toad was with his daughters, Sandra and Carol Ann, and members of their families. Toad, Sandra, Carol Ann, and T.O. (Carol Ann's husband), had come in the same car.

"I was walking along with Daddy, when he fell behind," Sandra recalled. "Carol Ann and T.O. were already in the car, so I crossed the street to join them. Daddy was visiting with someone."

"I was looking out the window and saw Daddy still on the curb," Carol Ann said. "Someone had stopped to give him a *chaw* of tobacco. The street was pretty dark. I looked away and then heard this terrible thud. I looked back and there was Daddy lying in the street."

The pickup that had hit Toad screeched to a halt. A teenage driver emerged. The young man was distraught. Carol Ann and Sandra were the first to reach their father. "I just *knew* he was dead!" Carol Ann said. She shouted, "Hey! Does anybody know CRP?" to the quickly gathered crowd that included the newlyweds in their formal attire.

"CRP?" someone asked, "You mean CPR?"

"Right, right," Carol Ann replied, wondering how she could confuse the government's Conservation Recovery Program for ranchers and farmers with the present emergency.

"Toad's breathing!" someone yelled.

"Well, I don't guess we need CPR," Carol Ann mumbled as she bent over her father. Then she saw a chilling sight—blood oozing from the corner of Toad's mouth. "Well, this is it, I told myself. He's got a head wound. I looked closer though and realized that what I thought was blood was fresh tobacco juice."

Sandra said 911 calls lit up a dozen cell phones. In no time emergency personnel were on the scene. It took considerably longer for the ambulance to arrive. Meanwhile, a groggy Toad had come to. His pain was considerable.

The emergency personnel had secured Toad on a board-like stretcher equipped to keep him from moving, especially his neck. "Daddy was trying to turn his head," Sandra said. "Mark Denton, his grand-nephew, kept telling him he couldn't do that. We had to be careful with his neck and back."

"You...don't...UNDERSTAND!" Toad stammered. "I'm about to DROWN!" I've...GOTTA...SPIT!" Finally, someone decided that Toad's "chaw" had run its course.

It was decided to cut across country and take Toad to Sid Petersen Memorial Hospital in Kerrville. A couple of CAT scans and plenty of other tests over the next two days revealed both good and bad news. Vital organs were unscathed, but his pelvis had suffered a two-inch split.

Still, he quickly became a celebrity around the medical staff. "They couldn't believe he was in such good shape at his age," Sandra said. "They were amazed that his only prescription was thyroid medicine."

"If some of our sixty-year olds were in as good condition and had the same attitude as Mr. Leon, they'd be out of here in no time," said Ann, one of Toad's nurses.

Still Dr. Allen informed Toad and his daughters that recuperation would be "a long haul." Surgery was ruled out because of Toad's age.

"I heard the pickup but didn't see a thing," Toad recalled of his brush with death. "It was such a great party and everybody was having so much fun."

"It wasn't the young driver's fault," Carol Ann said. He wasn't drinking and he wasn't driving recklessly, the police told her. And it wasn't Toad's fault either. "Daddy was wearing a dark blue suit and the street was pretty dark."

Early in the hospital stay, before much was known of what to expect of the unsinkable Toad Leon, friends and family came in and out wondering what the future held. One of them asked Toad if this would curtail his plans for the book.

"Not only NO, but HELL NO!" Toad growled through a morphine haze. "This is going to be the new last chapter."

Epilogue

To know C.D. (Toad) Leon is never to forget him. Or the people he has known during his ninety-one years plus (as of this writing) of trekking through dozens of business ventures stretching from the mountains of northern New Mexico, through tough-as-nails West Texas, and into the high life of cosmopolitan Dallas. Not to mention adventures, fun and games throughout much of the world.

My golfing buddy, Frank Sheffield, is a longtime friend of Toad's. He said it best. "I always thought that if I were going to write a 'Most Unforgettable Character I Ever Met' article for the Reader's Digest, it would be Toad. Not only for himself, but because he has known so many characters, and has such an unforgettable way of remembering them."

Toad is as much a social animal as anyone you'd ever meet. He truly likes people, and being around them. He thrives on being the center of attention and considers this role to be a duty not taken lightly.

No one ever had more fun with a joke or rehashed pun than Toad. Often buried in his one-liners and self-effacing humor are bits of wisdom he diligently tries to mask since far be it from him to be accused of being taken too seriously.

When asked, as a businessman who had made a buck or considerably more while buying, selling or trading farms and ranches, how one made money in real estate, Toad replied, "You find out where people are going to be going, and you get there first."

In spite of Toad Leon not having taken particularly good care of himself in his earlier years, at age ninety-one he was in relatively good shape, notwithstanding a pair of manufactured knees and a cataract operation that had worked as if it were from a textbook.

Family members have gone a considerable way toward making sure happiness takes its proper place in the health and well being of their patriarch.

Friends, of course, continue to be a vital function in his busy life. He has outlived his beloved wife, Donna, and his brothers and sisters, not to mention virtually all of his childhood friends from Rule; even most of his contemporaries in the film exhibition business headquartered in Dallas fifty and sixty years ago have passed on. In their place have come a couple more age layers of friends. There is no generation gap associated with Toad Leon.

No one knows the secret of that character mystique known as charisma. But everyone who has spent any time around Toad realizes that the man has it in double doses.

An active life, or at the very least a busy attitude, has contributed to his well being. "I don't expect to play golf anymore," he reflected, before adding with a sly smile as if to stave off unwanted sympathy, "unless you can find me one of those Callaway ERC2 drivers (outlawed by the USGA for spring-effect high performance) for two hundred bucks (an impossibility)." However, just a few months before, Toad had played a full eighteen holes, and taken every shot.

Never say the word "Go" around Toad, Frank Sheffield said, "or else he might run over you on the way to your car. I think he keeps a bag packed and stashed behind his couch, just in case."

As if Toad needed anybody to take him anywhere. By himself, he and his 2000 model red and white Cadillac Deville regularly burn up the highways and interstates between Abilene and Santa Fe, where Toad keeps a load of pals from a generation ago. Or to Midkiff, Texas near Midland, where daughter Carol Ann and her husband, T.O. Midkiff, live on their ranch.

His younger daughter, Sandra, and her husband Square Roberts reside just outside Abilene.

Toad never misses the annual Nickel Creek Music Festival David R. Ligon puts on in the Guadalupe Mountains of far West Texas. Or the Bennett Ranch Party celebrating its ties to the old Flying H Ranch near Mayhill, New Mexico, not far from Cloudcroft.

As he usually does to those, Toad also drives himself more than 500 miles to Harlingen, Texas, for the annual Life Begins at 40 golf tournament, and to Muleshoe, Texas, more than 200 miles into the Panhandle for the opening of the pheasant season each year.

Toad, the one-time big game hunter now limits his hands-on hunting to doves around Abilene. But any bird season is a good excuse to party.

To be in the presence of Toad Leon is to perk up, regardless of your station in life. That's part of his mystique. Here is a person whom you intuitively know will say something very funny one moment and perhaps be a bit profound the next.

Were I to develop a credo for Toad, it might be something like this: "Here is a man who knows how to enjoy life daily practices this knowledge, and considers it his duty to take others along for the ride."

–Bob Lapham

No urp from Wyatt this time. He just smiles.

Index

A

Allison, Bill, 236-237

Allred, Governor Jimmy, 35

Anderson, Harold, 74-75

Arrott, Jim & Tattie, 97-98

Anders, Audrey, 194

Autry, Gene, 52

B

Baca, Jose, 75, 92

Baca, Magarita, 75

Barker, Milton, 45

Barnhart, Claire, 227

Barnhart, Joe, 95

Barnhart, John Newhall, 68-69, 95-96,108-109

Barnhart, Nora Virginia (nee Leon) (niece), 22-23, 26-27, 32, 37,
	39-42, 68-69, 95, 228

Baucum, Marge, 227

Bennett, Bob, 219, 269

Bennett, Kay, 219

Bentley, C.E., 180

Bickers, Benny, 82

Black, John & Jane, 82-83, 111-113, 130, 157, 173, 183

Blackshear, Mildred Aylene (nee Leon) (niece), 13, 39-41, 68-69, 104

Blackshear, Robert ("Bob") King, 68-69, 104

Bourland, Gayle, 92, 148

Bourland, Marcus & Patsy, 224

Briggs, Hugh & Cris, 111-113, 130, 183-184

Brooks, Harold, 70

Brosseau, Ed, 178, 208-209, 212, 230

Brosseau, Roberta, 212

Brown, Guy, 268

Browning, Bill & Jane, 192, 212

Browning, Jeff, 133, 162, 178, 192-193, 212

Browning, Susie, 178, 192-193, 212

Bryan, Sonny, 194

Bucholtz, Bill, 81, 195

Burger King, 106-107

Burnstein, Natalie, 71-72

Butler, Pete, 57

C

Cain, John Paul, 135

Callas, Maria, 189

Callaway, Benjamin Claude ("Ben") (grandson), 236

Callaway, Donald Alphonso ("Al") (grandson), 195, 200

Campbell, Governor Jack, 144

Carter, Amon, Jr., 131

Childress, Major, 122

Clark, Ben, 110

Clark, Ron, 200

Cockerell, Dr. E.G. & Juanell, 80

Cole, Colonel, 50

Coody, Charles, 180

Coors, Henry & Judy, 219, 231

Coulson, Coony, 180

Cowden Jr., Jax M., 19

Cox, John & Virginia, 225-226

Crawford, Hershel, 52

Cree, Bill & Amber, 174-175

Creel, Eddie, 135

Curry, Ken, 238-239

D

Davidson, Jere, 227-230

Davis, Ben, 120, 196

Davis, Bonnie, 120

Dean, Dizzy, 131, 268

De Leon, Henry Joseph (father), 1-3, 6, 12

De Leon, Margaret Ann (nee Server) (mother), 1-3, 10, 12, 26

Denton, Chris & Jennifer (nee Welch), 247

Denton, Mark, 248

Denton, Velma Pauline ("Polly") (nee Leon) (niece), 13, 39-42, 99-101,
        224, 228

Denton, Edward D. ("Buck"), 99, 224

DiMaggio, Joe, 131

Dillinger, John, 29-30

Dobbins, Cecil, 144

Dodd, John, 190-191

Dysart, Cabot & Dorothy, 219, 242

E

Eplen, Mack, 144, 205-206

Estes, Bob, 136

Estes, Tommy, 180

Evans, Dale, 52

F

Fanning, Foy, 204

Falls, Horace & Margaret, 53

Faye, Alice, 70

Featherstone, Charlie & Glenna, 116-117

Fincher, Kenneth & Juanita, 172

Fogelson, Buddy, 145

Fouts, Bill, 9

Fleming, Ed, 72-73

Flowers, PeeWee, 129, 131

Flynn, Kathy, 226

Free, Jack, 138

Freeman, Wayne, 82-83, 103-104, 112

Frith, Houston, 208

G

Garner, James, 131

Garson, Greer, 145

George, Chief Dan, 203

Gerard, Gay, 243

Gerard, Jerry, 238

Goff, Tuffy & Liz, 159

Goldwater, Sen. Barry, 165

Grafton, Ed, 81

Griffith, H.J., 122

Gwinn, Bill, 166

H

Hale, Monte, 52

Haley, J. Evetts, 165

Haley, Jr., J. Evetts & Frances, 165, 212

Hancock, Libby, 212

Hancock, Nash, xi, 201, 208

Harrington, Lynn & Jere, 267

Harvey, Stu, 208

Hayter, Dub, 151

Henson, Mack, 234

Hill, G.S., 67, 72

Hill, Waddie, 18, 20

Hodge, Paul, 180

Holder, Margaret (nee Brooks), 14-16

Hollowell, Bill, 238-239

Holly, Horace, 67, 114

Hopkins, Ed, 135-136

Horne, Charlie, 208

Hubbard, Harold ("Snooky"), 112, 173

Hubbard, Jackie, 112

Hubbard, Morgan & Dodge, 112, 185-186

Hubbard, Ray, 186

Hudson, Dr. Fred (Doc"), 56-61, 63

Hughes, Betty, 148-150

Humphries, Joe, 164

Hunt, Bunker, 141, 196

Hunt, H.L., 169-170

I

Interstate Theaters, 44, 246

Isley Theaters, 50

J

Jack, Joe, 49, 54, 74 90

Jack, Nell, 49

Jackson, Estelle Mary (nee Leon) (sister), 1, 3, 17, 26

Jackson, Lester D. ("Jack"), 17, 19

January, Don, 204

Jarmon, Tom, 173

Jennings, Dick, 204

Johnson, Lyndon Baines, 116, 165

Johnson, Richard, 205

Johnson, Walter, 205

Jones, Foster L., 18

Jones, Jesse L., 2

Jones, Joe, 8

Jones, Mildred, 4

Jones, O.J., 179

Jordan, Harvey, 123

K

Karhan, Bob, 238-239

Kelly, Jim, 25

Kennedy, Claude, 38, 137

Kent, Buck, 205

Kirk, George & Ollie Faye, 212-213

Kittley, Martha, 8

Kittley, W.W. ("Pot Leg"), 4

Knaus, Ron, 238-239

Knight, Ruben & Florence, 112

Koontz, Jasper & Sis, 219

Kostas, Peter, 128

Kwalick, Ted, 131, 192

L

Lacy, Fran, 143

Lacy, Joe, 143

LaFarge, Oliver & Consuela (nee Baca), 75-76

Lambert, Mrs. Joe, 189, 204

Lapham, Bob, 180, 245, 251

Leddy, James, 129

Leon, Artie (nee West), 20, 21

Leon, Clarence Edward (brother), 1, 3, 13, 20, 22-25, 35, 39-40,
        42-43, 56, 58-61, 63, 72, 108-110, 114, 167-168

Leon, Harry Server (brother), 1, 3, 15, 20-21, 26-32, 36-37, 44-47,
        49-51, 121, 165

Leon, Henry Carroll (brother), 1, 3, 20, 21, 88, 108

Leon, Jerene (nee Ragan), 28, 40-41, 51, 64

Leon, Mary Frances (nee Settle), 108, 110, 130

Leon, Michael Timothy ("Mike") (brother), 1, 3, 6, 22-23, 93, 95

Leon, Morea (nee Patton), 22

Leon, Nora Myrtle (nee Cloud), 13, 23, 39-40, 42-43, 168

Leon, Wilbur Thomas (nephew), 21, 89, 108-110, 130, 171, 177

Levert, Frances, 236

Levitts, Phil, 201-202

Lewis, Buddy, 214

Lewis, Jeff, 214

Lewis, Tom, 236

Ligon, David, 219-220, 251

Life Magazine, 145

Lively, Cecelia, 1

Loper, Jerry, 238

Lowrey, Leroy, 162

Lumpkin, John, 128

Lumpkins, Bill, 78, 190

M

Mantle, Mickey, 131, 203

Marshall, Stan, 222

Martin, John, 199

Martinez, Celestino, 103, 146

Martinez, Senora, 146

Maxwell, Billy, 204,

Maxwell, Bobby, 204

McBee, Rives, 209

McCandless, Beans, 8

McDonald, Jr., Donald, 142

McGarvey, Mac, 56, 60, 65

McGowen, Carol Lynn, 144

McGowen, Ethelyn, 144

McGowen, H.C. ("Boy") (father-in-law), 32

McGowen, Dr. Henry, 155

McGowen, John, 32

McGowen, Johnnie Inez (nee Norman) (mother-in-law), 37, 39, 167

McLendon Theaters, 50

McNaughton, Bruce & Nancy, 232

McQueen, Jack, 118-119

Meek, Malcom, 71

Melson, Bobby, 216-218

Meredith, Don, xi, 195

Midkiff, T.O. (son-in-law), 219, 223, 232-235, 247, 251

Miles, Carl, 147-148, 185, 204

Monfree, John, 268

Monfree, Sadie, 155

Moore, Madge Ragan (nee Leon) (niece), 28, 39, 41, 228

Morrison, Lewis & Merle, 177, 226

Moser, Chuck, 116

Mundy, Bill & Ethel, 219, 231

Murphy, Ken, 205

N

Neff, Bob, 140

O

Oaks, Robert, 225

Otterman, Gus, 148-149

P

Packard, Al, 232

Parks, Hiram & Vivian, 267

Patterson, Pat, 238-239

Pendaries, Jean, 75-76

Perry, J.D., 180, 204

Petty, Jr., Ralph, 201-202

Pickett, Clyde, 93

Pitts, Ray, 56, 61

Polk, Jim, 245

Powell, Gary, 56, 59, 61

Pressnell, Gene & Willodine, 99-100

Price, Dr. Omer D. & Julie, 219

R

Rackley, John, 90-91

Ramsey, Dr. Wayne & Marie, 119

Rappe, Sibyl Annette (nee Jackson), 19

Rawlins, Bob ("Dark Cloud"), 209-211

Rawlins, Noni, 211

Ray, Harold & Grace, 267

Republic Pictures, 50

Reynolds, Jack, 109

Rice, Bob, 239

Ridgeway, Paul, 238

Riley, Jack, 199-200, 238-239

Ring, Bob, 130, 133

Ritter, Tex, 52

Robb & Rowley Theaters, 26

Roberson, B.C., 236

Roberts, Aubrey, 238

Roberts, Jack, 93, 95, 151

Roberts, Jimmy, 218

Roberts, Timothy Gerald ("Tim") (grandson), 200, 236

Roberts, W.C. ("Square") (son-in-law), 167, 194, 198-200, 222-223,
    251

Robertson, Dale, 118-119, 131

Rogers, Ernie, 93

Rogers, Roy, 52

Rose, Jim, 180

Ross, Jim, 56, 58

Roundtree, Martha, 17-18

Rule, R.O., 2

Rutledge, Gwen, 227-228, 230, 269

Rutledge, Paul, 227

S

Salmon, Col. Bill, 97-98

Scheef, Barbara (nee Leon), 21, 89

Schreiner, Louis, 197

Schulz, Malcom, 129

Seale, "Cowgirls", 35

Segal, Mike, 31

Server, James, 66

Severance, Lou, 66

Sheffield, Frank, 86, 119, 128, 185, 226, 245-246, 250-251

Shortly, Tom, 109

Shelton, "Stormy", 205

Sibley, Dr. Dub & Sanoma, 130-131, 206

Simons, Pollard, 203

Singleton, Tommy, 134

Silva, Eufracio, 80

Sivley, Rufus, 71

Slaughter, Betty Freeman, 82-83, 112, 133, 192-193, 232

Slaughter, George, 162-163, 192-193, 231-232

Sloan, Pat, 56, 59, 61

Smith, Cecil, 152

Smith, E.F. ("Smitty"), 180

Smith, Shelly, 118

Sommers, Joe, 141

Springer, Bob, 127, 142, 205

Springer, Bev, 127

St. Clair, Bill, 67, 132-133, 181, 208-209

St. Clair, Dorothy, 132, 230

St. Clair, Irvin, 67, 132-133, 230

St. Clair, Maureen, 133

Stephenson, Coke, 116-117, 165

Stillman, Patricia, 230, 269

Stovall, "Moose", 104, 180

Stroube, Jack, 104-105, 203-204

Sullins, Bob, 109

Swartz, "Mayor", 32

Swinney, Vince, 238

T

Tadlock, Maxine, 71

Thomas, Mack, xi

Tompkins, Jody, 173

Townsend, Irving, 37, 238-239

Trammell, Jim, 148, 187

Trujillo, Jose Maria, 77

Tucker, Howard, 114-115

Tucker, Jack, 114-115

Tune, Jim & Evelyn, 219

U

Underwood, Frank & June, 105

V

Vance, Vivian, 190-191

Varel, Barbara, 130, 169, 187-189

Varel, Dan, 130, 169-170, 187-189, 240

Vickery, Barbara, 221

Vickery, Don, 221-222

W

Watkins, "Windy", 179

Weaver, Elton "Leon" (nephew), 228-230, 236

Weaver, Hilland, 5

Weaver, Larry H. (nephew), 5

Weaver, Mattie Lee (nee Leon) (sister), 1, 3, 5, 26, 228

Welch, Tiffany Noel (nee Roberts) (granddaughter),

Westbrook Drug Store, 5

Wharton, E.B., 20

Wicker, Harold, 238-239

Wiggins, Ike, 93-94

Williams, Mack, 36, 137

Williamson, Buddy, 194

Winston, Nat & Martha, 219

Winters, Dan, 135-136

Wolf, Dave, 49

Wolff, Jr., Henry, 125

Woodard, Sam & Mabel, 148

Wylie, W.O., 32

Y

Yonge, Jack, 114, 155, 157-161

Yonge, Lois, 155, 155, 157-161

Z

Zachary, Linda Jay (nee Leon) (niece), 21, 88-89, 228

Party-goers at the Desert Inn in Las Vegas, Nevada in 1952 included (from left) Lynn Harrington, Donna Leon, Harold Ray, Vivian Parks, Toad Leon, Grace Ray, Hiram Parks, and Jere Harrington.

The 1969 Black and White Golf Tournament at San Antonio's Oak Hills paired Toad Leon and Guy Brown (two at left) with John Monfree and Baseball Hall of Famer, Dizzy Dean.

A stopover at Lake Tahoe by three couples on a four-week trip from New Mexico to northern California—from left are Hugh Briggs, Jane Black, Toad Leon, Cris Briggs, John Black and Donna Leon.

Newlyweds
C. D. and Donna Leon
in 1935

Patricia Stillman helped
celebrate Toad's 88th birthday
at the More or Less Ranch.

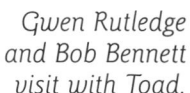

Gwen Rutledge
and Bob Bennett
visit with Toad.

A watercolor of Toad, ca. 1970, by renowned portrait artist, Bettina Steinke.